VERNON K. SCHUMANN

THE OCHRANA
THE RUSSIAN SECRET POLICE

A Maker of Bombs

THE OCHRANA
THE RUSSIAN SECRET POLICE

BY

A. T. VASSILYEV
THE LAST CHIEF OF POLICE UNDER THE TSAR

EDITED AND WITH
AN INTRODUCTION BY

RENÉ FÜLÖP-MILLER
AUTHOR OF "RASPUTIN : THE HOLY DEVIL"

WITH 47 ILLUSTRATIONS

PHILADELPHIA AND LONDON
J. B. LIPPINCOTT COMPANY
MCMXXX

CONTENTS

CHAPTER I

Functions of the Ochrana—The External Agency—Qualities required of Police Spies—Technique of Observation—Myednikov's School—His Special Section—Suppression of a Bomb Factory

CHAPTER II

Secret Collaborators or Assistants—Traitors by Conviction—Secret Rendezvous—Zubatov: his Work and his Death—Revolutionary Counter-espionage—Police Specialists in all Revolutionary Movements

CHAPTER III

Agents Provocateurs and Provocation (Direct Incitement)—The Tell-tale Misprint—Police Agents as Conspirators—Organization and Procedure of the Revolutionaries—Secret Printing-presses—Anarchists and Terrorists—A Frustrated Plot against the Life of the Tsar

CHAPTER IV

The Central Agency—The Azef Affair—The Chief of Police on Trial—Psychology of the Traitor—Murder of Colonel Karpov—Explosives in the Table-leg—Assassination of the Prison Governor—A Murderess with the Dynamite in her Corsage—Dreadful End of Stolypin, President of the Council

CHAPTER V

A Police Gazette for the Tsar—The Black Cabinets—Invisible Writing—A Master in Decoding—The Cipher of the Ochrana—Burtsev unmasks his Friends—Friends and Foes of the Ochrana

CHAPTER VI

The Government and the Jewish Question—The Part played by the Jews in preparing the Way for the Revolution—Were the Jews

CONTENTS

CHAPTER XXIII

CHAPTER XXIV

CHAPTER XXV

ILLUSTRATIONS

INTRODUCTION
BY
RENÉ FÜLÖP-MILLER

INTRODUCTION

O Dionysius, thy tyrant's robes are but a shroud!
Empedocles to Dionysius of Syracuse

MODERN man looks proudly upon the organization of the constitutional state as peculiarly his own creation. That the brutal elements in man have been able more rapidly and more skilfully to take advantage of even that institution than the humaner part of him has done must be regarded doubtless as one of the most characteristic traits of human nature.

In every political organism poor relief and the care of the sick were still in a state of anarchy, being left to the accident of individual compassion or the operation of pious communities, long after matters connected with spies, informers, imprisonment, torture, and execution had reached an admirably high degree of organization.

And it must be said that this officially sanctioned inhumanity has very rarely failed to justify itself in its own eyes by some 'lofty idea'; nay, it would almost appear that 'lofty ideas' are most intimately related to barbarity, and absolutely require for their realization hangmen and spies.

In subservience to the idea of the Roman Empire, the followers of the religion of love were tracked down in their catacombs and thrown to the lions. Again, the idea of Christian love seemed to demand the espionage system of the Inquisition: for his soul's salvation every one had to be put on the rack who had excited suspicion by singing Arab songs, by dyeing his finger-nails with henna, by indulging in too frequent baths, or even by too strict observance of the Sabbath. In honour of St Mark the secret tribunals of Venice called for their human sacrifices.

And in the name of reformed, evangelical Christianity Cromwell's police arrested all who took part in popular merry-making, all who frequented theatres and taverns, and all who had been guilty of swearing a full round oath. At that period strict Puritan authorities gave orders to burn all pictures in the royal galleries in which Christ or the Virgin Mary was represented; Greek statues were mutilated because of their sensual charm; adultery was punishable by death; an enactment ordered maypoles all over England to be cut down and playhouses to be destroyed.

An Austrian police administration, again, had the closest watch kept upon all persons who had aroused the distrust of the higher powers by their inclination toward philanthropy, for this, in the view of the Head of the Police at the time, was calculated only "to shake to its foundations the Christian religion."

While the French Revolution was putting an end to the intolerance and cruelty of persecution as practised by absolute authority in Church and State, it was at the same time spying upon, imprisoning, and guillotining all citizens who perchance were unwilling to believe in the ideas of the rights of man—liberty, equality, fraternity.

More than once, from such facts as these, thinkers have drawn the conclusion that cruelty constitutes a feature inherent in human nature. Just a short time ago Professor Siegmund Freud, on the strength of his profound knowledge of psycho-analysis and of the psychology of nations, expressed his conviction that cruelty, being one of the most powerful psychic impulses, has incontrovertibly taken a very large share in the creation of forms of social arrangements generally. In Freud's view man is not "a gentle being in need of love"; rather is he a being for whom his neighbour is always "a temptation to satisfy his aggressiveness upon him, to cause him pain, to torture

him, and to kill him." Whatever new paths may be taken by
civilization in its development, we shall have to expect, according to Freud, that cruelty—that "indestructible trait in human
nature"—will follow it everywhere.

But nowhere does this scientific deliverance find such direct
and striking confirmation as in the institutions of the Russian
State. Not that the propensity to cruelty has completely vanished from other lands; but in the West civilization—that
heroic struggle of the beast to reach the stature of man—has
already so far obliterated the savage traits that it requires the
keen eye of an expert still to be able to discern, in the sub-
limated forms of government and social institutions, the passion for torturing others and the thirst for blood.

In Russia, on the other hand, cruelty has preserved, right
into the twentieth century, its primitive and unadulterated
type. Maxim Gorky, one who possesses the most intimate understanding of his own people, is of opinion that the Russian
is by no means the good-natured, truly humble, and Christian
man that nineteenth-century literature was so fond of representing him to be; on the contrary, cruelty is just as much "the
most prominent feature of the Russian national character" as
humour is of the English character. "To whatever party Russians may belong, in their cruelty they are all alike."

Since the beginning of the eighteenth century the Muscovite
Empire has indeed made eager attempts to share in the achievements of the West. Peter the Great himself aimed at trans-
planting into his own land all the institutions he found in
European civilization; but what especially struck a chord of
sympathy in his Russian heart was the method of executing
criminals by breaking on the wheel, which he came across for
the first time in Königsberg and straightway introduced at
home.

When a few years later it was already beginning to be good

form for Governments to abolish the death penalty, the Empress Elizabeth, not wishing to be behindhand, declared that in future she would not have anyone executed. However, for this concession to foreign taste her Russian nature immediately found compensation in such an excessive use of the knout as must certainly have had the same deadly effect.

Catherine II was certainly among the few crowned heads of Europe who acknowledged the 'rights of man' and the doctrines of the age of 'enlightenment.' When Cesare Beccaria published his famous denunciation of secret judicial procedure, torture, and tyranny, Catherine had him invited to her Court and offered him an important office in her *entourage*. Even though it had required the murder of her husband to enable her to ascend the throne, and the exile and imprisonment of countless victims to keep her there, it cannot be denied that this Empress did show a certain sincere aspiration after humanity. This was perhaps all the easier for her, because she had not one drop of Russian blood in her veins.

Occasional moments of enlightened humanity are to be noted in later Tsars too. But in comparison with the seriousness and consistency with which they have always employed the most despotic means to maintain their authority, such humane decrees really look more like fleeting whims, excursions into a spiritual land in which these Russian rulers are not at home. In like manner Russian history has always been marked by compensation for any excess of humanity: Catherine was followed by the demented Paul, and Alexander I by the tyrant Nicholas I.

This Nicholas achieved the most truly Russian creation by endowing cruelty with definite form, with permanent machinery set up by the State and most exact in its working. In his reign arose the Corps of Gendarmerie, that mighty organization for the secret supervision of the whole Empire, in fear of which not only private citizens but all other Government departments trembled. The same Tsar also brought into being the now famous "Third Section" of his Court Chancery. All police matters were concentrated in that Third Section, the chiefs of which were in a position to decide at their own discretion the fate of every Russian subject.

Thenceforth any Russian might have the experience of receiving a call from a policeman and an intimation to set off within three hours for Archangel or Simbrisk. Such a decree issued by the Third Section admitted of no protest, no defence, and no appeal.

Then, in the eighties of the nineteenth century, under the influence of Liberal ideas, the Third Section was suppressed; but immediately its place was taken by the Ochrana, the rights and duties of which were only in name, but not in reality, less than those of its predecessor.

Nor was any change made in the use of the dreaded Trubyetskoy Bastion in the Fortress of Peter and Paul, the State prison in which, from the days of the Dekabrist [1] revolt, the actual or supposed ringleaders of revolutionary movements were kept in strict custody behind iron-bound doors, guarded by gaolers, double sentries with fixed bayonets, and gendarmes in their much-feared blue uniform. There were detained in cells, separated from each other by walls a yard thick, human beings who often, even after the lapse of years, had not been brought to trial, because the Government did not know what charge to bring against them.

Nor was there any change in the *katorga*—hard labour in Siberia—a punishment which had to be endured by the exiles with fetters on hands and feet. Right into the twentieth cen-

---

[1] This reference is to a military conspiracy that broke out in December 1825, at the very beginning of Nicholas I's reign.—TRANSLATOR.

tury prisoners' hands were shackled to the carts used for the transport of ore in the mines.

All that, although Alexander II soon after his ascension had made serious attempts to introduce into Russia modern forms of Western judicial procedure. At first, with admirable zeal for reform, he had published an edict that actually required legal proceedings to be held in public, substituted the oral method of conducting a case for the old system of working with documents only, and, for graver criminal offences, even called into existence trial by jury. But Alexander II would not have been a true Russian tsar if he had not very quickly added to these foreign institutions a national note.

Thus from the very start political offences were withdrawn from the jury courts, while publicity in such cases became very soon restricted, the courts being empowered "to close the doors." For ordinary crime the death penalty had indeed been abolished, but to make sure that revolutionaries should not happen to share in that benefit, the Government declared the greater part of the Empire to be permanently in an abnormal state,[1] thereby conferring upon governors of provinces the legal right to deal with all political crime by court-martial, which might at its discretion pronounce sentence of death.

Whenever, therefore, the Russian State brought itself to renounce some traditional form of barbarity, it immediately created new institutions in which the aggressive instincts of the Russian character could still find their expression.

If we have any confidence in psycho-analytic inquiry, and if we see in human sense of justice a system of psychic inhibitions set up against the brutal aggressive instincts that are innate in man, we shall not be astonished to note that Russian society, which has only rarely submitted to such inhibitions, has accordingly a defective appreciation of law.

[1] Practically equivalent to declaring it to be under martial law.—TRANSLATOR.

B. Kistyakovsky, the famous Russian jurist, refers expressly to the lack in the Russian people of any clear perception of the ideal of a person with legal rights, and draws the inference that the Russian, of whatever class he may be, does not in his heart respect the law and continually tries to break it, if he may do so with impunity. Even the *intelligentsia* (the educated classes), he says, have never fully realized the ideas of fundamental rights or of the constitutional state, and thus, in all the literature of jurisprudence in Russia, there is not one work that has championed any courageous thought in the realm of law. "Our public consciousness," he writes, "has never allowed the ideal of the person with legal rights to emerge."

Did not even Russian Socialism, first represented by Plechanov, proclaim from the very beginning the idea of despotism, and strive to introduce among its adherents a system of compulsion and oppression that corresponded exactly to that of government by the State Police? Within the revolutionary societies of Russia in this twentieth century there was continual talk of the "state of siege," and "special legislation to deal with waverers," while isolated protests like Martov's passed almost unnoticed. That is, even to those men who fought for *liberty* against autocracy in the state, the idea that the individual has an inalienable right to liberty in his own convictions and actions was absolutely strange and incomprehensible.

And, of course, the Russian system of illegality and violence can also appeal to a 'sublime idea.' With the Inquisition, the Council of Ten in Venice, the Holy Brotherhood in Spain, and the Committee of Public Safety in the time of the Terror, the Ochrana has likewise this feature in common, that it attempts to surround its informers with a halo and the place of execution with the odour of sanctity; it was "for the well-being of

Holy Mother Russia" that the Russian subject was kept under observation, persecuted, imprisoned, tortured, and executed by the Police.

This volume of the memoirs of the last Tsarist Chief of Police, A. T. Vassilyev, is accordingly permeated with the belief in the high calling of the Ochrana and its officials. That the author of the book was honestly convinced of the moral justification of the Russian Secret Police and its methods admits of no doubt whatever, for reliable witnesses vouch for Vassilyev's personal uprightness, and his private correspondence warrants the conclusion that his opinions were sincere. While many another ex-official of the Tsarist Police, not so scrupulous as he, entered the service of the new rulers brought into power by the Revolution, Vassilyev steadfastly declined such offers, which were made to him several times over, and preferred to spend the last years of his life in exile and in the severest privation. He was absolutely penniless when he died, on December 31, 1928, in the hospital of Houdon, having previously found refuge in his dire distress in a home for Russian refugees maintained by a philanthropic English lady in Sainte-Geneviève-des-Bois.

But to-day we know with equal certainty that almost all, and particularly the most pitiless, inquisitors of the Middle Ages were personally of sterling character, models of virtue in their life and conduct, and staunch believers in their own principles, and that, when they sentenced their fellow-men to be tortured, they did so in the assured faith that they were accomplishing a sublime mission.

And if Vassilyev, in his defence, seeks to prove that the Ochrana assisted the weak, and that the honest citizen never had any reason to fear it, we can find parallels for that too. Has not the Inquisition had its advocates, who can show how this institution was founded only to protect the weak and how much more humane and just it was than the practice previously in vogue of the right of the strongest, or of ordeal by battle or fire? Nor can it be denied that the great majority of the members of the French Revolutionary tribunals were genuinely convinced of the justice of their decisions and of the usefulness of their activities in advancing the public weal.

However, in face of such attempts at justification we shall never be able to command more than *historical* understanding, and, despite all the arguments advanced by Vassilyev, the operation of the Ochrana will always appear to us as a very low stage in the administration of law, as a relic of medieval times that, amid the civilization of the twentieth century, produces the disquieting effect of a foreign body.

It has to be admitted, of course, that a Secret Police service of the kind rendered by the Ochrana has, as a matter of fact, existed right down to the present day in all the other countries in the world. Nearly everywhere Figaro's saying still holds, "that the State keeps spies and pays traitors, ever concerned to palliate the pitifulness of the means by the importance of the end." As long as the democratic identification of the will of the State with the will of the people remains a fiction there will be secret societies and conspirators, and consequently also secret agents of the State employed to keep them in check.

But while everywhere else the powers of the Political Police had long since been limited to keeping suspects under observation, the Ochrana, of its own authority and under the thinnest of veils, took upon itself the punishment of accused persons by *administrative process*, thus preserving in judicial proceedings that secrecy which elsewhere had long been banished except from the actual supervision service.

In his *History of Russia* Michael Pokrovsky describes with sharp and telling irony the abuse that marked the practice of this secrecy in Tsarist Russia.

The proceedings of the court were strictly secret. Not only did they take place behind closed doors, but in the hall of justice there was neither defending counsel nor accused present. Only documentary evidence was placed before the judges, and on the strength of that the sentence was pronounced. Not judicial proceedings only were secret; the whole organization of the state was secret. All sittings of the higher authorities were held *in camera*; the most important ones were especially secret. Almost every official paper was marked "secret"; in the Foreign Office there were no documents at all that were not secret. If they wanted to indicate that something was really to be kept secret, it was marked "very secret," because the word "secret" by itself had lost all meaning.

In contrast, reflect that it was as far back as the beginning of the thirteenth century that England had won its Magna Charta, the provisions of which represented a far-reaching defence of personal liberty against undue interference on the part of police or autocracy, for does it not state that no freeman may be arrested, outlawed, exiled, or injured without legal sentence, pronounced in accordance with the law of the land? And even though this protection at first extended only to the classes of freemen, the signing of Magna Charta by King John was nevertheless a step of vital importance, for from that time onward the English people were unwearied in their efforts to extend these fundamental rights and to ensure the liberty and inviolability of the person by ever new guarantees. Whenever after that any attempt was made to tamper with those chartered liberties, the whole country reacted with such energy that the final outcome was never limitation, but rather some extension of those fundamental rights.

When Charles I ventured to betray absolutist leanings he was very soon obliged to accept the Petition of Right, recognizing that no one could be imprisoned without the legal forms being observed, or be condemned by any but the regular courts. On a similar occasion, when complaint was again being made of arbitrary imprisonment, Charles II had to sign the Habeas Corpus Act, according to the terms of which every prisoner must, within twenty-four hours, be brought before the appropriate magistrate, whose duty it is to decide freely as to the legality of the arrest.

These principles, which the English people in its struggle with autocracy had successfully affirmed, were cast into systematic legal form by English philosophy as far back as the seventeenth century. That was the famous doctrine of the rights of man, soon after to be adopted by the French Encyclopædists, who made it the basis of their whole political theory of the State. Locke, for instance, laid it down as a principle that the legislative and the executive powers must never be united in the same hand; and Montesquieu in his *L'Esprit des lois* sought to develop and to justify that teaching.

It must be admitted that, although the French Revolution set out to make the philosophic idea of human rights the basis of a new and better society, it certainly did not manage to dispense with the executioner. However, it did take a significant forward step, for, however barbarous their sentences may have been, the Revolutionary tribunals pronounced them after going through a form of public procedure. And it was the Revolution that, for the first time, expressly laid a constitutional foundation for the separation of the powers of the State— legislative, executive, and judicial.

By thus depriving cruelty of the right to secret activity, the breath was, so to speak, knocked out of it. In contrast to the vast pretensions of the Revolution, the publicity of judicial proceedings was certainly a very tiny achievement, but whoever has realized how very slowly the progress of civilization goes on will not underestimate even this little step. Since the French Revolution no civilized people has for any length of time tolerated the persistence of the secret and arbitrary administration of justice, and all attempts directed to that end have infallibly been broken on the indignant resistance of the nations.

More and more it has become an accepted principle that, apart from the legally determined relations between the State and its citizens, there is no power that can confer upon a Government the right to interfere with the liberty of the individual.

Untouched by this development, however, the Russian Ochrana, even in the twentieth century, clung to the system of arbitrary violence and the use of secret administrative penalties, and consequently the concessions made by it to European conceptions of freedom and justice remained, right down to the end, only apparent.

Even if all the assertions made by the Revolutionary and Liberal Press about the tyranny of the Ochrana were, to begin with, to be brushed aside as distorted and biased, it still admits of no doubt that the Russian police system, by its mere infliction of the sentence of "administrative banishment" without public trial, forfeited the right to repudiate the charge of being a detestable and reactionary institution.

But, further, many of the accusations made by parties hostile to the Government do bear the strictest examination. It is quite certain that the Ochrana adopted practices utterly irreconcilable with European ideas of freedom and law. It has been proved that in the Ochrana offices in Riga in the years 1905 and 1906 a great many persons suspected of revolutionary tendencies were tortured in the most barbarous fashion, with the knout, with pincers, with clubs, and with leather belts. Similar incidents occurred in Mohilyev, Smolyensk, and Yekaterinburg.

And the corporal punishment and the fettering of convicts were still permissible according to law even in the twentieth century. In the *Petersburg Weekly Medical Journal* the Russian physician Dr. Lobas reports:

Flogging with the knout is not the only dreaded chastisement in the prisons of Siberia; ordinary beating with rods is quite as harmful in its effects. That even people suffering from serious illness do not escape this infliction is unfortunately nothing but the naked truth. In the district of Korsakov a pregnant woman was beaten for so long that she died.

A. T. Vassilyev, it is true, endeavours in part to dispute such facts, in part to present them in a favourable light. According to his exposition of the matter, the Ochrana was an extremely humane institution within which deeds of cruelty and arbitrary acts never occurred. In his view the only admissible system in Russia was the Tsardom, and he was convinced with all his soul that, for the maintenance of that system, the Ochrana was indispensable, his only regret being that the Police did not proceed with such strictness as would have prevented the accursed Revolution. According to him, the use of the administrative banishment to Siberia was the kindliest form of self-protection that could be adopted by the State. The secret censorship of letters in the Black Cabinets of the Ochrana, whose existence is frankly admitted, he regards as being absolutely necessary in the interest of the common weal. And cases of infringement of the law and other irregularities brought home to individual Police officials do not affect the excellence of the system itself.

If such a presentation is frequently in contradiction of facts that have been proved, it is obvious that we must settle the conflict in favour of the facts. But even in cases where it is a matter of assertion against assertion we shall often be obliged to refuse credence to Vassilyev's statements. For, even though we do not desire to cast any doubt upon the honesty of this authority, we hear the evidence adduced on the other side by men like Alexander Herzen and Prince Krapotkin, who may lay at least equal claim to our confidence. And to believe these witnesses does not mean that we are charging Vassilyev with deliberate untruthfulness; it is enough if we ascribe to Herzen or Krapotkin a greater gift of observation, keener powers of discrimination. We read, for instance, in Vassilyev the touching anecdote of Tsar Nicholas I and Count Benkendorff. The Tsar, having just created the infamous Special Corps of Gendarmerie, hands to Benkendorff, the first Commander of the Corps, a white handkerchief with which to dry the tears of the unfortunate! The portrait of that same Count Benkendorff painted by Alexander Herzen will seem to us to carry much more conviction:

> I am disposed to believe, whenever I remember the insignificant expression of his face, that Benkendorff did not do as much harm as he might have done in his all-powerful situation; but neither did he do much good. He had neither the energy, nor the will, nor the heart for that. How many innocent victims passed through Benkendorff's hands, how many were ruined by his mere inattention and forgetfulness! To omit to say a word in defence of the oppressed is in itself a crime, especially with such a cold and merciless being as Nicholas I.

And how little do Vassilyev's statements agree with the testimony of Prince Krapotkin in his account of the doings of the Russian Political Police in the days of Tsar Alexander II, "the Liberator."

> The colonels of Gendarmerie had thousands of homes searched, without in any way troubling about law or justice. They made arrests as they chose, kept people as long as it pleased them in prison, and, by their own arbitrary decision or that of their superiors, exiled them in hundreds to North-East Russia or to Siberia.

Although, as has thus been shown, we cannot in every point implicitly trust the memoirs of Vassilyev, the Chief of the Police, his book provides nevertheless a very important contribution to our knowledge of the Ochrana, that system about whose working the public has till now heard little more than vague rumours and biased accusations.

The author's objective evidence concerning the organization of the Secret Service, the technique of espionage, the methods of working adopted by the "External" and the "Internal Agency," the practice of the "Black Cabinets," the action of the Police authorities during the World War, and finally the descriptions of his own experiences after the Revolution are undoubtedly of high interest and value.

But, quite apart from all that, what makes the publication of this book particularly important is our conviction that, in the investigation of the historical truth with regard to the Ochrana, nothing can be more essential than to be able to penetrate the spirit that animated its officials. The knowledge that we acquire in this way of the Ochrana is not merely information about an institution that belongs to the past. On the contrary, it puts us in a position to gain for the first time some proper understanding of Russian polity in general, and consequently also of Russia as it is to-day. For, even though the great Revolution may have destroyed all earlier forms in State and society, it has preserved unchanged the most characteristic feature in Russian methods of government—cruelty.

In the Museum of the Revolution, in Moscow, the visitor will find a room draped with black in which the Bolshevik rulers have collected relics of the Reign of Terror under the Tsars. There is arranged an exhibition of the most refined instruments of torture, of the most varied implements used for flogging, of fetters for hands and feet, of tools employed to prise open the nostrils of delinquents, of others to tear out finger- and toe-nails, of leaded clubs, of whips with lashes studded with screws.

The sight of this chamber of horrors cannot but call forth indignation and disgust at the methods adopted by Tsarist jurisprudence, and very few visitors will be able to avoid the conviction that a system which still made use of such instruments of torture in the twentieth century must be accused of

barbarous medievalism, and that therefore it was high time
that the Tsardom should come to an end.

But if we leave the Museum of the Past to look with open
eyes upon the Russian present, we shall be convinced by all we
see around us that the accursed past is still far from having
come to an end. In place of the old Tsarist fetters arranged
museum-wise, we hear the new fetters of the Bolsheviks clank-
ing, and if some day the rule of the Soviets should be replaced
by another system, the leaders of this new counter-revolution
will have no difficulty on their part in bringing together a
Museum of the Past with another Chamber of Horrors, the
contemplation of which will leave the visitor equally convinced
that the fall of the Communist dictatorship had been a necessity, if civilization were to stand.

The publication of this book should at once help to prepare
the way for recognition of that truth. For not until we have
quite familiarized ourselves with the truly medieval spirit of
the Tsarist Ochrana shall we become fully aware of the genetic
relationship existing between Ochrana and Tsheka or G.P.U.,
between Reactionary and Revolutionary tyranny. That perception will then keep us from being so misguided as to fall into
the snare of Bolshevik propaganda.

Bolshevism likes to appeal to the French Revolution, claim-
ing to have entered upon its inheritance. In the party debates
in Moscow members of the Government and of the Opposition are in the way of assigning to each other, as if they were
engaged in amateur theatricals, the *rôles* of Danton, Robes-
pierre, Saint-Just, and Marat. But even if the Moscow Reign
of Terror does in many respects resemble that of Paris, Bolshevism has not brought Russia one step nearer the rights of
liberty that France bought by shedding those torrents of blood.

The Soviet system has realized neither the principle of the
separation of the powers of government nor that of public

trial, and consequently cannot claim to be regarded as the heir of the First Republic. If we are to seek for prototypes of Russian modes of government, be they Tsarist or Revolutionary, we shall not find them in eighteenth-century France, but in the Spain and Italy of the Middle Ages.

Venice in the fourteenth century was ruled by an institution, the principles and forms of which recall the Tsheka to an astonishing degree. Did not the Council of Ten meet every evening to receive denunciations, to hear the reports of its spies, and to sit in swift judgment behind closed doors upon persons it had itself caused to be arrested? And just as the G.P.U. does, the Council of Ten kept under observation the whole population and the Government itself. Under its official purview came not merely conspiracies aiming at treason to the State, but criminal affairs, the policing of theatres, the control of masked balls and of churches. Even with the foreign policy of the Republic the Council of Ten interfered, by corresponding independently with the Venetian Ambassadors and by continually receiving from its agents confidential reports upon things done or left undone by Venetians abroad.

In his study of the Tsheka Vassilyev shows quite correctly that historically it arose immediately from the Ochrana. That is, the Secret Police of the Soviet *régime* constitutes in every respect a continuation of that last relic of medieval despotism; and this is a fact that, at the present moment if ever, needs to be recognized, for in Western Europe many a would-be Progressive, knowing nothing of Russian conditions or of their history, is ready to hail Bolshevism as a gospel of salvation containing promise of a freer and better future for mankind.

RENÉ FÜLÖP-MILLER

Vienna

THE OCHRANA
THE RUSSIAN SECRET POLICE

AUTHOR'S INTRODUCTION

THE 2nd of August, 1914, is a notable date in the history of Tsarist Russia. On the eve of that fateful day Count Pourtales, the German Ambassador, himself shaken with the deepest emotion and with tears in his eyes, had reluctantly handed to Sazonov, our Foreign Minister, the declaration of war. Thereupon, at two o'clock, a solemn religious service was held in the Winter Palace. The public proclamation of the state of war was made at that service.

A storm of patriotic enthusiasm swept over the whole population. All Petersburg was afoot, and from early morning long processions of men were seen marching through the streets. It was the various patriotic organizations, carrying pictures of the Emperor and national flags, making their way in countless ranks to the Kazan Cathedral, to gather on the vast square that extends in front of that noble pile with its spacious pillared interior. The Metropolitan delivered a solemn sermon that profoundly stirred his enraptured hearers, and after the service was over the crowd moved off, as though by word of command, to the Winter Palace, in order to salute the Emperor.

I was myself in the midst of the frenzied throng on that memorable day and allowed myself to be carried along to the Winter Palace. Wherever I looked I saw nothing but joyous resolve expressed in the faces around me; all seemed to share the feelings that were dominant within myself during those hours.

The immense host of the assembled people waited patiently till the service in the palace was over and the Emperor appeared to address them. The doors were flung open, the Tsar stepped out on to the balcony, and in the same instant the tens of thousands in the open space fell upon their knees. Along with Nicholas II the Empress also showed herself to the crowd. She appeared to be deeply affected, for she was covering her face with her hands and the convulsive movement of her shoulders suggested that she was weeping.

The Sovereigns were hailed with thunderous exultation. The Emperor bowed low in every direction in acknowledgment of the ovation thus expressed by the whole population of Petersburg.

How far away all that seems from the present, with its sordid and humiliating vulgarity! The memory of that day is both beautiful and painful for us who have been driven from the homeland we faithfully served and are obliged to live abroad as refugees, powerless to do more than keep alive our faith and hope that, to our poor Russia, happier days will return.

CHAPTER I

Functions of the Ochrana—The External Agency—Qualities required of Police Spies—Technique of Observation—Myednikov's School—His Special Section—Suppression of a Bomb Factory

MUCH that was mysterious, enigmatical, and dreadful was associated in the mind of the Russian people with the term Police Department. For great sections of the population this office signified frankly a phantom of terror, of which the most improbable tales were told. Many people seriously believed that in the Police Department the unhappy victims of the Ochrana [1] were dropped through a hole in the floor into the cellar, and there tortured.

Of course there was not the slightest foundation for such legends. The Police Department never perpetrated the bestial cruelties fantastically ascribed to it. On the contrary, its measures were always strictly legal. Nevertheless, this authority was really of terrifying import to certain people; but, of course, these were not the peaceful population. They were those adversaries of the Empire who, being not yet very numerous, were only tentatively but surely aiming at the diffusion in Russia of the poisonous gospel of Socialism.

It is to be ascribed to the propaganda of these scoundrels that the Secret Political Police acquired such an evil reputation, for the revolutionaries naturally did their utmost to bring discredit upon their bitterest enemy in order to hamper as far as possible its effective activity. They had once contrived to smuggle one of their agents, an individual named Voiloshnikov, into the Third Section of the Police Department, and consequently to bring about much confusion. Appropriate

[1] In the transliteration of the Russian names *ch* represents the sound of *ch* in *loch* and *tsk* the sound of *ch* in church.—TRANSLATOR.

37

measures were taken to prevent such things occurring again; and the revolutionaries, in their impotent rage, thereafter made it their business to accuse us persistently and at every opportunity of cruelty and illegality in our procedure.

However, I personally, and many of my predecessors, can most emphatically declare that these accusations were absolutely groundless. The correctness with which the Ochrana did its work is also vouched for by the testimony of that distinguished Public Prosecutor and model of uprightness, Muravyov, who after the Revolution acted as President of the Special Commission which investigated closely the conduct of the Tsarist authorities.

It would take too long if I were to set about tracing here the development of the Ochrana. I therefore confine myself to the statement that the first beginnings of a Political Police were made in the reign of Peter the Great. It was at that time that the Chancellor Biron set up a secret political office, whose functions in certain respects coincided with those undertaken afterward by the Ochrana. During the nineteenth century there finally arose the Third Section, since become so well known, from which the Special Corps of Gendarmerie and the Ochrana originated.

In the last decades of the nineteenth century the principal task of the Ochrana was to keep a check upon revolutionaries among the lower classes, and especially among the students, who had turned in large numbers to ideals subversive of the State. Later it was the active propaganda of the Socialists that assumed prominence, and with them were associated the followers of Tolstoi's Communistic teachings. The growth of revolutionary tendencies in the Empire obliged the authorities to increase the efficiency of the Ochrana and, for that purpose, to strengthen more and more its machinery.

The duties of the Secret Police were very exactly defined.

CHIEF OFFICIALS OF THE ST. PETERSBURG OCHRANA

They consisted in the investigation of all movements directed against the State, and in their destruction. Further, the Ochrana had also upon occasion to concern itself with various other crimes, such as murder and robbery, and, in time of war, with matters of espionage. In all its operations it was a question of police action pure and simple: the Ochrana's job was to discover the evil-doers. Their punishment was not its concern, but that of the judicial authorities.

Accordingly all investigations had to be handed over sooner or later to the Public Prosecutor. And the Ochrana had only the right to keep suspects under arrest for not more than two consecutive weeks. After the lapse of that period the prisoner had either to be released or to be transferred to the category of those undergoing regular imprisonment on remand. Attached to each Ochrana section were several public prosecutors, who followed the course of the inquiries and answered for the legality of all measures taken.

There was only one form of extra-judicial punishment, and that was *administrative banishment*; sentences of up to five years could be pronounced. This measure was, it must be admitted, frequently but leniently applied; and latterly exiles were allowed, if they desired, to go abroad instead of going to Siberia. If they took advantage of that option they were never permitted to return.

It is perfectly ridiculous to assert that the Ochrana ever, of its own authority, had a political prisoner executed. Without exception it was only the regular tribunals that could pronounce the death sentence, and this was nearly always in connexion with the crime of murder; the Ochrana had nothing at all to do with such sentences. Only in those districts where military law had been proclaimed could executions be carried out—as they are all over the world—without a regular judicial sentence, and by the order of the military officer commanding.

Thus the Governor-General of Warsaw once condemned a group of Anarchists to death; they had carried out a series of sanguinary crimes.

The supreme control of all investigations of a criminal or political nature was centred in the Police Department of the Home Office. This was organized in numerous sections, of which the Records Section was specially important. There were kept exact data with regard to all persons who had ever come under the observation of the Criminal or Political Police. Thus the authorities had at their disposal very carefully compiled archives containing not merely photographs, records of finger-prints and anthropometric details, but also the nicknames and *aliases* used by the conspirators among themselves.

The Chief of the Police Department occupied an extraordi-narily responsible post; and, considering the political im-portance of this office, the appointment of the Chief of Police for the time being was reserved for the Home Secretary (Min-ister of the Interior). Whenever this Minister retired, the Chief of Police relinquished his post at the same time, so that the new Minister might appoint a man in the enjoyment of his personal confidence.

The machinery of the Political Police embraced the centres stationed all over the Empire of the so-called Special Corps of Gendarmerie and the actual Ochrana, which functioned only in the larger localities. As a rule, Ochrana sections were brought into being in those towns in which the revolutionary parties had set up their committees. The Ochrana offices had at their disposal their special Records Sections and their own libraries containing all revolutionary and other prohibited printed works. For it is to be noted that all the higher officials of the Ochrana had always to be well acquainted with revolutionary literature, and to have completely at their command the history of all subversive movements.

Moreover, the Ochrana had at its disposal a staff of trained specialists; it had its photographers, its handwriting experts, and in many districts even its own Jewish specialists competent in all matters of Jewish faith, who supplied the Ochrana with many a valuable hint.

Suspected persons might be kept under observation by two fundamentally different methods, which were for the most part applied so as to supplement each other as far as possible. These were, on the one hand, the so-called system of External Observation, and, on the other, the Internal or Secret Agency.

The former consisted in the observation of all suspects by police spies or informers, who were officially designated Agents of the External Service. These agents formed special detachments under the command of officials trained expressly for this service. Their duties were to keep an eye upon suspicious characters in the streets, theatres, hotels, railway trains, and similar places of public resort, and to endeavour to discover all possible details concerning the mode of life of such persons and the company frequented by them.

The service of these informers was exceptionally exhausting and perilous. Only such men were adapted for it as were endowed with a considerable measure of staying power and of quick perceptive faculties, for the revolutionaries knew, of course, of the existence of the secret agents, and sought to baffle and mislead them by every conceivable trick. Frequently informers, recognized as such by the Terrorists, were murdered while they were performing their duty.

An official agent in the course of years acquired quite a peculiar capacity: once he had made a careful study of a photograph the features of the original were so impressed upon his memory that he never forgot them, and any person whom he had once seen would be infallibly identified by him among hundreds of others.

Of course, the secret agents generally assumed some sort of disguise: they served as porters, door-keepers, caretakers, newspaper-sellers, soldiers, officers, or railway officials. It was a special art to wear these disguises so that they might not be noticed. And the Ochrana kept for such purposes a regular store of its own, with clothing and uniforms of every kind, just as it maintained a permanent supply of horses and vehicles. In the headquarters of the Moscow Ochrana there was a special court for the numerous agents disguised as cab-drivers, where they were continually passing in and out.

The public has, generally speaking, entertained exaggerated ideas of the number of spies in Tsarist Russia. It was widely assumed that every town of any size was flooded with hundreds of secret agents, and that in St. Petersburg there were thousands. In reality the whole body of secret agents under the command of the Ochrana all over Russia did not number many more than a thousand men, and in St. Petersburg there were only about a hundred of them altogether. The Foreign Agency, the efficiency of which was so much talked of in revolutionary circles, had to carry on its operations with a very small personnel. Only when it was a question of observing perhaps a Socialist congress or a conspiracy abroad were a few agents occasionally sent out from the Ochrana in St. Petersburg and Moscow to strengthen the service in Western Europe.

The duties of the External Agency and the means to be employed in all cases by the agents are shown in detail in the orders of the Police Department. These orders were for a time kept strictly secret, but in spite of all precautions they came finally to the knowledge of the revolutionaries. This circumstance alone makes it permissible for me, in what I shall have to say in the following pages, to refer to these instructions, which provide in any case the most appropriate means of giving the reader authentic information as to the operation of the Ochrana.

The Police Department lays it down as a necessary preliminary to any successful piece of work that the agents should, above all, be able to impress firmly upon their memory the features of the individuals to be kept under observation. The spy is expressly recommended to take advantage of every opportunity of practising and developing this important faculty, and to cultivate the habit of calling back to mind, with his eyes closed, the characteristic features of any person, after having taken one brief glance at him. Along with the face, they were to observe accurately stature and build, gait, colour of the hair, and carriage of the shoulders.

All points noted were to be entered in the report book, and this was to be submitted every week to the head of the section to which the spy was attached. Special record folios, with red, green, and white leaves, afforded the chief official of the detective service added facilities in overlooking the materials that were continually coming in.

Every month the chiefs of the Ochrana sections drew up the lists of persons who were being watched, all known details about them being stated, as well as the reasons for keeping them under observation.

Written and telegraphic communications between spies and their superiors were never to be conducted in ordinary language, but chiefly in the jargon of business correspondence. If, for example, an agent wanted to report that the man he was tracking had gone to Tula, the telegram would run: "Goods required arrived Tula."

As for the personal qualities to be possessed by the agents, the instructions to which I have before alluded require all agents of the detective service to be politically and morally reliable, honest, sober, bold, adroit, intelligent, patient, prudent, upright, obedient, and of good health. Individuals of Polish or Hebrew descent were, on principle, excluded from any kind of employment in the External Service. All newly appointed agents were to have it explained to them how very important their office was for the security of the State, and then to be sworn in in the presence of a priest.

The first business of the new recruit was to make himself thoroughly acquainted with the town in which he was to be stationed, especially with drinking saloons, beer-gardens, taverns, and houses with an access to two or more streets. Then he must know all about droshkies and motors, their stances and their fares; the hours of arrival and departure of the main long-distance trains; times for beginning and stopping work in the various factories and workshops. He must memorize the uniforms of the various military units, of schoolboys and students. During his period of training he had, to begin with at least, to hand in daily a report in writing, showing his progress in those branches of knowledge. On these reports depended the decision whether he had, or had not, any aptitude for service in the Police.

Not till then was he entrusted with the execution of some actual observation work, and, to start with, even that only under the guidance of some older and more experienced official, whose duty it was to point out his faults. At the same time his political reliability was tested by other agents, who engaged him in conversation and sought to gain his confidence.

Nor was the private life of the secret agent a matter of indifference. He might indeed be a married man, but it was always regarded as rather an unfavourable circumstance if he showed any excessive devotion to his family. For dangerous and responsible commissions such men were just as ill-suited as those fellows who were inclined to form intimate associations with women of easy manners and with other doubtful acquaintances.

Of course, it was firmly impressed upon every agent entering the Service that whatever he got to know during the course of his duties was to be regarded as strictly official and secret, and must never be betrayed to anyone.

For certain reasons it had appeared expedient to indicate persons under observation not by their real names, but by certain nicknames. Whenever an agent was brought by his work into contact with a suspected person he had to give him at once some such nickname, which thereafter would always be employed to designate the individual in question. This nickname was to be short and characteristic, suggested, if possible, by some striking peculiarity in the exterior of the suspect.

If anyone were to be kept under observation for a fairly long period, the agents whom this concerned were to be frequently changed, so that the individual being spied upon might not thus become accustomed to seeing one particular face. By this means, too, the result was achieved of allowing all the agents to become acquainted with all persons under observation, which often proved very useful. Of course, every agent had to do his utmost not to be seen at all by the person he was watching, or, at least, to be seen only for a brief moment and from a distance. That demanded a peculiar technique by no means easy to acquire.

In pursuing a man in the streets exact knowledge of all houses with more than one entrance would often enable a smart agent to elude the notice of the person followed, to hurry on ahead of him by side-streets, and so to avoid producing that disquieting effect which often arises when a man feels that someone is dogging his every step. As far as possible a direct meeting with the suspect was to be avoided, and if it was quite unavoidable, the agent must never allow his eyes to be seen, as it was by them that he would have been most easily recognized.

If the person being watched showed by frequently turning round and hurrying his steps that he felt that he was being followed, it would sometimes be discreet to desist altogether from the pursuit; for it was nearly always of the highest importance that the shadowing should be so carried out that the object of it would be unaware that he was being shadowed. It was the agent's duty to make a very careful mental note of the route taken by the suspect and to enter the particulars in his notebook, indicating when he left home, the names of the streets he passed along, what buildings he entered, and how long he remained inside.

It demanded very great ingenuity to determine not merely the block or tenement, but the flat and exact door into which the quarry had gone. For this purpose it was of great advantage if the spy could stay up in the top storey and remain in hiding there, say, in the attic stairs, waiting till the man should take his departure. From the sound of the footsteps it would then be possible to judge which door had been used and so to determine the apartment visited. It was expedient that inquiries of that kind should be made by the agent in the uniform of a porter or postman, so that his presence in a strange building should excite the least possible comment. Sometimes it would be quite sufficient to lay aside quickly hat and coat, and to behave on the staircase just as if he were one of the tenants, who had just come out for a minute into the passage.

Many a time the uniform of a cab-driver proved of invaluable service to the spy; but, of course, it was imperative that the agent putting it on should really be able to handle horses and to drive properly, with due regard to all police regulations. He would have to possess a perfect mastery of the droshky-

A Bomb Factory Discovered by the Ochrana in Kuokala, in Finland

After the Explosion of a Bomb in the Armenian Bazaar in Tiflis

man's mode of speech, and to converse with other drivers on the ranks without giving himself away. In dealing with house-porters, the agent disguised as a cabman must always be ready to give some plausible explanation of his stopping at this or that house; in fact, he required to be an expert in the invention of such tales. Especially in the service of the Moscow Ochrana there were men who were simply past-masters in that line. When one of these assumed the *rôle* of cab-driver he was absolutely indistinguishable from his professional brethren: he spoke their jargon fluently, was a first-rate hand with horses, and was never the least bit embarrassed when he had to treat a revolutionary as a passenger and spend a few minutes with him haggling over the fare.

Generally, agents in the disguise of cab-drivers were not employed alone. More frequently they were in company with several other spies, who played the part of fares. If the person under observation was known to be in a certain building, the cab would usually stop at the door of a neighbouring public-house. The other agents would go and sit down in the inn, while the coachman on his box kept watch till the wanted man appeared again. The least sign of the hand sufficed to warn the agents seated within, whereupon they quietly and without making any fuss paid the score, took their places in the vehicle, and the pursuit was resumed.

A considerable degree of practice was requisite when it was a matter of hurrying after someone who had just got into a street car. In such cases it was specially difficult to avoid attracting attention; for, once inside the car, the spy could be examined at leasure by his victim, and from that moment there was a great risk of his being always recognized.

In theatres and similar establishments one agent was generally posted at the door, while another went in. If they discovered that their man had spoken to another person, then the latter had to be shadowed until they had managed to ferret out his name and address. The nature and duration of all such interviews between people already under observation and others was always to be exactly noted in the report books.

Sometimes it happened that, while watching a given house, the agents would notice in the course of a short period several suspicious persons already known to them entering the house after taking certain precautions. That fact would justify the assumption that a secret gathering was being held there. In such cases it was often expedient to send word at once to the headquarters of the Ochrana, so that the whole group of conspirators could be arrested. Such information was generally sent in the form of a note conveyed by a commissionaire. The document might contain some such sentence as this: "We are visiting at a certain house. Will you not join us? We should be very glad of your company." But it might also run: "Send so many men to fetch the goods."

Occasionally, when a house had to be watched in which the Ochrana suspected the existence of a secret printing-press, a bomb factory, or an arsenal, it would become necessary to find quarters for the agents in the neighbourhood of the suspicious building. They would take up their abode there as ordinary tenants, and would thus have abundant opportunity, by conversing with the caretakers and other people in the vicinity, and by means of their own personal observation, of collecting their evidence.

In all railway stations sums of money were always kept on deposit for the purpose of allowing agents of the Ochrana to undertake journeys at short notice, or no notice at all. For it might happen that a person under observation would quite unexpectedly drive to the station and board a train. In such cases the spy entrusted with the affair would draw the money lying at the superintendent's office, buy his ticket like any other passenger, and then endeavour not to lose sight of his man in the train, while himself remaining *incognito*. When they had to undertake any sudden journey of this kind the agents were to inform their superiors at the first opportunity, by telegram.

Every evening the agents of the Ochrana would meet and report to each other the new individuals who had come into the sphere of their observation during the day in question. In this way it could be determined to what extent the inquiries of the various agents completed each other. At these meetings, too, the spies' future course of action was decided upon.

As the detective activities of the Ochrana were, above all, devoted to the observation of Terrorists, Revolutionary Socialists, and other associations dangerous to the well-being of the State, one of their principal objects was the discovery of preparations for assassination, of secret printing-presses, and of those laboratories in which bombs were manufactured. The period during which individuals were kept under observation varied enormously; it was often only a few days, it often lasted for years. Important persons were watched by quite a number of agents, while only two of these sufficed to keep an eye on humbler folk.

A consequence of the arduous and dangerous service performed by these agents was that they generally aged quickly and suffered from nervous troubles. However, it was a comparatively rare occurrence for one of them to retire of his own accord from his profession, for, in spite of all the trials and perils it involved, these men were fond of the Service, probably not least of all because there was an element of romance about it.

One other peculiar feature of the External Agency of the Ochrana should be noted. Circumstances sometimes arose in which the desired end was to be attained not, as was usual, by keeping a person under secret observation, but by allowing the observation to become patent to all. This plan was adopted whenever the immediate object was to eliminate certain intermediaries between various revolutionary leaders, thereby obliging these leaders themselves to come out of hiding. For it sometimes turned out that a revolutionary organization would make use of a go-between, who was himself not initiated into the really important parts of the business and whose sole function was to maintain communication between the leaders. Now, if the Ochrana made it quite obvious to that person that they were shadowing him, the usual result was that the intermediary would become frightened and give up the job. When that happened the only line remaining open to the leaders was to get into personal touch with each other, and it was at that juncture that they were most likely to fall into the hands of the Ochrana.

The thorough organization and training of the Ochrana agents in all matters pertaining to so-called External Observation was, to a great extent, the work of the chief of the Moscow Ochrana, Eustraty Myednikov. He was in no sense a man of exceptional education, but he possessed a marvellous talent for the organization of the Secret Service, and was, above all, distinguished by the skill which he showed in dealing with subordinate officials. He had instituted a regular school for secret agents, and the men who served under him in the Moscow Ochrana developed, thanks to his excellent guidance, into real experts in their departments.

Myednikov's method of handling the whole of the Secret Service was the reverse of bureaucratic: he attached the highest importance to making himself personally acquainted with knowledge of all his good and bad qualities. The people he preferred as agents were retired N.C.O.s, whose army experience had given them the necessary sense of discipline.

It was he, too, who introduced the practice of assembling all the secret agents every night in a special apartment in the Ochrana buildings. He appeared there regularly himself, talked with every individual spy, took over the various reports, looked through them, and then gave appropriate instructions. Of course, he knew perfectly also all the revolutionary leaders, and was far better informed as to their conspiracies and policies than any other official of the Police.

Of those agents of the Moscow Ochrana who showed the greatest aptitude Myednikov then constituted a Special Section that was placed at the disposal of the Police Department and could be employed, when need arose, on important special missions. The agents of this Section were famous for their smartness. They were almost continually travelling, and were frequently sent abroad in order to strengthen the forces of the Ochrana stationed there.

Thanks to its excellent organization, the Moscow Ochrana did, as a matter of fact, score a series of brilliant successes in the struggle against the various societies aiming at the overthrow of the State. It prevented several criminal attempts upon the lives of members of the Imperial family. And it is chiefly to its efficiency that must be ascribed the destruction of that revolutionary group that called itself the Will of the People and for some considerable time displayed very disquieting activity.

In general, the results produced by the External Agency provided a valuable basis for the labours of the Political Police. The assistance of the secret agents many a time made possible the confiscation of prohibited books and libraries and the suppression of illegal printing-presses. Successes of this kind were often due entirely to the presence of mind of some agent who had sufficient initiative to come to a quick decision in a critical moment. Thus, too, on one occasion a Terrorist organization was laid bare by the smart work of an agent, who caught a person he was observing in the act of throwing away some fragments of paper. He at once got hold of a street urchin, gave him a small coin, and told him to pick up carefully all those bits of paper. Meanwhile the spy himself continued to follow his man. When, with endless toil and patience, the scraps of paper had been put together again, a letter was revealed which provided the key that opened up the ramifications of a dangerous society.

Another time a secret bomb manufactory was discovered by an agent who had been struck by the frequency with which a suspected person went walking in public parks and gardens. A bold association of ideas suggested to the spy that these continual walks were to be explained by the fact that the man in question was working most of his time with chemicals and therefore felt the greater need of fresh air. Acting upon this suspicion, the Ochrana stepped in, and did actually discover a regular bomb factory and a great stock of explosives.

Among the most significant and successful achievements of the External Agents of the Ochrana must be reckoned the suppression of the secret Seamen's Union, under Trotsky's leadership, which had assumed serious dimensions some years before the outbreak of the World War. The observations made by the External Agency led to a complete exposure of this organization and to the arrest of all the ringleaders, of whom more than two hundred were afterwards sentenced by the Courts.

CHAPTER II

Secret Collaborators or Assistants—Traitors by Conviction—Secret Rendezvous—Zubatov: his Work and his Death—Revolutionary Counter-espionage—Police Specialists in all Revolutionary Movements

THE gravest reproach that has been made against the Ochrana, and made over and over again, is that it employed the objectionable means of provocation, *i.e.*, direct incitement, first to drive countless numbers into political crime, and thereafter to send them to Siberia or even to bring them to the gallows. The irresponsible agitators whose work, after all, it was to compass the utter collapse of the Russian Empire have never tired of continually bringing up this reproach at home and abroad; and one result of their efforts certainly was that the Ochrana, out of mistaken consideration for public opinion, many a time showed too little energy and decision in its procedure.

This question of provocation was bound up in the very closest manner with that of the activity of the Ochrana in general and of its peculiar duties, which were quite distinct from those of the ordinary Criminal Police. Without having a clear comprehension of the position occupied by the Ochrana it is absolutely impossible to understand, in this much debated affair, what the real question at issue was.

When an ordinary crime, such as, say, murder or theft, is committed the authorities intervene, as a rule, only after the accomplished fact. The task of the Police is to follow up whatever clues may be found, to question witnesses, to employ all other resources available to the technique of criminal investigation in order to discover the guilty one, to arrest him, and to hand him over for judgment to the Courts.

The state of affairs is quite different, however, when we

are dealing with political crimes that are being planned and prepared by a group of conspirators. In this case the power of the State must not confine itself to bringing the guilty to punishment *after* the deed has been accomplished. Rather must it aim at spoiling the dangerous handiwork of the rebels betimes, and before they are ever in a position to realize their nefarious designs.

Every Government in the world, and not the Tsarist Government alone, was and is obliged to defend the maintenance of the order it stands for by all manner of provisions and measures. Everywhere, therefore, political authorities are all the time busily employed collecting information as to the projects of internal foes, with a view to intervening opportunely, whenever and wherever any revolutionary movement is being set on foot. Consequently, in all organized States there also exist offices having various designations but the same function, namely, to carry on, with as little noise as possible, an effective struggle against revolution and anarchy.

There is practically only one efficient means of becoming informed as to the intentions of the enemy. The Political Police must secretly get into touch with various individuals in the camp of the revolutionaries. It follows that the main part of the activity of the Ochrana was based on that fact. When this Secret, or Internal, Agency first came into being I cannot say, but I know that it must have happened a long time ago.

The Internal Agency was much more dangerous for the enemies of the State than the open spy service of the Ochrana, for by means of it the authorities got to know of the most confidential happenings within the various revolutionary organizations. Accordingly such secret co-operators, or assistants, drawn from the ranks of the enemy, were employed by the Police Department, as well as by the local sections of the Ochrana and by the Foreign Agency. The secret assistants in

POLICE ARREST A REVOLUTIONARY
Painted by Ilja Repin

Before the Police Arrived

the service of the Foreign Agency were entrusted with the task of watching the activities of the refugees and of supplying regular reports on all that happened in the inner councils of the insurgent groups settled abroad, and especially of the different Socialist sects. Sometimes the secret assistants would return to Russia, and would arrange there regular tours of inspection round the important centres of Russian conspiracy, giving themselves out as plenipotentiaries sent by the revolutionary headquarters staff stationed abroad.

The Ochrana included among its secret assistants members of all classes: people of the working class, prostitutes, students, as well as respected party leaders, and even members of the Duma. The motives that might induce a revolutionary to enter into secret co-operation with the Police and thus to become a traitor to the comrades of his own party were very varied. During the time I held office myself I came across men utterly devoid of character, who collapsed as soon as they were arrested and professed their readiness to supply the authorities with valuable particulars as to the doings of their group. With others again the officials of the Police were obliged to use their most skilful persuasive powers for quite a time before they induced them to co-operate. In such negotiations, of course, the most potent inducement was the prospect of having the punishment that otherwise awaited them remitted.

It sometimes happened, too, that individuals would present themselves to the Ochrana and quite spontaneously announce that they had become convinced that the organized rebellious activities of the group to which they belonged were highly reprehensible, and that consequently they were ready from that moment to assist the authorities in their struggle against the subversive elements. But often enough I have met people who, when I inquired why they were thinking of offering us their services, answered bluntly that they were doing it for the money's sake.

In general, however, material considerations did not play so large a part as might be supposed, for the remuneration which the Ochrana was in a position to pay must be described as very poor. If the Police Department were up against specially important personalities occupying a leading position in the revolutionary camp, it had no doubt to dip deep into its pocket in order to offer these people a reward commensurate with the magnitude of their treachery. Ordinary assistants in the Secret Agency, however, rarely received more than from twenty to fifty roubles per month.

I know many secret agents who for such meagre pay supplied us with a number of very valuable reports. The Jews especially—it is notorious that in every revolutionary movement in Russia the Jews have been well represented—were satisfied with perfectly trifling rewards for their traitorous services. After the Revolution of 1905 the sums placed at the disposal of the Police Department for such purposes were considerably augmented, but as the number of secret assistants increased simultaneously, the takings of these people remained approximately no higher than before.

Apart from the permanent secret assistants, there were also people who appeared upon occasion in the Ochrana and furnished information about this or the other society to which they or their friends belonged. Such occasional co-operators were paid a few roubles.

In their case it was often a matter of revenge of a personal character. It would occur that a revolutionary thought he had been insulted, slighted, or betrayed by members of his faction. In a fit of rage and spite he would then hurry off to the Ochrana and denounce his fellow-conspirators. Agitators, too, who had been promised a certain reward for their activity, and from whom their employers were withholding the money, would appear in our office, quivering with anger. They wanted to give vent to their feelings, and at the same time, by accepting the Police reward, to make up for the one out of which they had been cheated by the revolutionaries.

But there were also persons who co-operated with us out of pure interest in the work, and these were often the most efficient and capable auxiliaries the Police had. One of the most interesting figures of this class was a woman student named Zhutshenko, who for many years actively assisted the Moscow Ochrana, and in particular rendered extraordinarily valuable services in connexion with the unmasking of the fighting section of the Revolutionary Socialists. As a result of action taken in consequence of her communications, several assassinations planned by the Terrorists were prevented, and the prime movers placed under lock and key. For a long time the Revolutionary Socialists reposed great confidence in her, and once entrusted her with the execution of a plot against the life of General Kurlov, at that time Governor of Minsk. In agreement with the Ochrana, Zhutshenko undertook this commission and did actually throw a bomb at General Kurlov, exactly according to the scheme of the revolutionaries. Of course, experts in the service of the Ochrana had seen to it that the bomb was rendered harmless, so that it did not explode. It was not till some years after that that the revolutionaries discovered that Zhutschenko had been playing a double game, and from that time onward the bold girl was in perpetual danger of falling a victim to their vengeance. But she managed to escape all their snares, and actually still succeeded in sending in to the Ochrana valuable particulars concerning the Revolutionary Socialists.

Almost always extreme caution was observed by the Ochrana in carrying out any work along with these secret agents; and if at times rules laid down in this connexion were ignored, the consequences were nearly always disastrous.

It was a basic principle that, in all documents and reports and in oral communications, secret assistants must never be designated by their real names, but always by some pseudonym. In contrast to the procedure adopted in the External Agency, this pseudonym must not be derived from the family name, nor from the profession, nor from the place of residence, nor from the outward appearance of the individual in question; it was rather to be chosen quite arbitrarily.

Within the Ochrana itself only the chiefs knew the real names of the agents, so that even the officials who were in continual contact with the secret assistants did not, as a rule, know with whom they were actually dealing. Only in the Police Department were lists kept with the real names, and there, if need should arise, it was possible to discover the identity of the agents in question.

Whenever a nickname had become rather too well known in Ochrana circles it was at once changed, so that the same agent thenceforth went by another name, and no one except the chiefs of the Service was aware that the new assistant was identical with the old. At other times, too, all the assumed names in use were changed. This happened certainly when a new appointment had been made to the office of Chief of the Ochrana. The purpose of all these complicated measures was to make it as difficult as possible for the revolutionaries to unmask the secret assistants.

Interviews between the leaders of the Ochrana and the more important agents drawn from the hostile camp took place for the most part at so-called secret rendezvous, a large number of which were maintained by the Ochrana, and which played a very important part in this branch of the detective service.

These houses were situated in all parts of the town and were frequently changed, the aim being to fix appointments with the various agents, not in the same house, but always in different houses. The addresses of these quarters were, of course, kept strictly secret, and every building in which one of these meeting-places was situated was permanently watched by agents of the External Service. One particular official was entrusted with the supervision of these houses and carried the keys. Whenever an interview between a secret agent and a Police officer was to take place it was his duty to introduce each man separately into the flat, and, in the same way, to see him off the premises.

In spite of all precautions it did happen sometimes that the revolutionaries found out one of these addresses. Then they tried, on their part, to spy upon it, and so to learn who were the people that frequented it. By this means they occasionally managed to identify secret agents of the Ochrana. It was in order to avoid that that such addresses were changed as frequently as means allowed.

In carrying on the work of the Service it was also an important rule that the names of secret agents were, on principle, never made known to agents of the External System, and *vice versa*. The object of this measure was to guarantee that reports sent in by the External and the Internal Agencies should be quite independent of each other, and should, to the greatest extent possible, serve to supplement each other.

Reports from the Internal Agency were sent in to a special section of the Police Department and were treated as strictly private. Only the officials who worked in that section were allowed access to these confidential documents.

The real foundation of the Internal Agency, in the form which it assumed in the last decades of the Tsarist Government, is to be attributed to Zubatov, the last Chief of the Moscow Ochrana. He was one of the first to recognize clearly the serious dangers threatening the State through the growth of revolutionary movements from the later years of the nineteenth century onward. He also realized that the employment of secret assistants formed the only means at the command of the authorities that afforded them effective protection. By his personal influence he procured a number of valuable collaborators for the Ochrana, and always did his utmost to make his men into really convinced Monarchists and defenders of the existing order. Whenever the Ochrana had arrested a group of revolutionaries, Zubatov would seek out among their number those persons who appeared to him to be most amenable to influence. He would invite them into his private room and would begin to converse with them in a friendly way, explaining to them how detestable all revolutionary ambitions were, and how just was the defensive campaign waged by the Government.

In that way he often succeeded in winning for the Ochrana men who had merely been led astray by revolutionaries and now recognized their error. For these people Zubatov felt a sort of personal attraction and treated them, in a sense, as his special *protégés*. When their service with him was over, he took steps to see that his agents were settled in some respectable situation in civil life; and often used to say that it was the duty of the Police to turn revolutionaries into useful members of the State.

It was also Zubatov who introduced, in the Ochrana, the most modern methods of criminal investigation based on the Western European models. He instituted the up-to-date system of keeping records, and brought into being the anthropometric archives that afterward rendered the most precious services to the Ochrana. His work it was, too, that led to the establishment of branches of the Ochrana in numerous provincial towns.

The great successes his methods enabled him to achieve earned for him the intense hatred of all insurgent organizations. When, therefore, in the year 1917 the Revolution broke out, Zubatov knew what this meant for him, and shot himself as soon as the victory of the rebels was assured beyond any doubt.

Naturally we had to protect ourselves against the possibility that our agents might, deliberately or otherwise, supply us with wrong information. It occurred often enough that revolutionary bodies made attempts to smuggle their own responsible people into the Ochrana in order to mislead it, and especially in order to find out the names of the secret agents and then to wreak their vengeance upon these. It was, accordingly, absolutely essential that the reliability of all reports sent in by secret agents should be severely tested, which often demanded on the part of the officers of the Ochrana a very high degree of expert knowledge and of insight into human character. As a rule, an effort was made to have every revolutionary society watched, not by one agent, but by two or more men who were unacquainted with each other. Thus the officials would be in regular receipt of several reports on the same group, so that they could be collated, completed, and corrected.

A further check was provided by the fact already mentioned that the External and Internal Agencies acted separately and independently. As the regular informers and the secret agents did not know each other, the employees of the External Service reported, frankly and without bias, whatever they observed of the conduct of the secret agents; and those in charge of the Ochrana were enabled to satisfy themselves as to the trustworthiness of reports sent in by the secret agents, and, generally speaking, to form a fairly clear picture of the mode of life and real political attitude of these people. Then it must also be borne in mind that the higher Police officials had for long been specializing in the study of the various revolutionary tendencies. One official would busy himself with the doings of the Revolutionary Socialists, another with those of the Anarchists, others again with the disciples of Tolstoi, with the Democratic Socialists, and with other subversive associations. The officials concerned, therefore, had at their command exceptional knowledge of the facts, and were not easily taken in.

Simple-minded people, never having been initiated into the true state of matters and the technicalities of Police work, have often been offended by our entire procedure in the Internal Agency, and have made more or less well-intended proposals for improving it. For example, Count V. P. Meshtshersky, in his journal *Citizen*, once published an article calling for the suppression of the Internal Agency—that is, the abolition of the whole system of employing secret collaborators. He suggested that the Police should disguise their own officials and send them to the revolutionary meetings. It need hardly be said that such amateurish advice was undeserving of any serious consideration.

CHAPTER III

HOW little could really be accomplished without the technique elaborated by the Ochrana is perhaps most clearly revealed by incidents that befell after the Revolution of 1917. The Minister of Justice, Kerensky, applied to the former officials of the Ochrana, by that time in prison, for advice as to the best way of countering the intrigues of the Bolsheviks. General Globatshov, who had been Chief of the Ochrana in Petersburg, was one of those appealed to in this way. He had been arrested immediately after the Revolution, and it was at once suggested to him that he should place his experience at the disposal of the new Government in its fight with the extremists. I shall have to speak of a similar personal experience of my own.

But if co-operation with secret agents drawn from the ranks of the rebels certainly proved to be an imperative necessity for the Political Police, it is a long step from that to the provocation, or direct incitement, of which the Ochrana has always been accused. There was, as a matter of fact, only one mode of justifying that accusation; the enemies of the old *régime* simply and arbitrarily changed the meaning of the word provocation, and called every one an *agent provocateur* who secretly supplied us with information.

The true meaning of this much-abused term is, however, quite different. The *agent provocateur* is one who himself sets on foot some revolutionary movement and then betrays to the authorities the people he has befooled. If the term is taken in this sense, I can affirm that such real provocation was not merely never at any time encouraged by the Tsarist authorities, but was severely punished by them.

Moreover, the Ochrana unfortunately was never obliged to stage conspiracies of its own. The intellectual gentry of Russia considered it the smart thing to abandon themselves, with an utter lack of reason or restraint, to what they deemed Liberal ideas; and consequently the movements opposed to the Government were of themselves far too strong for them to require any artificial fostering, or to call for the organization of conspiracies and plots on the part of the Ochrana in the manner attributed to it. Those accursed mischief-makers and agitators, Burtsev, Gershuny, Balmashov, Kalyaev, Savinkov, and others, who worked together for decades to bring about the ruin of our country, have never to this day been able to produce any evidence to show that they had been *provoked* to their revolutionary activity.

It must not be concealed that here and there, owing to lack of experience on the part of local authorities, cases of provocation certainly did occur; but whenever the Police Department heard of such a case it always proceeded to punish severely the guilty parties. The men who were at the head of the Department, such as Kovalyensky, E. I. Vuitsh, M. I. Trusyevitsh, and myself, always took the greatest care to ensure that such inadmissible action was never tolerated, much less approved of.

That cases of provocation should have occurred at all was largely to be ascribed to the after-effects of the Revolution of 1905. The disturbances had proved that the Political Police was not numerically strong enough to tackle, with complete success, the seething turbulence of the rebels. To mitigate this evil, the Chief of Police, M. I. Trusyevitsh, had organized special Area-covering Sections, intended to strengthen the hands of those entrusted with political investigation. As, however, there was a lack of men suited for the leadership of these sections, Trusyevitsh had been obliged to appoint young army officers to positions of command. These officials were naturally very often lacking in the requisite knowledge and experience, and, to add to the difficulties, friction often arose between them and the Government authorities on the spot.

Further, the mistaken practice was for some time adopted in the Police Department of estimating the performance of the various Covering Sections rather mechanically, according to the number of reports of revolutionary intrigues submitted. Now, it might quite easily happen that, in a given area, the conspirators were not very active, and that the officer in charge feared, with more or less reason, that he would produce a bad impression in St Petersburg if he could not supply reports of some kind. This situation naturally suggested the tempting idea of manufacturing *troubles* by provoking them; then, by discovering them, the officer in question might acquire a reputation for special efficiency with the chiefs of the Police Department.

I have myself at various times had to inquire into such occurrences. Among them I remember particularly one case which happened in the year 1906, in Yekaterinoslav. I had been instructed by the Minister for Home Affairs, P. N. Durnovo, to go to that town, where I learned from the Public Prosecutor attached to the local courts that, shortly before my arrival, the Chief of the Ochrana had unearthed a secret revolutionary printing-press. The examining magistrate, however, who conducted a thorough search of the premises involved, soon discovered unmistakable proof that he was up against a job arranged by the Ochrana itself. This is how it was. In the printing-office several hundred complete copies of a highly treasonable pamphlet had been discovered, while the type corresponding had been found set up and in the press. The examining magistrate himself pulled a proof from this type, and it turned out that, in a certain passage in this proof, the little word 'that' was missing. But in the printed copies already completed that word was present. We all saw at once what this meant. The Ochrana had had the proclamations printed elsewhere, and had had them introduced into the printing-office by one of their agents, who had thereupon quickly set up the type corresponding. But for this man's little bit of carelessness in doing his part of the work the scheme would probably have succeeded, and the absolutely innocent printer would have been sent to Siberia. As it was, however, the Chief of the Ochrana section received a severe reprimand, the inquiry was stopped at once, and not a hair of the printer's head was touched. I reported the whole affair to the Minister, who, in his own hand, wrote in the margin of the document, "The officer in charge of the section must quit his office at once; the Commander of the Gendarmerie is to be informed without delay of his dismissal."

Another case of provocation occurred during the time that I was at the head of the Special Section of the Police Department. A commander of Gendarmerie attached to the railway service on the Far Eastern frontier, a man who probably had never before been engaged in a political investigation, sent word that some Russian revolutionaries were regularly meeting in a certain club in Tokio. To render these people harmless, he said, he had commissioned his agent there to blow up the whole club with a bomb. No sooner had I read this communication than I hurried to the Chief of Police and told him all about it. At once a telegram was dispatched to that officer of gendarmes, forbidding most strictly the execution of his mad enterprise. Fortunately the wire arrived in time, thereby preventing this bomb outrage that had been planned by one of our own people.

But with these I have exhausted the list of all the real cases of provocation that ever came to my knowledge. Indeed, to be quite plain, the Police Department was at all times almost too suspicious in looking into every case, in order to see that subordinate officials were not overstepping the bounds of their legal rights.

The work of the secret agents consisted solely in sending in to the Ochrana reports of the doings of the revolutionary groups; they were strictly forbidden to take any active part in deeds that were inimical to the interests of the State. Of course, the other members of the revolutionary group to which the agent ostensibly belonged would demand from him the performance of certain pieces of work, and he would not always be able to get out of that without exciting suspicion. Accordingly we granted to our assistants permission to take part in secret meetings and in the execution of minor acts which they might be ordered to commit. But whenever it came to serious and dangerous enterprises, the collaborator with the police was not allowed to obey the rebel leaders, and then the question was to find a credible pretext for the refusal to carry out instructions. The difficulty, therefore, for the agent was, on the one hand, to create the impression that he was zealously active in the party interest, and, on the other hand, to refuse any action that was really punishable as a grave offence. If in one respect the secret agent showed too little zeal, he incurred the risk of rousing the suspicion of his companions and of being murdered by them. If, however, his participation in the violence of the revolutionaries went too far, he might easily find himself in a situation which excluded any possibility of his ever getting back within the limits of the law.

It happened at times that our agents found themselves under the necessity of taking over from the revolutionaries, for safe-keeping, propaganda literature of a compromising character

and even explosives, especially when there was any danger
of a domiciliary search being made. In such cases our assistants,
according to their instructions, would bring such writings or
explosives to their superiors in the Police Office, and would
then declare to their party that they had been obliged to destroy the material in question because the landlady had become suspicious, or for some other plausible reason. It was
part of the duty of the head of the Ochrana section to supply
agents with such excuses for the consumption of the revolutionaries, and sometimes, with this end in view, even to arrange little comedies. By this means the authorities gained
possession of valuable documents, while the secret agent managed not to compromise himself in the eyes of the conspirators.

The reader may perhaps ask why the Police did not always
arrest at once the persons denounced to them by the agent;
why, on the other hand, they seemed to behave for quite a
long time as passive spectators of the machinations of dangerous conspirators. The explanation lay in the complicated structure of the revolutionary societies. To begin with, the Secret
Police agent would usually know only a few unimportant
members of those groups of plotters, while the real leaders remained entirely in the background. The truth is that the activities of the associations aiming at the overthrow of the State
in Russia were already so elaborate that they were not to be
countered by ill-considered measures of violence. If the Police
had always proceeded to make arrests immediately on the
receipt of the first reports furnished by their confidants, they
would have laid their hands upon merely insignificant tools,
who were not even well informed as to the details of conspiracies, and we should never have been able to discover the
whole extent of the organization in question. Our enemies
would have laughed in their sleeves if we had precipitately
arrested persons of little importance who had been thrust

into conspicuous positions, for it would simply have meant that we had, by our action, warned the real leaders.

For all the revolutionary societies were organized on a system as complicated as that of the Ochrana itself. The leaders occupying the more responsible posts showed themselves only very rarely to their comrades who were not of the initiated inner circle, and concealed their identity behind assumed names. And so it came about that the revolutionary usually did not himself know who his superior really was. All correspondence was carried on by the use of harmless-looking false addresses, which, in the jargon of those people, were called "blank addresses." Nearly all the leading personalities in the revolutionary camp possessed false passports, and they were so clever in preserving the secret of their identity that the authorities often had the greatest difficulty in determining whom they really had before them.

All written matter that might prove to be incriminating was either composed in complicated ciphers and in invisible ink, or preserved in very skilfully chosen hiding-places. Experienced revolutionaries always tried to make quite sure that they were not being followed in the streets, and special precautionary measures were arranged, to be taken in case of their being surprised by Police raids. If the Ochrana suddenly appeared in a suspected dwelling, the revolutionaries who happened to be present always managed, by drawing the window-curtains or by some such sign, to inform someone in their confidence who would be waiting in the street outside, and we could be quite certain that none of the conspirators would ever set foot again in the quarters we had unearthed.

The controlling powers in the rebel parties were, as a rule, abroad, and were by that very fact beyond the reach of the authorities. Switzerland, especially, was for long the centre of various Socialist and revolutionary organizations that used that country as a refuge from which to direct their systematic efforts to undermine the rule of the Tsar.

If a revolutionary were arrested, he, as a rule, refused to make any declaration. This was, it might be said, a principle acted upon so as to make the task of the authorities, right down to the last moment, as difficult as possible.

One of the most important means used by all these groups was the secret printing-press. These presses were most frequently installed in the cellars of old houses, or in out-of-the-way districts and side-streets. In them were printed appeals and proclamations intended to stir up the population against the lawful Government. To discover and render innocuous such hotbeds of revolution was one of the main problems of the Ochrana, and it could be solved, in the main, only by the assistance of secret collaborators. Whenever we succeeded in discovering one of these presses all the matter found on the premises was confiscated and destroyed; all persons who had had any share in the production of seditious pamphlets were transported for shorter or longer periods to Siberia.

The most dangerous enemies that the Ochrana had to contend with were the Anarchists, who were possessed by the blind lust of destruction, and sought to overthrow whatever in any way stood for the authority and order of the State. Among them there were many men who were betrayed by their fanatical faith in the rightness of their ideas into adopting such a pernicious line of conduct. But in the ranks of the Anarchists there were also members who sought simply an opportunity of indulging their diseased and criminal instincts.

The so-called "fighting group" of the Revolutionary Socialists also made a good deal of trouble for the Ochrana, for it was with them that many attempts upon the lives of members of

SAZONOV, MURDERER OF PLEHVE, AS A
CONVICT

KALYAEV, MURDERER OF THE GRAND
DUKE SERGYEI ALEXANDROVITSH

BODY OF PLEHVE, MINISTER OF THE INTERIOR, SHATTERED BY A BOMB

the Imperial family, of the Government, and of the Police originated. The number of victims who fell to the bombs or revolvers of this Terrorist association is very large. Even the life of the Tsar was often seriously threatened. We were continually hearing of plots to assassinate the monarch, and more than once a high degree of prudence and ingenuity was required to prevent the actual perpetration of these crimes.

How much depended in such cases upon the correct conduct of the Ochrana will perhaps best be shown by the story of the criminal attempt made by the Revolutionary Socialist Sletov. This Sletov had come to Petersburg along with some of his fellow-conspirators in order to murder the Tsar. He and his accomplices had disguised themselves as droshky-drivers, and first spent some time and much trouble in finding out exactly when the Emperor usually left the palace. By a lucky chance there was among Sletov's friends a secret agent of the Ochrana, who lost no time in warning the authorities of the designs of this dangerous company. The matter was brought to the notice of General Kurlov, then Under-Secretary for the Interior. For some time he was very uncertain as to what he should do. It would have been a simple affair to arrest there and then Sletov and his fellows; but we did not know exactly what ramifications of the society might still exist. If there were such, then we had to consider the risk that some other member of the group, unknown to the Ochrana, might after all carry out the projected outrage. After mature consideration Kurlov decided, for that time, to have Sletov quietly warned by the secret agent, and so to facilitate the flight of the whole band.

However surprising this step may seem, it was nevertheless, in the given situation, the best thing to do. The danger to the Emperor was averted. There was certainly the prospect that one of those conspirators might be engaged in some subsequent outrage, but now the Ochrana knew the identity of all of them. That materially increased the possibility of successful counter-action, while, if all the members of that band had been arrested, the Police would have been helpless in face of further conspiracies.

CHAPTER IV

*The Central Agency—The Azef Affair—The Chief of Police on Trial
—Psychology of the Traitor—Murder of Colonel Karpov—Explosives
in the Table-leg—Assassination of the Prison Governor—A Murderess
with Dynamite in her Corsage—Dreadful End of Stolypin, President of
the Council*

DURING the whole period of my service in the Police
Department I strenuously opposed the so-called Central
Agency—that is, the practice followed by the Ochrana of associating with itself, as co-workers, people who were themselves at the head of revolutionary societies. It may have seemed
to the Police rather attractive to win over the leader in a
dangerous conspiracy, and thereby to be able, at one blow, to
gain complete insight into the doings of the group in question.
Experience, however, has shown that, in that way, useful results could hardly ever be attained.

The man who is directing a treasonable organization can
never unreservedly pass on to the Police all he himself knows.
As he is the chief in his group, he alone will know their ulti-
mate intentions and projects. If he betrays these secrets to
the authorities, the inevitable consequence will be that he will
run the risk of being found out by his comrades and accomplices; he will certainly be compromised in their eyes. If,
therefore, such a man appears to have been won over by the
authorities, it is certain that he will put them in possession of
information that is far more likely to prove insignificant and
misleading than important and reliable.

Perhaps nothing so clearly justifies this view of mine as the
notorious Azef Affair. It was cited over and over again by the
Liberal Press in its irresponsible campaign of agitation against
the Government and its servants. It can certainly not be de-

nied that in this affair grave—nay, disastrous—faults were committed; but there was no ground whatever for the view of those people who would have deduced from such mistakes the conclusion that the whole Tsarist state system was based upon Azef methods.

It was about the year 1900 that Azef appeared for the first time in Russia, after living abroad, where he had been in touch with Ratshkovsky, the Chief of the Foreign Section of the Ochrana. The latter, however, soon began to distrust him and broke off all relations with him. In Russia Azef quickly got into contact with Zubatov, the Head of the Moscow Ochrana, while at the same time he occupied a position of increasing importance in the party of the Revolutionary Socialists, to which he had for years belonged. He was elected a member of the Central Committee of this party, and made use of his position to convey to the authorities information about Terrorist acts that were being projected by his comrades. But all the time he was playing a double game, and while he was in regular receipt of money from the Ochrana, he was, on the other hand, taking part in the preparation of crimes of violence, without giving any intimation of the fact to the Police. And so the authorities were lulled into a false sense of security, believing that they were really being kept fully informed by Azef as to the plans of the fighting group, which was then displaying such incessant and menacing activity.

Unfortunately, no precautions were taken to obtain reliable evidence to show whether the man who was being paid commission out of State funds was not himself helping to arrange attacks upon Ministers and Grand Dukes. The hope of at last being able to come upon the tracks of the widely ramified Terrorist conspiracies made the officials of the detective service who had to deal with Azef altogether too imprudent. For the

VLADIMIR BURTSEV

EVNO AZEF

A. A. LOPUCHIN, HEAD OF THE POLICE DEPARTMENT
His imprudence led to the revelation that Azef was a secret agent

latter took good care not to be found out by his comrades, and made sure that the Government was far from knowing all that was known to him. The authorities felt safe in the consciousness that the leader of their enemies was really co-operating with them; and their consternation was all the greater when political crime not merely did not cease, but actually began to assume ever more terrifying dimensions.

Within a short period W. K. Plehve, the Minister for Home Affairs, and the Grand Duke Sergyei Alexandrovitsh were murdered. In both cases the outrages had been conceived and planned by Azef's group, without Azef having warned the police betimes. The Liberal Press actually made the assertion that Azef had acted as an *agent provocateur* and had himself arranged these crimes. Even the former President of the Council of Ministers, Count Witte, apparently identified himself with this view, for in his memoirs he notes the rumour that the murderer of Grand Duke Sergyei Alexandrovitsh had been incited to commit the deed by "Azef, *the police agent.*" But it must be pointed out that Count Witte, who, after all, was at that time Prime Minister and, as he expresses himself, "ruled the country," did not put an end to the political intelligence service, which had thus brought about the murder of members of the Imperial Family by its own agents. On the contrary, it was then that the Count appointed as Minister of the Interior P. N. Durnovo, who clung most emphatically to that very system of political investigation. That fact alone suffices to characterize as devoid of seriousness Witte's condemnation of Police action.

In spite of all inquiries, newspaper articles, and speeches delivered in the Duma, no clear light has ever been shed upon the Azef Affair. Nor did I, during my whole period of service, ever set eyes upon any documents that might have been likely to clear up that mysterious business.

Unfortunately, when P. A. Stolypin, as Prime Minister, made his great speech in the Duma on the Azef Affair, he did not explicitly declare that it was a matter of an isolated blunder on the part of the Ochrana, for which those responsible were going to be called to account. Carried away by his oratorical enthusiasm, the Prime Minister spoke in far too general terms, and thereby made it possible for the opposition to continue its twaddle about the Azef System.

With this melancholy affair a certain trial was associated which made much stir in its time. It concerned my predecessor in office, A. A. Lopuchin, Chief of Police. Some time after his retirement from the headship of the Police Department he committed the grave indiscretion of communicating to Burtsev, in the course of conversation with this revolutionary, that Azef had been a secret agent of the Ochrana. It is altogether beyond comprehension how an experienced Chief of Police like Lopuchin could have been guilty of such a piece of imprudence. During the course of a railway journey abroad Lopuchin had by accident come across Burtsev, had become involved in an animated discussion, and in the heat of the argument he may have let fall the admission that Azef was in the service of the Police. Burtsev lost no time in publishing his conversation with Lopuchin in the Opposition Press. The result was not merely that Azef was branded in the eyes of the revolutionaries as a traitor, but that several other secret assistants of the Police began to excite the suspicion of the parties to which they belonged.

In the Government the episode caused the greatest dismay, especially as Lopuchin had been a friend of Stolypin in his youth and was on the most intimate terms with him. The Minister of the Interior, Makarov, summoned a special meeting at which Shtsheglovitov, the Minister of Justice, Kaminshansky, the Public Prosecutor at the Supreme Court of

Petersburg, and Kurlov, Under-Secretary, were present. Opinion as to whether Lopuchin should be put on trial was divided, but at last, in spite of weighty objections, the majority voted in favour of handing the matter over to the public Courts.

To my mind, that was a grave blunder: there was no serious basis whatever for the charge, which was founded on paragraph 102 of the Code, the paragraph that refers to participation in secret and prohibited associations. No doubt Lopuchin might have been punished by administrative process and even sent into exile; but, strictly considered, there was not the slightest justification for the institution of regular legal proceedings against him. I still remember how excited W. S. Korsak, the counsel for the prosecution, was during the trial, and, indeed, when only a few minutes before he delivered his address, I talked with him for a moment or two. He confessed to me quite frankly how difficult he found it to bring Lopuchin's conduct within the scope of the paragraph cited. Nevertheless, the guilty Chief was condemned and exiled to Siberia, a circumstance which, naturally, did not contribute towards enhancing the prestige of the Police Department.

Every secret assistant was, after all, a traitor to his comrades, and I always impressed upon my subordinates that they must never lost sight of the fact. This was all the more necessary because, unfortunately, many detective officers betrayed a degree of blind confidence in their agents that passed belief.

It can be easily understood that it was no simple task for the heads of the Police Service always to hit the right line in the treatment of their agents: firstly to make it possible for them to collect information, then to forbid them all active participation in punishable offences, and finally to shield them from discovery by their party. There is also to be considered a certain psychological phenomenon that almost regularly appeared among the secret assistants: they were continuously in touch both with the Police and with the revolutionaries, and consequently found themselves in an extremely unnatural position, which exercised the most harmful influence on the state of their nerves. The treachery which they were practising all the time toward their real comrades in political opinion, and which quite frequently led those comrades to imprisonment or exile, weighed upon the consciences of these people; while, on the other hand, they must always have been in terror lest they should be found out by the revolutionaries, and murdered. Therefore, in the life of every secret agent there would almost certainly come a moment when he regretted the double game upon which he had embarked. This critical phase led many a time to a sudden blazing up of fanatical hatred for the Ochrana officer who controlled the agent's activities. Upon him the whilom revolutionary would wish to avenge himself for his own moral lapse. That is the explanation of the fact that Police officials were so often murdered by agents in their service who had till then proved absolutely trustworthy.

Experienced leaders in the Secret Agency were able to detect at once when such a crisis was approaching in the mind of one of their agents, and would then seek to anticipate a catastrophe by withdrawing the man from active service, and by finding him occupation of another kind more easily reconcilable with his conscience.

But not all the officials of the detective service were conscious of these difficulties. Very often, too, the affairs of the Secret Agency were treated with endless red tape, on thoroughly bureaucratic lines, as if the one thing that mattered was the multiplication of documents. Time was wasted on such futilities, and meanwhile the most precious results produced by secret observation were lost or remained simply unused. It might, and did, happen that in some districts, though the Secret Police were quite well informed by their assistants of the abominable practices of the revolutionary societies, the people in charge of the Sections in question would calmly go on piling up papers, and never make up their minds to intervene in any energetic fashion. Such bureaucratic methods were, in the Ochrana, even more out of place than in any other branch of the State service, and the situations to which they gave rise were sometimes too grotesque.

Once, when I was making a tour of inspection in the Government of Penza, I came upon a very curious state of affairs. For a year past the Ochrana officer in charge of the district had been keeping a careful watch upon the proceedings of the rebel groups, and I was absolutely astounded at the fullness and the minuteness of the intelligence he had collected. Not only were all the plans of the revolutionaries exactly detailed in the records, but there was a long list of persons known to the authorities as having been for some time addicted to seditious practices. I asked the officer in command if he would explain to me why, with such complete evidence at his disposal, he had not six months before, set about restoring order by arresting the whole band. To this question I received the artless reply that there were still lacking one or two particulars about a few of the agitators, whose personal characteristics were rather inadequately described in the existing documents. Naturally I gave immediate instructions to proceed without further delay to the arrest of the ringleaders, suggesting that, if some unimportant folk got off with a rude shock, that would not be of such serious consequence as the continuance of an attitude of silent toleration toward that dangerous group. I gave the officer commanding to understand that, if he did not take steps, and at once, he would soon find it impossible to act at all, for one of those days the garrison, whom the revolutionaries were inciting to mutiny, would be arresting him and the whole Police Force.

The inability of many of the Ochrana officials to recognize in time the crisis in the temper of their collaborators, no less than the blind confidence which those officials, in general, showed with regard to their agents, led frequently to fatal catastrophes. Such a case was the murder of Colonel S. G. Karpov, who, in his capacity of Chief of the Petersburg Ochrana, had entered into most intimate association with one of his men in the Secret Service, and paid for his ill-advised trust by the loss of his life. I was myself a personal friend of Karpov's, who used often to look me up and tell me very frankly all that was on his mind: I was at that time serving in the office of the Public Prosecutor of Petersburg, and consequently had nothing directly to do with the Secret Police. One evening Karpov had again called upon me and said to me very mysteriously as he bade me good-bye, that he was just on the point of laying bare a great Terrorist conspiracy, and that, on that very evening, with this in view, he was going to meet a secret agent in a specially rented little flat, where the latter was to reveal to him all the threads of the plot. With pride and satisfaction Karpov expressed the hope that, within a short time, thanks to the reports brought in by that agent, the lives of Ministers would cease to be endangered. In answer to my question whether Karpov had known the man long, the Colonel said he had not, but that the agent had been very highly recommended to him and that he had no grounds whatever for doubting his trustworthiness and loyalty.

"Sergyei Georgyevitsh," I warned him, "One may be brave, but there is nothing to be gained by foolhardiness! It is, after all, a very risky business to share the occupancy of rooms with an individual who, when all is said, can only be described as a traitor!"

He replied frankly and cheerfully that he had no fear, and was ready to do anything to check the revolutionary terror.

He added that, by doing what he intended, he would prevent the assassination of the Prime Minister, Stolypin, General Kurlov, and other high-placed public servants, whose lives were being seriously threatened. With these words he took his departure.

After midnight an official attached to the Ochrana called at my place and inquired whether his Chief was still there. I immediately had an uncanny feeling that something was wrong, but when I asked a question I received a perfectly colourless reply. Not more than an hour later, however, I knew of the dreadful end of my friend.

I shall briefly narrate the events that led up to this tragedy, and how it actually happened. In the spring of the year 1909 the Ochrana had received numerous confidential reports concerning a projected attack on the life of the Tsar, and these intimations sounded all the more serious, because at that time the Emperor was proposing to undertake long journeys through Russia. The information that the Ochrana had been able to obtain about this conspiracy against the life of the Monarch was, however, very scanty; and the most exalted personalities, right up to the Prime Minister, felt very insecure and were really in terror lest some disaster should occur. It was just at the critical moment when the Tsar was about to leave Petersburg that the Commander of the Gendarmerie in Saratov sent in word that a revolutionary named Petrov, who was imprisoned there, had offered to make communications about the plot, on condition that he should be set free.

The Ministry of the Interior, in view of the exceptional importance of the matter, decided to accede to Petrov's suggestion and to facilitate his escape from prison. From that moment the revolutionary was under the supervision of the Ochrana and especially of Colonel Karpov. He supplied various pieces of information which, however, proved to be partly of no consequence and partly not altogether reliable. Meanwhile the Tsar's journey passed off without incident.

A few days before his death Colonel Karpov had again had an interview with Petrov, who had, as I have already related, promised to reveal to him details of some new plot. The Terrorist had succeeded in gaining Karpov's complete confidence; and finally it was resolved that the two, Karpov and Petrov, should for some weeks live together at a secret address, a flat having been hired for the purpose in Archangel Street. Petrov had insisted on this arrangement, declaring that only thus could he remain in touch with Karpov, without exciting the suspicion of the revolutionaries.

But surely the limit of carelessness was touched by the Ochrana when they allowed Petrov to look after the fitting up of this flat. The first thing he saw to was the installation of electric bells. The flat consisted of three rooms and a kitchen, all of which opened on to a corridor. The middle room was intended for the common use of both tenants, and Petrov procured a sofa and an old-fashioned round table with a broad, heavy base.

The bell system fitted up consisted of a wire from the street door and one from the door of the flat; the former was controlled by a special switch and could be thrown out of action. Then Petrov procured a large quantity of dynamite, which he concealed in the hollow leg of the table and connected to another set of electric wires so arranged that they passed unnoticed.

It was on that last evening when Karpov called on me that he was to go for the first time to meet Petrov in the new flat. Meantime the latter had connected up the wire from the street door with the circuit that was to ignite the charge of dynamite; and then, by means of the switch provided for the purpose, he had temporarily cut out the front-door bell. When, therefore, the Colonel arrived, the bell was not working, and it was only by calling out that Karpov could make his presence known. Petrov opened the door to him, showed him into the flat, and then, on some pretext or another, he left him. He turned on the fatal switch, went out to the street, and pressed the button at the front door. The dynamite exploded, and Karpov was, in the most literal sense of the word, torn to pieces.

Only by a lucky chance was the treacherous agent seized in the street, just as he was getting into an ordinary Finnish sledge, which was there in readiness to secure his escape. He was condemned to death and executed, without his having given the slightest hint as to the real motives for his horrible deed.

General Kurlov told me afterward that, from the very start, he had always entertained the gravest doubts as to Petrov's trustworthiness, and had over and over again advised Karpov to test very carefully all data supplied by that agent, and never in any way to trust the man himself. Just before Kurlov went to the Crimea, in order to supervise all precautions being taken in connexion with the Tsar's journey, Colonel Karpov had submitted to him highly improbable reports sent in by Petrov; and Kurlov had once more emphasized his opinion that this agent was a very shady customer. But the Colonel had merely asserted that he would answer for Petrov with his head.

"Take care that you do not lose your head," General Kurlov had answered, and subsequent events were to show that he was unfortunately only too near the mark.

In a similar manner Radom, the Commander of the Gendarmerie, fell, in the following year, a victim to a Terrorist who had managed to procure access to his person under the guise of an agent anxious to assist the work of the Secret Police. The official, with misplaced confidence enough, received him without witnesses, in his own home, whereupon the Terrorist suddenly whipped out a revolver and fired several shots at his victim, killing him outright.

Among the most exciting experiences of my life must be reckoned the murder of A. M. Maximovsky, a prison governor. I shall relate some of the dramatic circumstances accompanying it. One evening a woman appeared in the central office of the prison and requested to be allowed to see Maximovsky. No sooner had the governor stepped out of his room into the waiting-room than the stranger produced a pistol and fired several times at him. He collapsed at once, streaming with blood and mortally wounded. The murderess thereupon tried to throw the instrument of death through the window on to the street, but was prevented from so doing by an official who happened to come upon the scene. It turned out later that the throwing out of the revolver would have served as a sign to the other members of the conspiracy—the criminal was not acting alone—that the outrage had been successfully carried out. For it was discovered that the Terrorists had planned to kill also the Minister of Justice and the Chief of the City Police of Petersburg. As soon as the signal agreed upon had been given other conspirators would have hastened to the houses of those two personalities, and there waited until they started for the scene of the first crime. In the general confusion it would probably not have been difficult for the scoundrels to shoot down both those exalted personages.

Accompanied by General Kurlov I betook myself as soon as the news arrived to the prison, where Shtsheglovitov, the Minister of Justice, the Chief of the City Police, and a few other high officials had already arrived. The murderess refused persistently to give her name, and mockingly declared that it was the business of the authorities to establish

DESTRUCTION WROUGHT BY THE EXPLOSION AT STOLYPIN'S VILLA

After the Unsuccessful Attempt on the Life of Stolypin—Shattered Carriage Used by the Conspirators

her identity. General Kurlov ordered her to be searched by women attendants who were present. A remark made by the woman, however, made us suspect that she had explosives about her person; and I must admit that, at that moment, we all felt very uncomfortable. Some policemen held the woman firmly by hands and feet while First Lieutenant Komissarov, who had been formerly in the Artillery, set about examining her. And he did really find in the criminal's corsage a quantity of dynamite that would have sufficed to blow the whole house to atoms. It was a miracle that Komissarov was able to deal with this terrifying charge, so that it did no harm and that we were not all utterly destroyed.

A propos of the relations between the Police authorities and the revolutionaries, I should like finally to add a brief account of the assassination of Stolypin, the President of the Council of Ministers, as statements have been frequently circulated about this lamentable occurrence that are absolutely false. Some irresponsible busybodies have even had the effrontery to accuse certain members of the Imperial House of being indirectly to blame for this crime.

As far back as August 1906 a sinister attempt was made on Stolypin's life. The Minister himself escaped as by a miracle, but some members of his family and numerous other persons were victims of this plot. The crime was committed in the days when Stolypin lived in his villa on Apothecary Island, and used to entertain on a lavish scale. Four conspirators drove up in a carriage to the door of the Minister's house, behaving as if they were among the invited guests, and entered the house. One of them was in uniform and was wearing a helmet, inside which a charge of dynamite was concealed. When he threw down this helmet there followed a terrific explosion, which at once transformed the house into a heap of ruins. Several guests and a number of servants were killed; Stolypin's son and daughter were severely wounded. The insane assassins were themselves blown to pieces by their bomb.

This horrible event contributed largely to the change in the direction of the Minister's policy, which dates from that time: to begin with, his inclinations had been rather toward liberal views, but now he adopted an attitude of energetic opposition to all radical tendencies in the country. Having had a miraculous escape from one assault on his life, he thenceforth set his face firmly and decidedly against every revolutionary movement, and stuck to his post unmoved, until he was laid low by another attack.

It was in the summer of 1911 that he was at last overtaken by the fate that he had so often felt to be at his heels. The Tsar was then on his way to Kiev, and in his suite, along with other eminent personages, was the President of the Council. The authorities had taken comprehensive measures to protect the Tsar from attack, and at Stolypin's behest the supreme control of the Police Service had been entrusted to General Kurlov.

A few days after the Court arrived in Kiev a former secret agent, named Bagrov, presented himself at the office of the local Ochrana, with the information that he knew the details of a plot against the life of the Tsar that was being hatched by a certain group of conspirators who intended to carry out their plans in Kiev. What Bagrov had to report sounded very definite, and therefore the authorities made their precautions even more complete than they were already. Nothing of an exceptional nature took place, however—for a time.

The programme of festivities included a performance in the Kiev Theatre, and it goes without saying that, on this occasion, when the Emperor and all the high officials in his train were gathered together, most particular care would be taken in checking the identity of all the guests. General Kurlov had been very wary in the steps he had taken to ensure that not a single person would find admission who was not far removed from the least breath of suspicion. Consequently everyone thought he could afford to keep his mind easy for that evening; no one had the slightest foreboding that, during the performance of the play itself, the Prime Minister would be murdered.

It was none other than that secret agent Bagrov who did the work. Under some pretext or other he appeared in the theatre while the play was going on, and delivered to First Lieutenant Kulyabko, the head of the Special Police Service in Kiev, some quite insignificant piece of intelligence. Thereupon Kulyabko was guilty of an act of great imprudence, and one which was to involve the most serious consequences: after Bagrov had given his message Kulyabko did indeed tell him to be off home, but neglected to make sure himself that the agent had obeyed the order. Without troubling further about Bagrov, Kulyabko devoted himself to the other duties that fell to him, so that Bagrov found an opportunity, during the interval, of slipping unnoticed into the auditorium. Suddenly several shots were fired at Stolypin, who fell down severely wounded. He died two days later in hospital as the result of his injuries.

This affair provided the enemies of General Kurlov with a welcome pretext for making out that he, as supreme head of the Special Police Service, was solely responsible for the disaster. His Majesty commanded that an inquiry should be held, which was to be conducted by Trusyevitsh, the Chief of Police in Russia; and although Trusyevitsh was not very kindly disposed toward General Kurlov, this inquiry led to nothing, and it was in the end stopped again at the command of the Tsar.

What the circumstances were that induced the secret agent Bagrov to murder Stolypin has never been quite clearly made out. It may be that, from the outset, he had intended to commit the crime, and that for this purpose he had wormed himself into the confidence of the authorities by supplying false intelligence. More probable, however, appears the assumption that the band of conspirators to which he belonged selected him only at the last moment to kill the Prime Minister, and that he did not dare, for fear of their vengeance, to refuse to carry out the order received.

In the years subsequent to the first Russian Revolution the Polish Socialists distinguished themselves by their sanguinary Terrorist fight with the Government. Under the leadership of Pilsudski, afterward President of the Republic, this party waged savage warfare especially against the Ochrana. They slew mercilessly every secret agent whose name they managed to get to know. Thus it came about that, within a short period, more than a thousand informers and Government officials fell by the assassin's hand; and the criminals, for the most part, carried out their plans with such masterly skill that, once the deed was done, they made off without leaving a clue.

Another special line of the Polish Socialist Party was the organization of surprise attacks upon railways trains, banks, and post-offices, by means of which these dangerous rebels were able to provide themselves with means of support and funds for the continuance of their detestable practices. At these raids it often happened that all officials who endeavoured to offer any resistance were ruthlessly cut down. It called for the utmost efforts on the part of the Ochrana to put an end to this

The Cross Worn by Stolypin Shot Through by the Bullet

Dimitry Bagrov, the Murderer of Stolypin

Murder of Colonel Karpov—Secret Rendezvous After
the Explosion
See page 80

scandalous state of matters; but it was stopped at last, to some extent, thanks chiefly to the ingenuity of the Moscow Ochrana.

The examples I have adduced show clearly enough how difficult, how responsible, and how perilous service in the Ochrana was, and how complicated were the relations that subsisted between the Police and their secret agents.

CHAPTER V

*A Police Gazette for the Tsar—The Black Cabinets—Invisible Writing
—A Master in Decoding—The Cipher of the Ochrana—Burtsev unmasks his Friends—Friends and Foes of the Ochrana*

IN ORDER to supply their officials with the latest news
of all that was going on in the revolutionary camp, the
Ochrana issued its own Service periodicals. To begin with, it
published an annual volume describing the state of the various
seditious parties at the moment, with details of their pro-
grammes and publications, and including lists of their members. Later on, between the years 1902 and 1905, a regular
Ochrana Gazette appeared, generally twice a month, in litho-
graph; copies were sent to all the chiefs of the local Ochrana
Sections.

In this sheet everything was contained that had come to the
knowledge, for the time being, of the Ochrana. It embodied
the substance of the reports sent in by the External and the
Secret Agencies, and dealt with the most recent activities of
the revolutionary groups. Strict attention had to be given to a
point mentioned before: the avoidance of all reference to the
secret agents under their own names, so that if by chance a
copy of the journal should find its way into the hands of the
revolutionaries, it might not lead to the identification of the
agents. If one of these secret assistants had distinguished
himself by bringing in peculiarly important evidence, recognition of his services and the due meed of praise were conveyed to him, under his assumed name, in this gazette.

Another publication of the Ochrana deserves mention. This
was a journal of which only a single copy of each issue was
produced; it was intended for the personal use of the Tsar. In
this way the Secret Police submitted to the Emperor twice a

month a sort of statement of accounts, and the Tsar used to read this with great interest and to annotate it in his own hand. The Minister of the Interior would then expressly direct the attention of the Ochrana to those passages marked by the Tsar, and give instructions to have most careful inquiries made in connexion with the affairs in question. Thus the Ochrana always knew exactly, when their gazette was returned to them, which part of their investigations had particularly attracted the Emperor's notice.

His Majesty was always very desirous of being minutely posted in all the details of the revolutionary movement and of the fight being waged against it. He attached great value to complete accounts of the discovery of secret printing-presses, of plots, forbidden libraries, and other seditious organizations. Whenever the Ochrana had succeeded in confiscating proclamations issued by the agitators, these were always appended to the gazette. This was also done with revolutionary pamphlets, and with the tickets for lotteries that had been got up for the benefit of the revolutionaries—for such lotteries *were* sometimes arranged.

The Ochrana was also responsible for the secret censorship of letters, which had been practised in Russia for a very long time. Even in the eighteenth century Chancellor Betushev had been able to reveal the insidious intrigues of the French Ambassador by having his correspondence and dispatches closely watched, and then bringing to the notice of Empress Elizabeth the evidence of that diplomat's hostility to the interests of our land. When, in the reign of Nicholas I, the Corps of Gendarmerie was instituted, the Commandant pointed out in an early memorandum the necessity of maintaining a censorship of correspondence, and made arrangements for the establishment of a secret censor's department in all the important post-offices in Russia. Tsar Alexander III also signified his emphatic approval of this procedure, and, by a special edict, empowered the Minister of the Interior to open private correspondence, as a measure of protection to the State. This edict was, from its first coming into force, treated as strictly confidential, and was handed over in a sealed envelope to the Minister of the Interior for the time being. When the new Minister had taken cognizance of the contents, the document was sealed up again and preserved till the next change of Ministers.

The Police Department kept the heads of the Post and Telegraph Office regularly informed of the names of persons whose letters were of interest to the Government. Moreover, most letters coming from, or addressed to, foreign countries were censored. During the last years before the Revolution, in the post-offices of Petersburg, Moscow, Warsaw, Odessa, Kiev, Charkov, Riga, Vilna, Tomsk, and Tiflis there were so-called "black cabinets" regularly at work; and, in addition, when circumstances made it seem expedient, a temporary censorship was set up in other towns.

Every office of the kind had at its disposal a number of specially competent linguists and the requisite technical equipment for the opening and closing of letters. Generally, the envelope would be held over steam until the gum had melted; then the contents would be copied, replaced in the envelope, and posted again. The employees of these "black cabinets" acquired such a *flair* that they often opened letters whose writers were not on the lists of the Police Department: little signs, such as dots, dashes, or crosses, on the envelope were sufficient to awaken the suspicion of the censors.

This whole procedure will perhaps appear surprising, as it is in conflict with views that have become accepted in certain democratic States. But I should like to point out that this censorship of letters many a time enabled the Russian Police to prevent robberies, murders, and Terrorist crimes. The advantages of the system were therefore undoubtedly very real, and I do not believe that the disadvantages were ever worthy of serious consideration. The right-minded citizen certainly never had any reason to fear the censorship, for private business was, on principle, completely ignored.

Of course, in spite of all precautions and of the strictest secrecy with which the system was surrounded, the revolutionaries were quite well aware of the existence of the censorship, and endeavoured by all sorts of ingenious devices to avoid having their schemes discovered by its agency. With this end in view they would often send each other quite harmless letters written in ordinary ink, but between the lines of the apparently innocent communication would be written the message that really mattered, in invisible ink. In such cases the Ochrana found itself on the horns of a dilemma: either the invisible script was to be brought up, or the job must be left definitely alone and the letter of interest sent on unread to the addressee. It was, naturally, not a very difficult task to make such sympathetic inks visible; generally all that was needed was to treat the paper with lemon juice, chlorine water, or milk, or else to apply gentle heat. If, however, such a piece of secret writing had once been revealed, the letter in question could not, of course, be delivered. On the other hand, it was a hard thing to decide not to try to bring to light messages that were possibly of the highest political import.

A solution to this puzzle was hit upon by First Lieutenant G. G. Metz, an officer of Gendarmes attached to the Police Department. Being a very intelligent and cultured man and an enthusiastic photographer, he devised a method of deciphering such letters by photographic means that left not the slightest mark on the letter itself. From that moment it was possible to read messages in invisible ink without the receivers having any idea that the correspondence had been tampered with.

The task presented to us was a harder one when we were faced with letters drawn up in cryptic writing or in cipher. For the decoding of such messages a special official was appointed, who had peculiar gifts for this work, and whose real name, for various reasons, I do not wish to mention. I shall therefore simply call him Nezlobin.

He had an uncanny talent for divination and reconstruction, and was able to find the key to the most complicated ciphers. An insignificant act of aggression had been committed in Sebastopol, and during the course of a domiciliary visit made immediately after a sheet of paper was found covered with figures and without a single letter upon it. When this document reached my department I handed it over to the said Nezlobin, with a request to set to work at once on the decoding of it. On the following day Nezlobin called upon me and suggested that I should telegraph to Sebastopol for a list of all the books that had been found during the search. I certainly had not the haziest idea what this was for, but I acceded to the wish of my collaborator, and at once received a detailed report enumerating a number of quite harmless literary works. A short time after, Nezlobin placed before me the decoded text of the sheet that had looked so incomprehensible. In reply to my inquiry, he explained that the key to the cipher had been provided by page thirty-two of a book by Kuprin, *Poedinka*. The numbers signified the line and the letter in each line on that thirty-second page. That is to say, each pair of numbers indicated a letter, and so the mystery was solved. I admired the genius or instinct of Nezlobin which had been revealed in this case very clearly, and obtained for him a certain order and the increase in salary that went with it.

On another occasion, when he was likewise employed on a

sheet covered with arithmetical figures, he inquired of me what was the price of a pound of dynamite. I was rather astonished and asked him why he was taking an interest in such a matter. He replied very modestly that he thought the cipher referred to explosives. This time again he had got the right inspiration, for the price of dynamite did actually lead him to the solution of the cipher.

The man had an incredibly sure sense for everything that was designed to mislead, and more than once, after taking merely a quick glance at a document in cipher, he was able to say that this or that line was of no importance whatever and was simply to be ignored in decoding. Or he would at once point out the intervals at which meaningless groups of figures were introduced merely to add to the difficulty of finding the key.

Moreover, the Ochrana made use, for its own dispatches, of a cipher which was very difficult to work out. It was based on the principle of two movable scales, placed against each other in such a way that the letters in alphabetical order corresponded to a sliding scale of figures arranged in a special order; the scales had, however, to be adjusted properly to each other on any given occasion in order to make it possible to read the message, which was drawn up in figures instead of letters. As the key varied not only from one dispatch to the next, but also several times within the same text, the decoding of such a message was almost impossible for the uninitiated.

The Journal of the Ochrana prepared for the Tsar, to which reference has already been made, frequently contained materials supplied by the "black cabinets." For some time, for example, all letters by Leo Tolstoi were opened and photographed by the censor, and some of his writings in which Tolstoi had given expression to his anti-militarist views, were submitted to the Emperor.

Before I leave the subject of the detective service I should like to say one word more about the expression *provocateur*. This designation, which, as has been already suggested, was employed in seditious circles for all assistants in the Secret Agency, was first used, if I am not mistaken, by Burtsev. Burtsev, a base but able journalist, who had in a sense risen to be controller of the press for the Revolution, was very anxious on one occasion to learn which members of the various revolutionary groups were maintaining secret relations with the Ochrana. He attained this object by the very simple process of drawing up a list of persons who appeared to him to be suspicious characters and whose names he published in a series of articles, calling them *provocateurs*. Then he waited quietly till the people in question had cleared themselves in the eyes of their organizations, or had by them been declared guilty.

This was by no means displeasing to the Government, and I, personally, was highly delighted at this unmasking campaign of Burtsev's. For it gave rise to the greatest confusion among the revolutionaries, who fell to suspecting each other, so that in the end no conspirator could trust another. In consequence, the activities of the rebels were seriously hampered for quite a time.

From all that I have said so far the reader has now probably obtained some little insight into the operation and methods of the much-maligned Ochrana. At the same time, if he is able to take an unprejudiced view of things, he will have been convinced that the action of that body was never directed against orderly subjects of the Tsar who knew their duty and attended to it, and that these had no reason whatever to fear the Ochrana. Like the Political Police in all other lands, the Ochrana fought only the disastrous agitation carried on by seditious elements in the population, and did its utmost to prevent those things happening which, after all and in spite of the efforts of its conscientious officials, did come to pass. Perhaps much might have turned out otherwise, perhaps the lives of many thousands might have been saved, if the Tsarist authorities had not shown such strict consideration for existing laws, and had in many cases intervened more sternly and more energetically than they actually did.

The real honest Russian has always had respect for power that was power, and he bowed before it, without asking questions, or meditating upon the reasons there might be for commands given, even though these were often difficult to fulfil or to endure. The explanation was that the Russian, in the depths of his soul, knew and understood that the authorities had been appointed by the Tsar in order that they might serve him faithfully and advance by all possible means the welfare of Russia. So that the peaceful and patriotic inhabitants of the Russian Empire were really proud of their Police and were indignant when they heard of isolated examples that occurred here and there of corruption and neglect of duty. It is only now, having learned from the bitter experiences of the Revolution and of the Bolshevik *régime*, that we emigrants are in better position than ever to make a just comparison between the political conditions of the Tsardom, much decried as they were, and those that prevail under the Soviets. In the light of such facts, no doubt, many a Russian who once inveighed against the Ochrana will have arrived at a more correct estimate of that institution.

CHAPTER VI

*The Government and the Jewish Question—The Part played by the
Jews in preparing the Way for the Revolution—Were the Jews in
Russia oppressed?—The Problem of Settlement—Evasion of Military
Service—Disillusioned Emigrants—The New York Council of the
Jewish People—Intrigues in America*

CLOSELY related to the accusation of provocation is the
assertion, made over and over again in Liberal and Socialist quarters, that the authorities of Tsarist Russia not
merely showed benevolent toleration toward the persecution
of Jews and the *pogroms* (riots) organized against them, but
actually arranged such manifestations themselves. Especially
the former Minister of the Interior, Plehve, who was so shamefully done to death, was widely regarded as an instigator of
Anti-Semitic excesses. The responsibility for the *pogrom* that
took place at Easter 1903 in Kishinyov was particularly ascribed
to him.

Now, everyone knows that Russia was by no means the only
State in which the aversion of the population for Jews gave
vent to itself from time to time in tumults of violence that
no one certainly would care to defend. But while similar incidents occurring abroad passed almost unnoticed, stories of
this kind affecting Russia were told, in ever new varients and
thousands of times over, in the Press of the extreme Left, so
that they obtained the widest publicity throughout the world.
The notorious fact is that certain persons were so consumed
with zeal for the ruin of the Russian Empire that, for them,
it was a necessity to fabricate the base slander that the Imperial Government took a share in staging the *pogroms*. For
that reason it was never allowed to die down, but was continually revived, until our glorious Russia was really destroyed.

After the Revolution the Provisional Government rummaged the archives of the Ochrana from top to bottom, in the hope of discovering documents that would compromise the old régime in this respect. But nothing of the kind was found; on the contrary, many orders were brought to the light of day forbidding, under threat of very severe penalties, all participation by Government officials in Anti-Semitic movements.

No doubt the archives of the Police Department yielded many an interesting document that went to prove that the Government was not always what would be called kindly disposed toward the Jews. At the same time, however, these documents indicated the grounds for this attitude, and they were doubtless cogent enough.

From of old the Jewish element had notoriously played a very important part in preparing the ground for the Revolution. As far back as the year 1897 the General Union of Jewish Workmen had been founded; and it soon developed into one of the most dangerous of the revolutionary associations. In this so-called Alliance magnificent organization was combined with typical Jewish fanaticism and hatred of the existing Government. The secret organ of this group, styled *The Will of the Workers,* became within a short time one of the leading revolutionary papers in Russia. It was by this journal proclaimed to the whole world that in the Empire of the Tsar the Jews were shamefully oppressed, that they were not treated as citizens having the same rights and privileges as others, and that *pogroms* were organized against them.

But were the Jews, then, really so oppressed that for decades on end the attention of the whole civilized world should have been directed by excited newspaper articles to the conditions prevailing among us? Was there any justification for that? It is, no doubt, true that long ago the so-called Pale was created in Russia—that is, certain governments (provinces) were reserved for Jewish settlement, while in others they were not permitted to reside. But we can all testify that this law was continually evaded, and that countless Jews, with the consent of the authorities, lived in towns that should have been closed to them. The Police looked upon the fact with benevolence and shut both eyes. A few figures will serve to show the reader what the real truth of the matter was with regard to this question of the oppression of the Jews. In Russian Poland, for example, the Jewish population in the year 1856 amounted to a bare ninety thousand, but by the year 1908 it had risen to over half a million. In Warsaw at the beginning of the nineteenth century the Jewish element had embraced only 12 per cent. of the inhabitants; in the year 1913, on the other hand, it represented 37 per cent. In other words, while the whole population of that city had been multiplied by twelve, the actual number of the Jews had multiplied forty-fold during the course of a century.

In other Russian towns very similar observations might be made. In Odessa, for example, the Jewish element increased within the last twenty years of the Tsardom by fully one-third. In Petersburg, which, according to the strict letter of the law, should really have been for Jews a forbidden city, there were living, all the same, more than twenty thousand persons confessing the Hebrew faith.

No one can deny that throughout Russia the medical profession, the bar, the merchant class, the banks, the Press, and the Exchange were swarming with Jews, not to mention other lines of business, such as music, watchmaking, tailoring, and many more that were at least profitable, though not always honourable. On the other hand, no one ever observed that the Jews had understanding or inclination for agriculture, or had devoted themselves to that calling.

The Emperor Alexander I had already expressly granted permission to the Jews to acquire property in land and to farm it. His successor, Nicholas I, strove again and again, devoting considerable State funds to the purpose, to induce the Jews to settle on the land. To those who professed their willingness to do so he granted special privileges, such as exemption from compulsory military service. But it soon appeared that colonies of agriculturalists founded in this way could not maintain themselves. The Jewish population could simply not be accustomed to earning its livelihood by any means other than business or trade. So the well-intentioned attempt had to be given up, and a path was entered upon that led in the very opposite direction.

It was just in this unfortunate inaptitude of the Jews for healthy productive work that the core of the evil was to be found. The Government would never have had the slightest reason to adopt measures directed against the Jews had not these been rendered imperative by the necessity for protecting the Russian population, and especially the peasants. For the Jewish traders, speculators, and usurers constituted, for those people, the most serious economic danger. The Russian peasant was far too artless and credible to be able to defend himself with his own resources against the intelligence and the unscrupulousness of the Jews. The authorities had to come to the assistance of the people in this struggle for life by means of legislation, and this was the sole purpose of all the prescriptions and measures adopted to deal with the Jewish problem.

I can still remember how, about the year 1900, two governors from the Volga country complained of the activity of Jewish middlemen and monopolists in the Rudinsk corn region. The honest Russian traders could hardly hold their own, as the prices were fixed by a ring of Jewish profiteers, who were able to cut out all competition. And yet the two governors alluded to had no means, as they regretfully affirmed, of placing a check upon those practices, for in Old Russia the Government was run on the basis of legality—officials being prohibited from doing anything not sanctioned by the law and from using their own discretion, however appropriate such action might have seemed. In another case the Government intervened in the shady activities of those Jewish exploiters who had enmeshed all the bread supplies in the toils of their spider's net. The result was the long-drawn-out *Bread Case of Nizhny-Novgorod*, during which the Jews made every effort to drag through the mire the honourable name of the most exalted Government official of the district.

There *was* a certain kind of oppression of the Jews in Russia, but, unfortunately, this was far from being as effective as it ought to have been. The Government did seek to protect the peasants from the ruthless exploitation of the Jews; but its action bore only too little fruit, because, despite all prohibitions, the Jews used to go out from the small towns into the open country, and there buy up the harvest, practising the most outrageous usury. They were quite willing to take up any such business, but hard physical toil they took good care to avoid. Nor did I ever meet a Jew in the situation of a servant.

Another matter which led to continual disputes was that of military service. The Jews fought shy of serving in the army, and at the time of the calling up of the conscripts the Police had to carry on a regular campaign against those Jewish doctors, who, in consideration of generous cash payments, were always able to diagnose in their co-religionists some kind of ailment—it might be inflammation of the ear or chronic disease of the knee. A popular device was the wearing of glasses that were far too powerful and led to temporary defects of vision. The military doctors did not, it must be admitted, allow themselves to be taken in for very long, and kept a particularly sharp look-out when they had to do with Jews, so that many cases of malingering were successfully dealt with.

A series of trials before the courts that arose from affairs of the kind led the Jews to think of other means of escaping the detested military service. They endeavoured to make their way abroad in plenty of time; and as official permission to cross the frontier was not easy to obtain, they would secretly flee to Austria. That soon called into being a new profession that, of course, only Jews could follow: there grew up regular secret emigration offices, which worked hand in hand with smugglers living near the frontier. The latter were perfectly acquainted with all the bypaths along which they could take whole bands of deserters into Austria without ever being noticed. In order to put a stop to this state of things the Ministry of the Interior issued an order by which Jews who were occupied in smuggling out of the country young men of military age were expelled from the frontier governments.

After some years, however, there began an organized movement to encourage the emigration of Jewish families to America. It was carried on by the aid of false papers and other illegal means. It was the United States that proved most attractive to the Russian Jews, who hoped to enjoy a freer life there and, above all, to find opportunities of getting rich quickly. The other side of the picture, however, was not long in showing itself. In America every one who wants to make money must really work for it, and in this respect the Yankees admit of no compromise. In that country there has existed for a long time past a definite tariff for the payment of brokers, middlemen, and other agents, so that people of that class had no prospect of making great sums of money quickly and without effort as they had managed to do fairly easily in Russia, where they had had to do with ignorant peasants.

Hence there soon arose among many of the Jews who had migrated to America an ardent desire to return to Russia. The oppression under the Tsarist rule now seemed to them a more agreeable condition than the 'freedom' that reigned in America. This mood became so strong that the Council of the Jewish People sitting in New York determined to initiate action in the matter.

At the head of this Council sat the Russian physician Jakob Schiff, who had been one of the first to leave his home. He rendered many valuable services to his co-religionists and laid the foundation of that active Jewish policy that was to lead later on to such far-reaching and disastrous consequences.

They began, then, to sound the Russian Government as to its probable attitude to returning Russian Jews. These quondam deserters were, of course, already American subjects, and in Russia would have claimed all the rights of American citizens, and would, consequently, not have been amenable even to the special laws enforced in the Empire of the Tsar against the Jews. Our Ministry of the Interior, however, recognized at once the danger inherent in this assumption. Under the protection of their American citizenship these returned Jews would have been able to do with impunity the very things that the special legislation of the Empire had been intended to prevent. With these considerations in mind, the Ministry answered that the authorities would pay no attention whatever to the American citizenship of the returned emigrants and would treat them exactly as if they were Russian subjects.

Thereupon the Council of the Jewish People determined to bring pressure to bear upon the Russian Government. And, to this end, they set about using all possible means to effect the denunciation of a trade convention that had existed for more than a century between the United States and Russia, and that had proved very advantageous to both sides. They got the length of inducing the then President of the United States, Taft, to receive a deputation, who conveyed to him their lamentations over the alleged injustice of the Tsarist Government. It must be admitted that the President lost little time in replying to the deputation that the statements of the Jewish leaders were rather exaggerated. He also refused to undo the trade agreement which had always been observed by Russia with the utmost strictness and honour. The leader, Schiff, was so vexed by this snub that he would not shake hands with the President when he went away.

Then the Jewish Council had recourse to the most varied intrigues, and set about bringing all its influence to bear upon the world of finance. Within a year it was able to call into being a political situation that actually obliged President Taft to give way; under the extraordinary pressure exerted by the international power of the Jews, the commercial treaty with Russia was denounced. This unfriendly act on the part of the American Government took place in the year 1911, but it did not achieve the success the Jews had expected. The Russian Government was far too well aware of its own strength to yield to such pressure; it allowed the Liberal Press to storm as it would and troubled no more about it.

Still, the Jews were able to boast that they had revenged themselves on Russia, and could therewith satisfy that evil propensity which is so characteristic of the Jewish spirit. Or perhaps it was not thirst for vengeance when an orator at the Zionist Congress of the year 1904 proclaimed that the Tsar would have to pay with his blood for the *pogroms* he had instigated.

All these statements are not products of my own fancy. No; they are supported, from beginning to end, by documents which came under my purview while I occupied the post of

Chief of the Police. These documents also afford statistical proof that, for all offences of a political character, the majority of the accused have always been of Jewish nationality.

After the Revolution the Jews did indeed have abundant opportunities of exacting vengeance, and these opportunities they took care not to neglect. It is they who, through the Revolution, attained to power and wealth, so that when the question is asked, "Who, then, should bear the blame for the collapse of the Tsardom?" we may well answer in the old Roman phrase, "Is fecit cui prodest"—*i.e.,* he did the thing who profited by it. To-day there are lying in the Soviet Embassy in Berlin thirty pounds' weight of diamonds stolen in Russia and destined to serve the purposes of Bolshevik-Jewish international propaganda. Not till you have properly considered such facts, and many more, is it possible to grasp the meaning of that Roman proverbial saying and to recognize clearly who, above all others, are responsible for the downfall of the splendid Empire of the Russian Tsars.

A worthy representative of the new *régime* was that Jewish commissary who, after the Bolshevik Revolution, made himself notorious for some considerable time in Petersburg by his scandalous behaviour. This young fellow had been a seamen's barber in Odessa, and conducted himself after his promotion with such shamelessness that he excited the indignation even of the Communist Party. He abused his office for the purpose of instituting domiciliary investigations in all clubs, and of appropriating not merely whatever monies he found on hand, but even the stocks of wine. They subsequently discovered in his quarters a regular cellar, full of alcoholic beverages, which he had thus acquired by wholesale theft. He was finally handed over to the Revolutionary Tribunal, which, of course, acquitted him, as it was almost always in the way of doing with thieves and murderers.

CHAPTER VII

Russian Dissenters—Church Dispute over the Spelling of the Name of Jesus—The Tsar as Antichrist—Communist Sects—The Gospel of Sin —Shocking Self-inflicted Mutilations—The Dissenters and Leo Tolstoi— The Sect of Tramps

MY POLICE experience, especially the period of service spent in several provincial towns, brought me frequently into touch with Russian sectarianism, that peculiar side of the life of the people in Russia of which Western Europe knows very little, and of which, therefore, I shall say something in the following pages.

Perhaps nowhere outside of America does there exist such a plethora of religious sects as in Russia. And certainly in no part of the world is there to be found that strange mixture of religious fanaticism and political radicalism which is characteristic of many of the Russian sects. Owing to the circumstance that many of these brotherhoods indulged in ardent political propaganda, the Police of the Empire was obliged to take a fairly close interest in these Dissenters. The authorities could not ignore the activities of zealots whose whole teaching tended to forbid obedience to both the temporal and the ecclesiastical powers, and to insist that the rule of the Tsar meant the rule of Antichrist.

Probably the most widespread of these sects is that of the Old Believers. The history of their rise is very typical of much in the spiritual make-up of the Russian peasant class. In the sixteenth century the Church, under the guidance of the energetic Patriarch Nikon, set about purging the Liturgy and the sacred books of numerous errors that had crept in in the course of ages. But the reform met with violent opposition on the part of the people. It was especially a change made in the spelling of the name of Jesus that excited most bitter feeling in the minds of men: the uneducated people, deeply attached to tradition, actually believed that the change of one letter in this word sufficed to turn the Saviour's name into the name of Satan.

All attempts made by the Church authorities to convince the people of their mistake proved fruitless. In the country every innovation in the forms of service and in the prayers was obstinately resisted; and when the Church ultimately had recourse to forcible measures, threatening everyone who refused to accept the new liturgy with excommunication, the only result was that great numbers of convinced Old Believers banded themselves together in open opposition. The Solovyetsky monastery, for example, which was a stronghold of the Old Believers, defended itself for seven years against the reforms, until, on the command of the Tsar, it was taken by assault.

This sect continued persistently to stand out against all the measures of compulsion adopted by the Government. Some of them fled over the nearest frontiers; some concealed themselves in bands in the impenetrable forests, to issue forth again in all manner of disguises, appearing among the people in order to spread their peculiar tenets. More than once it happened that one of these communities, rather than fall into the hands of its persecutors, voluntarily chose death by fire, men and women shutting themselves up in their huts and then setting light to them.

The whole movement was at that time directed quite as much against the Tsar as against the Church, for, to the ignorant people, the reforms instituted by Peter appeared to be the work of the Devil, and the Emperor himself as the Ambassador of Antichrist. Nevertheless Peter the Great allowed the Old Believers to be persecuted only so long as they constituted a danger to the State, and afterward granted them, under certain conditions, the privilege of observing their own rites and customs without let or hindrance.

The Tsarina Catherine carried this policy of toleration even farther, for she actually invited the Old Believers who had fled abroad to return to Russia. From that time onward the Government adopted toward them, for the most part, a more or less indulgent attitude, and made an attempt to stop only the most blatant excesses of the Dissenters.

In the course of time there developed among the Old Believers several varieties, some of which showed greater inclination to compromise with the existing order. The most radical group, however—they were called the Priestless—continued to maintain their irreconcilable views, steadfastly rejecting the Church in every form as well as the State. It does not require to be said that the authorities were often enough compelled to intervene with appropriate energy against the consequences of such senseless ideas.

No less strange were the teachings of some other bodies that had grown up in the course of the nineteenth century. The Stundists, who were widely disseminated, especially in the south of the Empire, preached a sort of Puritanism, affirming that the Orthodox Church with its ceremonies was nothing else than pagan idolatry, while the true Christian should believe only in the Gospel. This sect itself may have been harmless enough; but a brotherhood, sprung from it and calling itself the New Stundists, soon evolved a sinister Anarchist programme. These taught that on earth no other power must rule than the power of God, and that we need neither Government nor any other authority; the land belongs to the community; all property must be subservient to the general weal; all private ownership is sinful. That is to say, the views of these New Stundists amounted to nothing else than Communism coloured by religion, and against that the Government had to defend itself as against any similar aspirations of a purely political nature.

Other sects, such as the Non-Prayers, refused steadily to pay taxes or dues of any kind, and likewise preached Communism under the guise of religious claims. In the Caucasus there arose the sect of God's People, whose ambition it was to realize heaven here on earth; and they too insisted upon the common ownership of property. One group of these God's People, calling themselves Duchobors—they denied the divinity of the Holy Ghost—combined to form a kind of independent State in a pathless mountainous region. The centre of the community was formed by the Orphan Home, where their leader dwelt. As these Duchobors were otherwise a quiet, orderly folk, the Tsarist authorities nearly always managed to come to a peaceful understanding with them.

Much less innocent were certain other sects, still numerously represented in Russia: the Chlysty, the Skoptsy, the Molokany, and the Stranniky. The first-named trace their history back to a certain Daniel Filipitsh, living in the seventeenth century, who, having been enlightened from above, recognized the 'only true doctrine,' which consists simply in the belief that man, even in his lifetime, can be united with God, and that Christ is ever receiving a new incarnation and continually walks upon this earth in the form of a peasant. From this belief the Chlysty arrived at the dangerous opinion that man must sin in order to attain to God, for without sin there can be no repentance, and without repentance there is no redemption. This doubtful view of morals led them to all manner of extremely grave sensual excesses, which over and over again brought them into conflict with the authorities of both Church and State.

The Skoptsy again are a sect that was, and is still, widespread. The name means 'eunuchs.' For certain sayings in the Gospel according to St. John they believe that there is only one interpretation: if a man is ever to join the company of the elect he must maim himself. This cruel ceremony is carried out at secret meetings held by night, and is followed by dancing and revelry continued until those taking part are in a condition of absolute frenzy. The amazing fact is that this body, whose practices can only be described as religious insanity, counts many adherents not merely among the peasants, but among townspeople, the merchant class, and even officials.

The Molokany do not indulge in such sexual abnormalities, but they evince a violent hostility to the State and all its measures. Consequently, under the Tsardom, they were in a state of permanent and stubborn conflict with the authorities, striving continually, by every possible device, to escape their control. Their views were closely related to the teaching of Leo Tolstoi and exercised a strong influence upon him.

Finally, the Stranniky represent the out-and-out Anarchist element among the Russian peasants. The Strannik ('pilgrim') wanders restlessly and aimlessly through the country, carefully avoiding all contact with the representatives of the State and the order it stands for. He possesses either no identification papers or else false ones, he conceals his real name with the utmost persistence, and thus succeeds in avoiding all social obligations. At the beginning of the twentieth century there were still thousands of such Dissenters wandering over the Empire. In the villages there were people holding the same views: their task was to conceal the migrants from the authorities and to supply them secretly with food and lodging in dark cellars. So the Stranniky were really in a way an organized guild of tramps, the suppression of which, in the interests of public order and security, was indeed highly necessary, but as a rule, in practice, uncommonly difficult.

The Government of the Tsar tried again and again, by indulgence and toleration, to come to a peaceful accommodation with the various sects; and in part it succeeded. But those fanatical sects that, on principle, denied not only Church, but State as well, aiming at a Communistic world order and regarding all possession, nay, even the foundation of a family, as sin, had of necessity to be kept within bounds by force. Thus it came about that the struggle with these Dissenters had to be included among the duties of the Russian Police, and it was certainly not one of the easiest.

CHAPTER VIII

Spy-fever—Campaign against People with German Names—The Suspected House-porter Witte—Kaiser Wilhelm's Aides-de-camp in Petersburg!—Ineptitude of the Army Command—Senseless Severity, Equally Senseless Leniency—Ochrana and War Espionage—Jealousy between War Department and Police—Disorganization of the Transport System —The Spy-fever and the Suchomlinov Case

WITH the outbreak of war came a wave of patriotic enthusiasm; but along with this appeared a most unwelcome phenomenon in the form of hysterical fear of spies. This 'spy-fever' ran through the whole Russian population like a plague.

Innocent people who had been settled in Russia for years and years, bakers, butchers, shoemakers, and tailors, were all of a sudden regarded as agents of Kaiser William; and the suspicion extended even to many absolutely loyal Russians, who merely had the misfortune to bear German surnames. This morbid temper was stimulated by the sensational Press, and led to the formation in the Duma of a special anti-German group under the leadership of Chvostov, which soon became very influential.

Many persons changed their name at that time, including men in very distinguished positions, like V. K. Sabler, the Chief Procurator of the Holy Synod, who received special permission from the Emperor to assume the name of Dezyatovsk. People whose name was Kaiser were peculiarly hard hit. Certainly there were individuals who showed themselves superior or indifferent to all that mass of prejudice and who did not change their names, preferring to prove their patriotism rather by their courageous bearing in face of the enemy. One of these was General Zimmermann, who afterward fought bravely also in the White Army against the Bolsheviks.

Even the lower class of people sought everywhere for German spies. In the very first days of the War a man called at my office in a state of great excitement, and reported that he had heard from the neighbouring flat the noise of a typewriter and the voices of the members of a "secret association"; he was sure he had discovered a nest of spies. Although from the start I was disposed to be sceptical with regard to such tale-bearing, my duty compelled me to have investigation made. The result of the inquiry was to show that the "secret association" consisted of some friends of the Chief Secretary to the Senate, while, as for the typewriter, the over-zealous citizen must have dreamt of it, for there was not one to be found in any flat in the whole building.

Another time I received a letter warning me to keep an eye upon a person having the well-known name of Witte. This man was a house-porter on the Petersburg Side. When I had looked through his papers and had, as a matter of precaution, ordered observation to be kept for a time upon his comings out and goings in, I came to the conclusion that this Witte was a more trustworthy and patriotic man than his famous namesake.

Unfortunately, there were also highly placed officials in the State service who had fallen victims to this dread of spies, and who, in consequence, committed many an act of injustice against loyal Russian subjects. Among them must be included my former superior, General Junkovsky, in other respects an exceptionally honest and conscientious officer. Certain men of the most pronounced patriotic way of thinking he had prosecuted as spies, for no other reason than that they had been employed, many years before the War, as journalists on the staff of a review published in Germany. At his instigation these unfortunate persons were banished to the remotest governments of the Empire, although there did not exist a shred of evidence to prove their guilt.

As late as the beginning of 1917 an episode took place which was quite characteristic in this respect. One day I was summoned by the President of the Council of Ministers, Prince N. D. Golitsin, who confided to me in very mysterious tones that, according to information he had received, two aides-de-camp of Kaiser Wilhelm were residing in Petersburg: they had been seen, a few days before, walking along the Nevsky-Prospekt, dressed as civilians, of course, and "with their coat-collars turned up." I answered that I was already acquainted with that legend, and knew also the member of the Duma who had told the Prime Minister the dreadful tale. Then I named Colonel Engelhardt.

Count Golitsin, who till then had been very reserved and apparently quite calm, looked at me, you might say, in terror and utmost amazement, asking me how on earth I knew that. I did *not* tell him the sources of my information, but I managed to convince him of the senselessness of the rumour, to which even he had given credence.

In itself this whole incident would not have been of such importance as to call for special reference. The story of the German officers walking in the streets of the Russian capital might have been told everywhere and after a few days forgotten, to be replaced by some other equally ill-founded tale. But as a matter of fact the invention was quoted as a proof of the slackness of the Government, and of its inability to defend the Empire from the external foe. What kind of police was that that allowed the most dangerous spies to move about unmolested even in Petersburg? It was such idle gossip that gave rise to the parrot-cry, soon in everybody's mouth, "Things cannot go on like this!"

During the War much disorder was created by the inde-

pendent action of the military authorities, who had had conferred upon them the right of removing, without formality of
any kind, from the war zone all persons whom they deemed to
be suspicious. Governors representing the Civil Power were
obliged, in matters of this kind, to submit to the instructions
of the military commanders and to carry out their orders. The
officers commanding the various army groups would send
whole bands of people away from the territories under their
jurisdiction. The exiles had to look out for a place of residence somewhere else; and an untenable state of things arose,
for hundreds of persons thus driven from home, being free
to choose, took refuge in towns where their presence was
essentially as dangerous as in the war zone itself.

For quite a long time the Army proceeded thus independently, the civil authorities having no say at all in this matter
of the expulsion of undesirable elements from the war zone.
At last an understanding was arrived at; and from that time
onward, whenever the Army Command decided upon a case,
the facts were sent at once to the Police Department, and
the Ministry of the Interior determined the locality where
the undesirables were to reside. The effect of this new regula-
tion was that the exiles were equally distributed, and were
absolutely prohibited from entering those governments where
there were important munition factories or similar industries
connected with the supply of the materials of war. That was
how the Ministry of the Interior did at last succeed, by peaceful means, in taking over again from the Army Command the
functions that properly belonged to it.

Hundreds of such cases of expulsion from the war zone
came under my personal observation; and many a time I
could not but shake my head over the primitive methods
adopted by the military authorities in making the necessary

inquiries, and the summary fashion they had of dealing with innocent persons, dubbing them simply spies.

The most irresponsible denunciations were listened to by some military officials with a willing ear. There was a certain two-faced rascal, a suspicious character if ever there was one, who long before had been dismissed from the Secret Service of the Ochrana. He got into touch with the Commandant of the Military District of Dunaburg, whom the adventurer imposed upon with a fantastic tale of his own invention, stating that he had come upon the tracks of a widespread conspiracy, aiming at the blowing up of all the bridges and the munition-dumps in the district. The Commandant fell blindly into the snare, and set all the machinery in motion to make sure that the structures and points alleged to be threatened were protected from criminal onslaughts. It was not until General Kurlov was referred to—he recognized at once the name of the notorious informer—that it came out that there was not a word of truth in the whole story of conspiracy.

General Kurlov complained to me frequently of the amount of trouble he was caused, in his capacity of Civil Governor of the Baltic Provinces, by false reports of espionage and sabotage. The German-speaking population of the region was continually being accused of co-operating with the enemy and of supplying them with news of the movements of our troops. Information was coming in all the time to the effect that the tower of this or the other castle owned by some German Baltic baron was being used for the purpose of transmitting signals to the German army, or even to the German fleet. Wireless stations were being scented out everywhere. In the end, General Kurlov found it necessary to adopt the plan of having every estate in the country visited by commissions appointed for the purpose, whose business it was to determine whether any illegal work was going on.

An old savant who had had a small observatory erected on his property near Riga suffered severely through the universal *spy-fever*. Police, military, and naval authorities visited this observatory not once but many times, and ransacked it from top to bottom.

Kurlov laughed as he told me how an old Lett (Lithuanian) had called upon him, and stated that he and others had seen a German military aeroplane land in the estate of a German baron. The proprietor had received the flying officers and entertained them hospitably. Not satisfied with that, the Lithuanian peasant added that, on their departure, the German airman had seized a cow and carried it off. It was with reports of that kind that the highest authorities had to waste their time in those days!

And it happened often that the Military Intelligence officers themselves perpetrated the most incredible blunders, so that they were hardly distinguishable from the ignorant country-people in their panic fear of spies. Thus there were many cases in which the Staff insisted upon the expulsion of certain people, and justified their demand by asserting that these persons were far too well informed as to the positions occupied by units of the enemy's troops. Closer investigation brought out the fact that these were our own spies, who had already been the means of keeping us accurately posted in everything connected with the movements of the German army. The ill-founded dread lest such spies should be working for the enemy as well induced the army commanders summarily to interrupt the activities of these people, invaluable as they were, and to banish them from the war zone. And no doubt, in taking that action, they never stopped to reflect that, after all, experienced spies could not be replaced as easily as housemaids or clerks.

I was well acquainted with a Frenchman named J. R. Kurz,

who had been settled in Russia for a very long time. He taught at the Petersburg Commercial School and was also a correspondent for the Associated Press. Being a journalist, he had been received by many Ministers and other persons of high rank, and so, when the War came, it had not been a very difficult matter for him to secure a post in the Intelligence Service on the Southern Front. His knowledge made him of great value to us, for, as his mother had been a Hungarian by birth, he spoke Magyar fluently. After one year of service it was recognized that the results of his work were really splendid, and Kurz was decorated with the Cross of Vladimir of the Fourth Class.

When he was spending his leave in Petersburg I met him and he related to me some details of his experience. He had penetrated quite a long way into Hungary to spy out the conditions prevailing in the country and the strength of the Austrian Army. Shortly afterward I was visited by Count Ignatiev, his superior in the Service, who requested me to tell him frankly what I thought of Kurz. I said all the good I could of him, for I guessed the reason for the exceptional interest that was being taken in him. I specially stressed the complete absence of any kind of suspicion against him, pointing out that, not even in the most confidential talks I had had with him, had I observed anything peculiar about him.

How great therefore was my surprise when, a few days later, Kurz was arrested by the order of the military authorities, under the suspicion of espionage. At my request the case was personally investigated by the Procurator attached to the Court of Libau, A. A. Tshernyavsky, who declared to me, after making a careful study of the documents, that there was not a particle of evidence that Kurz was guilty of treachery. The whole affair ended in smoke, and Kurz was set free after five months' detention. Of course, along with the Order he had received for special merit, he was now wearing the indelible mark that stamps the suspected spy.

In strange contrast to the senseless severity shown by the Military in this case was their attitude on other occasions, when energetic measures would have been appropriate. When Russian troops had driven the Austrians out of a Galician village a curious find was made in the garret of the cottage where the enemy's G.H.Q. had been quartered. In one of a number of documents belonging to the Austrian Intelligence Service was a list of five Jews, who were employed as permanent agents receiving a fixed monthly allowance from the Austrian Espionage authorities, to whom they had furnished valuable reports concerning the positions of our troops. All this was exactly stated in the Austrian papers, which even included a detailed account of the sums paid to those five Jews. They were arrested, but instead of bringing them at once before a court-martial the Staff merely decided to expel them from the war zone.

When the record of the proceedings reached me, I submitted a report to the Ministry of the Interior conveying my view that this case was not one to be punished by administrative expulsion, but should be dealt with by court-martial and sentence of death. The Ministry did memorialize in this sense the General Officer Commanding, Brussilov, but I do not know how the affair ended, for the documents never came back to me. I hope, however, that those five spies did not escape their well-deserved fate.

In another case of espionage and communication with the enemy the military authorities showed similar ineptitude. Near the Riga front an officer's wife was denounced. She was said to be entertaining nightly officers on furlough, encouraging them to drink heavily, with a view to getting them to betray important points of strategy, which information she passed on to the enemy. The woman was a German by birth, and the charges against her, which had come to the knowledge of the Intelligence Department of our Army Command, sounded very definite. This time again, to my amazement, the military authorities did nothing more than recommend the woman for deportation from the war zone.

The question arises why the Military Intelligence people, as soon as this wasps' nest of German espionage had been discovered, did not have the sense to make the most of their opportunity. It would surely have been easy enough to unravel in a very short time the threads of this business, and to track down all the accomplices. If, on the other hand, thorough investigation had revealed that there was no foundation whatever for the accusations made against that officer's wife, it would have been the duty of the authorities to bring the informers in question to a sharp account for spreading such slander. Instead of doing that, they decided upon half-measures, and simply suggested the deportation of the suspect.

The explanation of such vagaries may perhaps be found in the haste with which the Intelligence Sections of the Army were improvised. Almost of necessity they consisted of inexperienced people, who were often quite unable to understand the supreme importance of the duties entrusted to them. Many of the officers now responsible for the safety of the troops had been, in time of peace, engineers or teachers at the Military Academy, and had had no training of any kind to prepare them for their new office.

All the more disastrous was the blunder committed by General Junkovsky, Under-Secretary for Home Affairs, when he decided upon the suppression of the Ochrana agencies in the Army. It was just at that time, once the War had come, that the revolutionary agitators began to devote particular attention to the Army, and to employ any and every means to work upon the minds of the soldiers through their poisonous propaganda; and the military authorities, lacking in the requisite experience, were practically helpless in face of those sinister machinations.

It was still more serious that most of the military commanders, one might almost say deliberately, closed their eyes whenever it was a question of revolutionary intrigues among their units. These officers simply refused to admit, either to themselves or to anyone else, the barest possibility of there being anything like indiscipline or political ferment among the men under their command. So it came about that they looked askance at any intervention of the Ochrana in Army affairs, and strove so persistently for the abolition of all Ochrana establishments in the Army that they succeeded in achieving their aim by having those offices closed. For General Junkovsky made the great mistake of relying upon the assurances of the Staff that he could quite safely leave the necessary political supervision of the troops to their own officers. It was then that he issued the circular which categorically prohibited the Ochrana from taking any interest whatever in the internal concerns of the Army.

General Kurlov had prepared a scheme for opening booths and refreshment huts in the neighbourhood of the barracks, under the management of Ochrana agents, with a view to exercising some measure of observation and check upon the state of feeling among the soldiers. But that plan was not carried out either.

From the papers that came into my office daily I could not but notice, with growing sorrow and concern, what unfortunate results were ensuing upon that unwise attitude of the Ministry of the Interior. For the Ochrana agents, who in the performance of their duty still came into contact with military men of any rank, did not, of course, fail to report what they observed, so that, although the secret agencies in the Army had ceased to exist, we continued all the same to receive regular information as to the temper of the soldiers, and that information became more and more disquieting.

More than once during the War the Ochrana had to deal with affairs of espionage. On one occasion the activity of the "black cabinet" led to the discovery of a nest of German spies in South Russia. The correspondence of these people was conducted in cipher, but we managed to find the key and consequently to suppress the whole company.

In a similar way the Ochrana unearthed a group of German spies in Ismail. All the written evidence in this case was in cipher. But as every one of the members of this organization that we arrested had the same calendar upon him, it was almost obvious that the calendar contained the solution to the mystery. And, as a matter of fact, it did enable us to decode the whole of the records of this group; and they proved to be important.

It often happened that in espionage affairs the Ochrana and the Military were following the same clue; and unfortunately it was only rarely possible to achieve anything like useful co-operation. As a rule, the military authorities showed a certain jealousy of the Police, a circumstance which frequently made the inquiries considerably more difficult and reduced the probability of success. One way in which the Ministry of War showed this jealousy was to ignore systematically communications received from the Ochrana. Of reports derived from the most reliable sources the Minister of War would declare that, after thorough investigation, the information in question had proved to be wrong. It is certainly not my desire to make the General Staff alone responsible for various mistakes that were made at that time, but justice demands that it should be plainly stated that, with few exceptions, the military authorities fell far short of what was expected of them in these police matters. In making this observation I wish to rebut the baseless accusation, so often made against the Ministry of the Interior, of having been remiss in the measures it adopted to counter the revolutionary agitation and to ward off the general collapse.

I still remember the conversations I had with General P. K. Solovyov, then Chief of the North-western Railways Police. He complained to me of the frequency with which the Army Staff insisted upon the immediate dispatch of trains with war stores, pointing out that it was through the execution of those orders that the so-called blocks in the railway traffic arose. Repeatedly Solovyov had to go in person to some important junction or other in order to clear away the jam: slow trains had to be kept waiting, so that trains carrying munitions and other goods for the Army might get through faster. A particular reason for complaint was that wagons sent off to Warsaw never came back to the points of departure, which led to increasing lack of rolling-stock at these stations, and rendered it difficult to make up new trains. What the military authorities were doing in Warsaw was to unload the trains, shunt them into sidings in order to clear the main line, and then to leave them to stand there to all eternity.

"All order is upset, and it can hardly be restored again," declared General Solovyov. "And this has come about mainly, because those in command of the Army are entirely unacquainted with the rules and the technique of the railway service. Then the task falls to me, a police official, to sort out these blocks; I have continually to act as an intermediary, endeavouring to reconcile the demands of the military with those of the railway management. In cases of urgent need for the Army, even food trains have to be kept waiting for days."

There, perhaps, we have the first cause of the rapidly increasing dearth of necessities, the consequence of which, in its turn, was the universal economic collapse. Of course the traders were anxious to exploit the exceptional conditions for their own advantage, and, once prices had risen, did not want to bring them down again. Officials and workmen, on the other hand, basing their claims upon the increased cost of living, were continually crying for higher salaries or wages.

When I was still Assistant Chief of Police I received a call, on one occasion, from the President of the Moscow Association of Merchants and Manufacturers, G. P. Guyon, a shrewd, staid, Russified Frenchman, whom I had never met before. In great detail and with much ability he expounded the view that was generally prevalent, that the irregularity in the goods and passenger traffic might lead to dangerous excitement among the people, and that timely steps should be taken to meet such an emergency. One example he quoted was this: important raw materials intended for Moscow, and coming from towns in the north, were kept lying for weeks in the stations for want of trucks to take them, while there were standing in the same stations empty trucks, which, however, were reserved for the Ministry of War and were not allowed to be used. According to Guyon the failure to secure delivery of raw materials was reducing the productivity in the factories, thus causing unrest and discontent among the workmen, which provided a favourable soil for the undesirable agitation of the Socialists. Guyon concluded his speech by affirming that, as representative and head of the Association, he had at heart only the commercial interests of the manufacturers, and that these were making it their object to keep down the number of dismissals. But he said he was afraid that, in the very near future, all their efforts would be absolutely fruitless, for none of the attempts made to convince the General Staff of the necessity for introducing some kind of regularity in the train service and an orderly distribution of railway wagons had so far met with any success.

The exceptionally serious points that arose from my conversation with Guyon I passed on to my Chief, Briand de Saint-Hypolite, with the request that he should submit them to the Under-Secretary, W. O. Junkovsky. But the steps that were taken were quite inadequate to secure any result whatever, for the Army, in the person of the all-powerful General Yanushkyevitsh, showed absolutely no consideration for the plight of the interior of the country. In the consciousness of his power, Yanushkyevitsh gave orders to the men at the head of the War Department as if the general condition of things within the State was a matter of complete indifference.

The universal spy-fever led in two cases to results which, even with respect to their influence upon the repute of the Russian Army, were extremely grave. I have in my mind the trials of Colonel Myassoyedov and of Suchomlinov, the Minister of War.

It was a Member of the Duma, Gutshkov, about whose personality I shall have something to say later, that raised the hue and cry against Colonel Myassoyedov, by asserting that he possessed overwhelming proofs that Myassoyedov had committed high treason. Inspired by Gutshkov, the *Evening Times* began its 'revelations' about Myassoyedov, and demanded that legal proceedings should be instituted against this officer. It was characteristic of the spiritual corruption of the so-called "cultured circles" in Russia that this indictment, brought by a disreputable newspaper, should have found at once a willing public and have been generally believed. If anyone still asked sceptically whether all that was really true, he would generally receive the reply, spoken with conviction, "It must be true when it is in the papers!"

Very soon, by order of the Higher Command, Myasso-

yedov's case was taken up by a military court of inquiry; but
the Yellow Press was now not to be satisfied with that, and
was already demanding roundly the condemnation of the
alleged traitor. At G.H.Q. they happened to attribute far too
much importance to the Petersburg press and, generally speaking, to whatever took place in the Capital. So it came about
that politics turned the scales in circles that ought to have
been attending exclusively to questions of strategy. Colonel
Myassoyedov was first of all acquitted by the court-martial.
Thereupon, however, at the express command of the Grand
Duke Nicholai Nicholayevitsh a second trial was held, and it
ended with a sentence of death for the accused. The sentence
was executed shortly after it was pronounced. I am informed
that Myassoyedov, in despair, tried to commit suicide by opening an artery with a fragment of the metal frame of his eye-
glasses. This attempt was, however, discovered in time, and
from that moment till his execution the unhappy man was
in close company with a warder.

In the official records the condemnation of Myassoyedov
is justified by the statement that the Colonel had been con-
victed of espionage and pillage. The second accusation was
based upon the fact that, when he was on the East Prussian
front, he had sent to some near relative a lamp and a picture. But the prosecution had been quite unable to prove that
Myassoyedov had acquired the articles mentioned by *pillage*
and not by legitimate purchase. As for the other count, espionage, the officer was alleged to have received ten thousand roubles from the enemy as the price of his treachery, but there
was no clue whatever as to the whereabouts of the money.
Indeed, neither in the possession of Myassoyedov, nor in that
of his wife, nor in that of his relatives, could they discover
any sums of money worth mentioning.

After the Revolution, Myassoyedov's case was reopened, and

everybody involved at the time in this affair was acquitted. Of course the unfortunate Colonel had been executed long before then, so that he could not take advantage of this rectification of the miscarriage of justice.

Almost at the same time as the campaign against Myasso-yedov, the outcry against the Minister of War, Suchomlinov, was raised. This also was the work of Gutshkov and his acolytes. This time it was a definite act of vengeance originating with General Polivanov, Gutshkov's most intimate friend. Polivanov occupied the office of Assistant to the Minister of War (Under-Secretary), and had for some time been on very good terms with the Minister, until he began to throw in his lot with the Duma. Suchomlinov did not like this and sought to force him more and more into the background. It was for that that Polivanov, an ambitious man, was now avenging himself in this barbarous manner.

Suchomlinov was accused of treason. What amount of truth there was in the evidence adduced I had excellent and direct means of judging. In those days I was Assistant Chief of the Police Department, and was closely associated with the members of the Court that had to try the Minister. Now, the Examining Magistrate, Kotshubinsky, showed me one day in triumph a document which he characterized as a "convincing proof" of guilt. It was a letter posted in Carlsbad and addressed to the wife of the War Minister by a merchant, named Altschiller, belonging to Kiev. The letter conveyed the information that it was raining in Carlsbad, that the roads were bad, and that, consequently, long walks were out of the question. When I asked the magistrate in amazement, how such a letter could possibly serve to prove Suchomlinov's guilt, he said that it was quite certain that the words contained a hidden meaning: the reference to the rain and bad roads really covered something different. In reply to my inquiry as to the mysterious significance of the letter he waved his hand as if to suggest that my question was rather silly, for the hidden sense was there all right, but answered, "The devil knows what the man meant!"

It was upon such evidence that the monstrous charge was built up, that Suchomlinov, the Imperial War Minister, had been guilty of treasonable practices in order to assist the enemy! And meanwhile, the extraordinarily valuable services rendered by him in the reorganization of the Army were forgotten. It had been due to his work that the mobilization was carried out with such astonishing rapidity: he had raised to a high level the efficiency of the Remount Department in the cavalry; he had brought about the re-arming of the Artillery; he had organized the Military Air Service; he had created the Motor Service, which was so important in the War; he had fundamentally reformed the internal administration of War Office business.

The Chief Public Prosecutor, V. P. Nossovitsh, who conducted the case against Suchomlinov throughout the whole trial, failed to produce the slightest evidence to show what had become of the monies which the Minister must have received for his treachery; yet these sums of money must have been large. Despite this obviously serious lacuna in the structure of the proof led against Suchomlinov—and it was shaky enough anyway—he was condemned, certainly, as I have already indicated, a victim of faction and intrigue. It is shameful enough that the aged General had to wait for his release from severe imprisonment till the coming of the Bolshevik Government. After the general amnesty granted by the Soviets had liberated him from prison, Suchomlinov ended his life in dire poverty. If he had really been a traitor and had received large sums of money from the Germans, things would probably have been otherwise.

After thinking these matters over for many years I am to-day still firmly convinced that neither Colonel Myassoyedov nor General Suchomlinov ever committed criminal actions. They were perhaps thoughtless and imprudent, but that they were guilty of deliberate treachery I find as difficult to believe as ever. Even among Russian refugees I have often been told that I was wrong in my opinion; that it was absolutely impossible to imagine what incredible sums the Germans had spent during the War on bribery; that positive proofs were to be found in the archives of the German Staff.

But even this argument does not convince me, for I know from my long years of experience that often *amounts of money were entered as having been paid to certain individuals without those persons having actually received them*. That happened, for example, in a case of espionage which my superior, General Junkovsky, handed over to be dealt with by me personally. As it is typical of the situation I have in mind, I shall give a brief account of it.

One day we received from our Foreign Agency a long telegram, in which Krassilnikov, who was in charge of our service abroad, communicated a very interesting piece of news: the Germans had approached a political refugee with the proposal that he should assist them in carrying out certain schemes they had formed for doing deliberate damage in Russia. Unfortunately, the Germans had applied to the wrong man, for this refugee was one of our secret agents, and immediately got into touch with the Foreign Department of the Ochrana. For some considerable time I had heard nothing more of this business when, one day, that refugee appeared in person in my office. He described in detail the enemy's plans and then took from his pocket thirteen thousand roubles in banknotes. The money he handed over to me, saying that it was the amount the Germans had paid him to meet travelling expenses.

General Suchomlinov, Minister of War in 1914

RASPUTIN

They had promised him a much larger sum if he managed to blow up a bridge, a railway-line, or a factory. The agent, you see, had accepted the money, but, being the loyal official that he was he passed it over, according to instructions. I am convinced that, in the papers of the German Intelligence Service, he is noted as having received that bribe, so that in the eyes of people who do not know the real facts of the case he must seem very seriously compromised.

CHAPTER IX

Rasputin—His Behaviour in Society—His Debauchery—The 'Healing' of the Heir to the Throne—Rasputin's Political Influence and its Limitations—Petitioners who appealed to Rasputin—His Relations with the Tsar and the Tsarina

OF THE countless lies that have become current about the last years of the Russian Tsardom the majority are associated with the name of Rasputin. Therefore I feel that I am under an obligation to treat this subject at some length, and, making use of the information and the notes that are at my disposal, to sketch a truer picture of that much reviled person and of his significance in Russian politics.

The Rasputin Affair bears no little resemblance to the famous Necklace Affair that, in a sense, started the French Revolution. In France the people who were preparing to bring about the Revolution found in that scandal the means to lower the prestige of the Royal House and thereby to undermine the Throne. The men of the Russian Revolution made use in a similar fashion and for similar ends of the famous peasant monk. But the saddest thing about this episode is that even members of the Imperial family took part in the calumny directed against the Tsar and the Tsarina; this feature distinguishes the Russian catastrophe from the fall of the Bourbons.

Who was Rasputin? A simple, illiterate, Russian peasant, but, at the same time, one endowed with great natural sagacity. He came from the little village of Pokrovskoye on the Tura—that is, from the nearest part of Western Siberia. His father was a carter there, and he himself had followed this calling until, like so many Siberian peasants, he had been seized with a certain religious ecstasy, and had left his home to wander all over Russia as a pilgrim.

After he had visited Mount Athos, his path brought him at last to Petersburg, where he attracted the interest of several dignitaries of the Church by his sensible and edifying addresses on religious matters. By their intermediary he made the acquaintance of the Grand Duke Nikolai Nikolayevitsh, whose wife introduced him to the Tsarina.

From that time onward he frequented various circles in the highest ranks of society in the capital, and was often made too much of. But he was under no delusion as to his own abilities: he was fully aware that he was not intellectually equal to the part that was now being thrust upon him. His complete want of education prevented him from grasping even the main lines, much less the details, of things he was expected to accomplish by his influence. However, he had enough natural intelligence to be able, in many things, to form a sound judgment. Wherever he might be, he used to observe attentively all that was said and done; and from what he had perceived with his innate peasant wit he was often able to make very intelligent deductions. Hardly ever did he put questions which would have revealed his lack of culture, and this circumstance it was that led people so generally to overestimate his knowledge.

Many a time I had the opportunity of meeting Rasputin and of conversing with him about a great variety of topics. On these occasions I was struck over and over again by the care and patience with which he sought to grasp the essentials of the matter of discourse; every speaker he listened to with an attention that was almost too strained, in his obvious endeavour not to lose the thread of the discussion. It was only now and then that he himself made a remark, and when he did it was, as a rule, very much to the point. More than once I heard him break in upon some highfalutin ravings with a matter-of-fact interjection that had the effect of bringing the babbler down from his airy talk to sober reality.

His political views, so far as he possessed any at all, were simple enough. He was nothing more than a plain Russian patriot and a genuine Monarchist, but not in the sense given to that word to-day: he was neither a Left, nor a Right, nor a Constitutional Monarchist, for Monarchy meant for him rather a kind of religion. Russia without a Tsar was something he could not conceive of. The subtleties of so-called higher politics went far beyond his horizon, and he was quite unable to comprehend what the various parties, or the groups in the Duma, or the newspapers were ultimately aiming at. His fundamental principle in politics consisted simply in the *pacification,* as far as that was possible, of the enemies of the Tsar. In this sense he once explained to me with great ardour his view, that the Ministers should devote all their energy to the pacification of all internal foes. He said he was sorry for the latter, for they knew not what they did; all that was needed was to show them the error of their ways, and at once all disorder would come to an end.

However artless he was in politics, he took a very great interest in all that appeared to him to be of practical importance and value for the people. Even in Petersburg drawing-rooms he still remained enough of a peasant to be able to sympathize with the peasants and to understand their needs. Thus in the months preceding his death he was very actively occupied with the problem of the food-supply, which was becoming daily more and more urgent. As I have already indicated, various circumstances had created certain difficulties in the provisioning of the country, and Rasputin considered it to be one of the most important duties of the Government to provide remedial measures. His opinions on this point he did not, like so many of the politicians, dress in a cloud of beautiful phrases, but said simply, "You must feed the people; then they'll be quiet." He was right when he declared that the task of victualling the country should be entrusted to the Minister who was in the best position to distribute the food supplies. And that was the Minister of the Interior.

Before I had become personally acquainted with Rasputin, I had been told repeatedly of his boastfulness. People were particularly indignant because of the way he bragged, in and out of season, of his intimate relations with the Imperial family. I had heard a lot of talk, too, about the reputed hypnotic power of his eyes; indeed, the wildest legends were current on this subject. Consequently, when I did meet him, my chief object was to test the truthfulness of those statements. So I would sit right opposite him whenever the thing was practicable, and try to impress upon my mind every one of his gestures, every tiniest change in the play of his features, every word he uttered. What I saw did not correspond at all to the reports that were in circulation. There was not the least sign of self-satisfaction about him. The impression I received was rather, that he was fully aware of his inferiority in the matter of education to those around him. If he did occasionally make some allusion to the Tsar or the Tsarina, his utterance was unusually respectful in tone and wording, and was spoken in an awkward, halting manner. Never did I hear him boast of his intercourse with the Imperial family; nor did I on any occasion see him the worse for liquor. As often as he spoke of the Ministers, it was merely to stress his opinion that they must assist the Tsar with all their powers in this difficult task of ruling the country.

In spite of all that, I know, of course, very well—better perhaps than most other people—that there was a basis of truth for the rumours concerning the bumptious mode of expression he sometimes adopted in gay society. After all, was I not in a position to look at any time into the Police records bearing upon this matter? In this connexion, however, it should be considered that no one in an elevated condition is quite master of his tongue, and that his enemies often laid themselves out to get him a little fuddled, when they would ask him provocative questions, to which he did return many a thoughtless answer.

Certainly Rasputin had a weakness for wine and women, but it was not his peasant breeding that had developed such inclinations in him. Before he enjoyed the *entrée* to Petersburg society he was not guilty of such excesses, so far as inquiries have shown; rather was it the new and sophisticated environment of town-dwellers that deliberately set about corrupting and debauching him in order thereby to discredit the Tsar and his consort. Once those people had succeeded in besmirching Rasputin's name, then they wove their stories round it, told of his influence in the appointment of the highest officials, of his secret dealings with the Germans, and of his efforts to bring about the conclusion of a separate peace; and it was all designed to tarnish the glory of the Imperial House.

Rasputin did not thrust himself into the foreground of the political arena; others pushed him into that position, people whose object it was to shake the foundations of the Russian Throne and Empire. He himself never quite understood what was going on. If he said that with his death Russia too would perish, he failed to recognize that he was merely a puppet in the hands of those vile schemers.

These harbingers of the Revolution had to make an idol of Rasputin in order to realize their satanic projects. So then they spread abroad the most absurd rumours to the effect that it was only through the intermediary of this Siberian peasant that it was possible to attain to office and dignity. The more soiled Rasputin's name became and the more his influence was exaggerated, the easier was it to compromise the bright

THE SON OF NICHOLAS II

PLAYING-CARD CONFISCATED BY THE OCHRANA
Tsar above—Rasputin below

figure of the Tsarina, by this means to turn the Russian people into slaves of the Internationale and to transform the once mighty and glorious Empire into a wilderness.

No doubt Rasputin was commanded to appear now and then before the Empress, who, with the cordiality so becoming in Her Majesty and perhaps, too, from a certain inclination toward mysticism, received him with a considerable measure of kindliness. She firmly believed that he would never tell her what was not true, and the accident that his visits often coincided with an improvement in the health of the Heir to the Throne strengthened still more the friendship she felt toward him. That the alleged healing of the Tsaryevitsh by Rasputin rested entirely upon accidental coincidence is my firm and immovable conviction. I never believed for one moment that Rasputin possessed hypnotic powers, or was able to work miraculous cures. Chance willed it that once or twice after Rasputin had visited the sick-room of the Tsaryevitsh the patient seemed to be better, and perhaps the soothing influence that certainly emanated from the person of that healthy peasant may have played some obscure part in bringing about such improvement.

Nor did I believe that the Tsarina regarded Rasputin as a worker of miracles. He did often betray a sincere and honest interest in the fate of the Tsaryevitsh, and that is sufficient to provide an adequate explanation of the benevolent attitude of the Empress toward him. She was far too noble-minded to hurt the feelings of that good man, who was so absolutely devoted to her, by yielding to vulgar and offensive gossip.

It may even have happened that the Emperor did on an occasion discuss Government affairs with his consort in the presence of Rasputin, and that the sovereigns did then ask what Rasputin's views were. But it is perfectly foolish and altogether too naïve to assume that the Tsar, in coming to a decision, allowed himself to be influenced in any way by the haphazard remarks of a mere peasant. In those circumstances it was doubly wrong when even various persons in Government circles and high-placed officials began to take Rasputin's 'influence' into account, instead of doing what would have been much more sensible and more in keeping with the actual situation—that is, simply ignoring Rasputin. Really, how absurd was the belief that the wise and lawful recommendation of a Minister required the support of a peasant before it had any likelihood of being approved by the Tsar!

However, the idle chatter of society proved more powerful than rational consideration. So it came about that, within a short time, people throughout Russia believed in the omnipotence of Rasputin, and spoke of it in drawing-rooms and restaurants, as well as in barracks, kitchens, and servants' quarters, as of a matter of fact that had been proved. The revolutionaries naturally used this to work up the population against a system in which, as they affirmed, Russia was being ruled by a dirty monk.

In reality all that was far removed from the truth. If Rasputin played any part at all in politics at the Court, it can have been only an extremely limited one, and not in the least to be compared with that performed by any high official. His intelligence and insight enabled him sometimes to form a tolerably shrewd judgment with regard to persons he had once met. This too was known to the Tsarina, and therefore she would ask him sometimes what he thought of this or that candidate for some high Government post. But from such entirely harmless inquiries to the reputed appointment of Ministers by Rasputin is a very long step, and this step the Tsar and the Tsarina quite certainly never took.

It may seem at first that this assertion of mine is in conflict with the known fact that once or twice Rasputin used the telegraph to propose certain candidates to the Empress for important Government appointments. These telegrams are generally regarded as incontrovertible proofs that Rasputin did exercise very real influence at Court. I, however, maintain that the existence of these telegrams proves nothing more than a regrettable lack of tact on the part of Rasputin. Whether these recommendations met with any success is a very different question. Only if this had been the case, would anyone have had a right to speak of his 'influence.' It appears, on the other hand, that in many cases Rasputin's advocacy was of no avail. Once or twice it did happen, it must be admitted, that the candidates favoured by him were really appointed; but in these cases the decisions had been made long before, on quite other grounds, and would have been carried out without Rasputin's having stirred a finger. These cases were, indeed, just as truly accidental as the alleged relief to the Tsaryevitsh effected by the monk.

In one single connexion Rasputin was able to render real service to petitioners who appealed to him; that was when it was a question of granting a reprieve to condemned prisoners. But here again I should like to note a certain important observation which I often had occasion to make in the course of my service. It was the Emperor's practice to mark all reports read by him with a blue pencil, to signify that the matter was settled; but I never saw a death sentence to which this mark had been affixed. The conclusion to be drawn from that is that the Tsar systematically never read death sentences, but rather left the Minister of Justice to deal with them. That being so, even when it was a question of granting such an amnesty, it was not with the Tsar that Rasputin's influence can have been effective.

As to Rasputin's life and conduct I was very accurately informed, for the Chief of the Petersburg Ochrana used to call upon me every morning with a report, in which was a detailed list of all persons who had appeared at Rasputin's quarters the day before and of all the people that he had visited. It was often really funny to see who the petitioners were that did resort to the magician. He faced them all with the equanimity of a professional soothsayer or fortune-teller, bent only on satisfying his customers. When anyone was detailing to him all the particulars of some complicated case he would listen to the tale very quietly, and then generally ask only one question: Which Minister did the business concern? Thereupon, without saying a word, he would hand the suppliant a note consisting of a phrase or two and addressed to some exalted personage in the Government. His letters, as a rule, would run:

> MY DEAR GOOD SIR,
>   Help if you can.
>   GRISHA RASPUTIN.

Provided with such recommendations, people from the provinces would generally seek an audience with the Minister in question, firmly convinced that their request would be fulfilled at once. How great was their amazement when, despite the intervention of the almighty monk, they received a refusal!

A petition which in itself was justifiable and which, after adequate examination of the facts, proved to be practicable, would naturally be dealt with in a sense pleasing to the applicant, and it would be a matter of indifference whether he possessed an introduction from Rasputin or not. And, *vice versa,* in spite of the monk's intermediary, unjustifiable wishes or complaints would not be considered by any of the Departments. And yet people imagined that it all depended on that bit of paper with a few words in Rasputin's hand. It is true that people have asserted over and over again that he did successfully exercise his patronage in doubtful affairs, but I have never believed this, and although I have frequently investigated such rumours I never managed to convince myself of their truth. I am therefore, in this matter too, still of the opinion that, as with so many of the assertions about Rasputin, such reports were idle gossip.

Almost one-half of the visitors who called on Rasputin consisted of poor people who hoped to get some material assistance from him. Their expectations of this kind were not disappointed, for Rasputin never once refused to help anyone with money. Whenever a well-to-do caller left behind him a sum of money Rasputin distributed it among the next poor petitioners who were waiting, so that of all such monies he never kept a rouble for himself.

Very often it happened, too, that simple country-people would call on him for no other reason than that they were impelled by curiosity, and wanted very much to talk with the man who, though an ordinary peasant, had found access to the Court. Rasputin generally received such visitors and made them doubly welcome, talking with them at length and with much sympathy about their affairs, and thinking nothing of keeping much more fashionable people waiting. And it was especially such visitors from the country who were sure to go away with a present.

The things I am here setting down are not, as some may be tempted to think, sentimental inventions of my own; they are supported by the testimony of Ochrana agents, who for years acted as servants in Rasputin's home and consequently knew his daily life to the last detail. Those officials noted repeatedly too, with what hesitation Rasputin always got ready for his journeys to Tsarskoye Syelo; he was frankly nervous whenever he was summoned there by Mme. Vyrubova. The agents testify that whenever he knew he was about to have to meet the Tsarina he became extraordinarily excitable and ill at ease. It is therefore utterly false when people talk, as they do continually, of Rasputin's cynical self-assurance in his intercourse with the Imperial family.

The means he had at his disposal were quite exactly determined. From the Tsarina's private purse he received an annual allowance of ten thousand roubles. And during the time I was at the head of the Police Department the Minister of the Interior, Protopopov, once ordered a thousand roubles to be paid to him. Larger sums than this he never received from the Ministry of the Interior.

I have already spoken of his fondness for wine and women. But it should be observed that he was never a soaker in the proper sense of the word. As a typical peasant he probably drank on occasion more than was good for him, especially when he was invited to some carousal at which they would encourage him to immoderate indulgence. But I know beyond a doubt that on the following morning he would nearly always reproach himself bitterly when he became aware that he had allowed his tongue to wag too freely while he had been in a state of intoxication. This was possibly one of the reasons why he fell into such a peculiar state of mind whenever he was called upon to appear in Tsarskoye Syelo. He was afraid that, in the interval since his last visit, reports about his excesses might have reached the Emperor's ears and that he ran the risk of being severely reprimanded. For it did indeed happen several times that the Tsar remonstrated with him in no uncertain terms about the error of his ways, which never failed to cause Rasputin deep remorse. Unfortunately this repentance was not of very long duration, and he had not the necessary will-power to resist the next temptation offered him to indulge in fresh orgies.

CHAPTER X

A FRIEND of Rasputin was Peter Alexandrovitsh Badmayev, and, like Rasputin, he was often made the subject of the foulest calumnies. I should therefore, at this point, like to say something of that remarkable man, unique in his way, whom I knew very well.

Badmayev came from Mongolia. He had acquired the secret lore of the Tibetans in the use of medicinal herbs, and then, at the time of the Russo-Turkish War, he had become an Army doctor. He was a man of strong will-power and endowed with a great love of righteousness.

With a view to improving the lot of the East Siberian population he undertook to act as leader of one or two deputations, and to appeal directly to the Imperial Court. On these occasions he attracted the attention of Tsar Alexander III, who, at his request, expressly authorized him to practise his knowledge of the Tibetan healing art. On subsequent occasions, too, Badmayev was received in audience by the Emperor, when he spoke on behalf of his Siberian fellow-countrymen. But he was never really in close contact with actual court circles, and as a convinced and loyal Monarchist he would never have dreamed of exploiting in any illegal way his connexion with the Tsar and the governing class.

Nevertheless, shameless journalists have caused him to be suspected of participation in all manner of mysterious court intrigues. They even affirmed that, in collusion with Rasputin, he had induced the Emperor to take Tibetan infusions of herbs that had paralysed the ruler's mental powers.

I still remember very well a dinner at my house at which Kurlov and Badmayev were present. We learned from the newspaper that the Heir to the Throne was again suffering from an attack of internal hæmorrhage, and the news had an extraordinarily depressing influence on Badmayev; his previous talkativeness and his cheerful mood vanished, so to speak, at a stroke. When we had retired to my private study, Badmayev turned to Kurlov and myself, begging us to obtain for him permission to treat the young prince with Tibetan remedies; he said he was able by the means at his command to cure completely the Tsaryevitsh's trouble, while European doctors were helpless in dealing with it. After discussing the matter for some time, we decided to telegraph to General V. A. Dyedyulin, then Court-Marshal, and I myself composed the message. Two days later we received a reply from Dyedyulin by letter, intimating that Fyodorov, the Physician-in-Ordinary, and the other medical men in attendance had expressed their disapproval of Badmayev's being called in, and that the sovereigns had finally declared their agreement with that refusal. This incident is surely the clearest proof of the essential inaccuracy of the statements made about Badmayev's professional activities at court.

What so attracted me to Badmayev was my conviction that his medical powers were exceptional, as well as the esteem I felt for his Monarchist opinions and his extraordinarily wide culture. I have been told that he studied the Orthodox religion for twenty years before he resolved to go over to it. Desire for revenge was entirely foreign to his nature. His constant effort was to help those in distress to the utmost of his powers. To the multitudes of people who appealed to him

General Kurlov, Commander of the Gendarmerie, with Dyedyulin, Controller of the Imperial Household, and Gerardi, the Chief of the Palace Police

№ 22

Государственный преступникъ Надежда Еписова Смирницкая, дочь Священника.

ПРИМѢТЫ:

Лѣта *31*

Ростъ *2* арш. *4* вер.

Лицо *чистое*

Глаза *спрае*

Волосы на головѣ *черные*

Бакенбарды ——

Брови *черные*

Борода ——

Усы ——

Носъ *умеренный*

Ротъ *обыкновенный*

Зубы *цѣлы*

Подбородокъ *круглый*

Особыя примѣты: *1, На первомъ спинномъ позвонкѣ на 2 сантиметра влѣво отъ середины его родимое пятно коричневаго цвѣта величиною менѣе горошины. Второе такоеже*

EXILED ANARCHIST'S PRISON CARD

The woman is the daughter of a priest. Age, height, face, eyes, hair, brows, nose, mouth, teeth, chin are indicated; and as a special mark are mentioned two brown birthmarks rather less in size than a pea and situated two centimetres from the middle of the first segment of the spinal column, on the left of it

for assistance he unfailingly presented gifts of money, which were sometimes considerable in amount.

The fate of Badmayev after the Revolution was interesting and characteristic too. When he was making an attempt to find his way to Finland he was arrested by Revolutionary seamen and kept for some time in prison. While there he made no effort to conceal from his guards his frank opinion that the deposition of the Tsar had been an act of folly. The sailors, generally so uncompromising, listened in silence to what Badmayev had to say, finding nothing to reply. Before long he was released from confinement and sent back to Petersburg, where he resumed his medical practice. Hundreds of patients flocked to him again, and in conversation with them he expressed openly his Monarchist views, letting them know that he thought Russia had fallen into the hands of unworthy men who would bring it to ruin.

Later, when the Bolsheviks were already in power, an agent of the Tsheka (literally Extraordinary Commission, actually Secret Police) called on Badmayev as a patient, and set about involving him in a political discussion. It was no difficult task, for Badmayev was neither to hold nor to bind when it was a matter of comparison between the old and the new *régimes*; so he started off at once in violent abuse of the Communist system. The agent visited the doctor two or three times after that, and finally the Tsheka had Badmayev's house searched. They slit the sofa, ripped up all stuffed articles of furniture, and sought in every hole and corner for the supposed secret correspondence between Badmayev and the Tsarina. As such correspondence had never existed, all the attempts of the Bolshevik agents to find it naturally remained fruitless. Nevertheless Badmayev was arrested and lodged in the Militia Building.

Two days afterward three seamen rang his front-door bell.

Badmayev had known them before and they wanted to consult him about various ailments. His servant told them that his master had been arrested and was being held a prisoner by the Tsheka. The seamen lost no time in hurrying back on board their ship to give the alarm to their comrades; then they all took their arms and made straight for the headquarters of the Tsheka. On their arrival they administered a sound drubbing to their comrades who were officiating there, set Badmayev free, and led him back home in triumph.

It was in Badmayev's house, too, that I met Rasputin for the first time in person, though I had long known all about him through the documentary evidence at my disposal. One evening, on my way home from the office, the thought occurred to me to call at Badmayev's to get his advice about a certain indisposition from which I was suffering. The maid showed me into the dining-room, where I found the master of the house at supper with Rasputin, the latter's friend Marya Golovina, and some other guests. Badmayev invited me to take a seat opposite Rasputin, and so I had an immediate opportunity of observing him closely without making the fact too obvious. I heard Rasputin inquiring of Badmayev who I was, and Badmayev explaining to Rasputin my identity and my official capacity. The information appeared to satisfy the monk, for he smiled cheerfully and took part again in the general conversation, which had rather flagged at my entrance. Later on Kurlov and Protopopov also turned up, for they were both convinced supporters and regular patients of the Tibetan doctor. After some talk of a general nature the conversation turned into a discussion of *the* questions of the moment—the carriage of food-supplies on the railways and the distribution of the refugees from the evacuated districts. The Imperial Duma also was referred to several times, and we were unanimous in coming to the conclusion that the action of that body was of no use whatever, and that it was directed mainly to hampering the work of the Government by political intrigue and by criticism as ill-founded as it was malicious.

However, I should like to emphasize the fact that all the conversation we had on that evening, and on other occasions, on these subjects, was purely academic in character and was in no sense directed, as was often asserted at the time, toward the end of getting Rasputin to take an interest in the person of Protopopov and of swaying him in that sense. Just then— that is, the end of October 1916—the Imperial Duma had begun its fateful Autumn Session, when every sitting was accompanied by fresh outbursts against the Government and by attacks on the ruling house, that grew daily more and more open. It was therefore not to be wondered at if in our circle too we discussed the things that were at the moment preoccupying all Russia.

At that, my first meeting with him, Rasputin gradually got into a state of visible excitement. He rose from the table and strode to and fro in the room, raising his hands to heaven in obviously genuine despair. "Why do the members of the Duma not love the Tsar?" he exclaimed several times. "Does he not live only for the well-being of Russia?" Then, in his awkward mode of speech, he began to talk of the various slanders that were current about the Tsarina. I did not for a moment doubt his sincerity when he bitterly lamented that the Empress was being more and more plainly accused among the people, in the Army, and by the Duma members, of treasonable practices in favour of the Germans, nay, even of maintaining a secret correspondence with Emperor William. He said he could not understand at all how such senseless reports had arisen, as every one, after all, who knew the Tsarina must be well aware how sincerely and how intimately she felt herself bound up with the Russian people and its fate.

That very first evening which I spent in company with Rasputin convinced me that all the stories of his hypnotic powers were pure twaddle. Several times he addressed me directly, looking straight into my face with his piercing eyes. But his glance had not affected me in the least in such a way as to make me think of suggestive influence on his part, nor did the expression of his face resemble in any way that of a hypnotist. His eyes conveyed nothing more than strained attention. You could see plainly what an effort he was making to understand all that was being said, and how his brain was working the while, to think over and to get ready an answer. And further acquaintance served merely to confirm that first impression.

With all that I am saying I do not wish to create in the reader's mind the idea that I was irresistibly carried away with enthusiasm for Rasputin. I was, and still am, far removed from that attitude. But I do regard it as my duty, in view of the innumerable calumnies associated with the name of this man, to bring out the good sides of his character. In any just and dispassionate estimate of Rasputin we must not leave out of account his genuine Russian nature, any more than his steadfastness or his passionate love of his country, which admits of no doubt whatever.

Concerning the relations between Rasputin and Protopopov, who a little later was to become the last Minister of the Interior under the Tsarist system, countless lying statements have been made. I shall return to them again. Meantime I should like to point out that from the beginning there certainly existed a strong bond of mutual sympathy between them. Protopopov took a deep and lively interest in Rasputin, because he appeared to him to be the real representative of the soul of the Russian people. Protopopov believed that he could learn much about the prevalent state of feeling among the peasants from the utterances of Rasputin. Of this Protopopov expressly assured me several times, and I have no reason at all to doubt the sincerity of that most honourable man.

My first meeting with Rasputin was soon followed by many more, and so I had abundant opportunity of making a careful study of him. By that time he had already been, to some extent, corrupted by his environment; and, further, he had become involved in the intrigues of the Under-Secretary Belyetsky, which led him to take many a step that it would be hard to justify. At the same time, and unfortunately too late, he had begun to have a dark foreboding that he had grown to be a plaything in the hands of a group of adventurers. The vague realization of this fact both oppressed and confused him. The cunning Belyetsky, in association with the Minister Chvostov and a very shady individual named Andronnikov, had succeeded in drawing Rasputin into the net of their self-seeking political scheming. In his honour sumptuous feasts had been regularly arranged, during the course of which the plan was to influence Rasputin in a definite direction. Without suspecting it, he had allowed himself to be used as a tool in the most varied and sometimes unscrupulous manœuvres.

After some time the complicated intrigue was wrecked on the distrust and petty jealousies existing between Belyetsky and Chvostov; the positions of the two men became untenable; and only then did Rasputin recognize in what a dangerous game he had been taking a hand. From that moment onward he was in perpetual fear lest his lack of experience and education should again be taken advantage of, to involve him in some other equivocal affair. To this dread was added the dissatisfaction naturally caused by the attacks on him made in the Duma.

In this mood of depression he said to me once quite frankly that he did not understand at all why such importance was so generally ascribed to his person. "After all," he said, "I am not a minister, and I just speak as my peasant wit tells me. If the Tsar asks my opinion, I tell him honestly what I think, and that is all. What have I done to these Duma men that they should hate me so?"

In spite of that, he was by no means in favour of dissolving the Duma. On the contrary, he often declared that, as the Tsar had founded the Duma, it must continue to exist. He could not and would not understand that this body had long since ceased to wish to co-operate with the Tsar and his Government; that, rather, it had one goal before it: the complete destruction of the Tsardom. If, then, it was pointed out to him that, not only in the public sittings, but in the party meetings and in the lobbies, the Members of the Duma were discussing him in urgent and not very kindly terms, he would fall into a curious state of confusion and begin to speak in detached phrases, gesticulating with excitement.

"Leave them alone. They will talk and they will be quiet again. They must be shown the right way, so that they may get on with their work and not bother about me. What am I then? A simple peasant. The Tsar and the Tsarina, in their love, have been too good to me, and I tell them the truth when I am asked. I believe in God, and I tell the truth in the presence of the Tsar, as I would before God. The Duma-men must not be vexed—they have many things to think of—they must be pacified. When they have talked as long as they want to, they will be sure to stop again of themselves. What is it they want of me? After all, they are Russians anyway, and will understand what they have been called to do? Surely not to busy themselves with Grigory Rasputin, but to help the Tsar in his Government. On no account must the Duma be dissolved!"

He used to speak to me quite frankly about such things, for he knew that I understood him well. If I took him to task about his disorderly and often improper behaviour he would reply with an awkward and somewhat embarrassed wave of the hand, "What would you have, my dear man? Who is innocent before God is also innocent before the Tsar."

I was quite aware that one of Rasputin's scandalous affairs, in the summer of 1915, had led to the fall of General Junkovsky, at that time my superior. On one of his numerous journeys to Siberia Rasputin had stopped in Moscow and had been invited to the home of a merchant of that city, with whom he was on friendly terms. While there he had, by very unmistakable signs, made known his intentions with regard to a pretty maid-servant, although she had several times most energetically repelled his advances. The Chief of the Moscow Ochrana had sent in a secret report of the occurrence, and I had forwarded this through the Chief of the Police Department to General Junkovsky, the Under-Secretary for Home Affairs. Junkovsky thought it necessary to inform the Emperor of what had happened, and, to tell the truth, he appears to have been rather tactless in his procedure. For, soon after, the Minister of the Interior, Prince Shtsherbatshov, received a communication from the Tsar suggesting that he might find another more suitable post for his Assistant. General Junkovsky naturally drew the proper deduction from this Imperial reprimand and went into retirement.

Meanwhile Rasputin, accompanied by the agents who were keeping him under observation, had been making his way to his homeland. He had not had the slightest idea of the whole incident, and consequently could hardly have had any influence upon Junkovsky's fate. Yet in these days it was generally affirmed that Junkovsky had fallen a victim to Rasputin's vengeance; the latter was said to have exerted his utmost influence at Court in order to compass the fall of the General who had dared to inform the Tsar of his misconduct. Of course

I was now interested to hear what Rasputin himself would have to say about this affair, and therefore, at the first opportunity that presented itself I managed, by a few adroit turns, to bring the conversation to this Junkovsky business. He immediately took up the topic. He confessed, without any more ado, the sin he had committed that time in Moscow, and denied emphatically that he had taken any part whatever in the dismissal of Junkovsky. He asserted that it was some time after the event that he had been told about his retirement and the cause.

Altogether, so far as I gained any insight into his character, I should say that Rasputin entertained no sort of vengeful feelings against those who took up a hostile attitude toward him. Whenever he spoke of any one of his enemies, he nearly always used to characterize him by the simple sentence, "He is a bad man!" On the other hand, I never heard threats or curses upon his lips.

As I have already mentioned, in the last months before his death he allowed himself to be involved too deeply in the schemes of political intriguers whose aims he was quite unable to grasp. It was simply flattering to him to be able to associate with rich and fashionable people and to observe how attentively they listened to all he had to say and tell. The semblance of special importance which that attitude conferred upon him went to his head, and he did not notice how he was being systematically drawn into boastful forms of speech. When in the society of people who spoiled him with nightly orgies he soon adopted the airs of a man in the enjoyment of power and honour, a man with whom it was not permissible for the first person that came along to converse, as if Rasputin were an ordinary peasant.

One man alone saw clearly and plainly the approaching fall of Rasputin, and sought to warn the monk. That was

Badmayev. He once had a long talk with me about the disaster that seemed to be threatening to overwhelm Rasputin. At my behest he went himself and implored Rasputin to cease from allowing himself to be dragged from one scene of debauchery to another, and especially to give up indulging in dangerous and compromising talk. In his affectionate and touching way he concluded this moral lecture by falling on his knees before Rasputin and beseeching him to be a sensible man. Unfortunately this well-meant warning came too late, for, only a short time after, Badmayev's fears were realized: Rasputin was murdered by a group of his enemies.

UNLESS it be kept in mind that systematic and prolonged preparations were made by certain circles, it would be impossible to understand the crime that finally brought about Rasputin's death. The method pursued has already been indicated: it consisted essentially in inducing the unsuspecting peasant continually to drink to excess, and in encouraging him to indulge in boastful and compromising talk, while, on the other hand, his influence was grossly exaggerated. By these means the opinion was created that this dissolute, arrogant fellow—for that was what Rasputin was represented to be— was really the omnipotent ruler of Russia, that the fate of the Empire of the Tsars depended upon him alone.

It was almost inevitable that this calculated agitation should, in the end, lead to a catastrophe. But the individuals who actually carried out Rasputin's murder are almost of less importance than those plotters and schemers whose work it was to stir up the general feeling of hatred for the man. The truth is that this murder was not decided upon in the councils of the mere doers of the deed, but months beforehand in the lobbies of the Duma.

One of the murderers was V. N. Purishkyevitsh, a man whose natural inclinations were morbid enough to make it an easy thing for him to yield to the inflammatory atmosphere around him. That is the only possible explanation of the fact that this Deputy, till then a Monarchist of the strictest kind, suddenly mounted the orator's platform to make a fierce attack upon Rasputin and the Tsarina.

After this first departure from the straight road it was, as it were, only a step farther along the crooked path that turned him into a murderer. You can imagine what a triumph it was for the instigators of the crime, men of the extreme Left, when they managed to have the deed they so much wished to do actually performed by a leading member of the Right wing of the Duma.

However one may judge the motives that induced Purishkyevitsh to commit the crime, it was certainly inexcusable and in the highest degree dishonourable on his part to drag the Grand Duke Dimitry Pavlovitsh, a special favourite of the Tsar, into the plot. As a loyal Monarchist it would have been his duty even to prevent the whole wicked scheme by all the means at his command, if it were only to keep the Grand Duke from any sort of participation in such a deplorable deed of bloodshed. But what are we to think of his action after the murder had been committed? For he had the audacity to compose a letter in the name of the Grand Duke addressed to the Tsarina, in which he shamelessly lied to her. During the many years of my legal practice I have, I must admit, come across many a similar case of cowardice and untruthfulness, but always among people from a very different social class. Probably Purishkyevitsh was not quite capable of estimating the full import of his act.

In that respect he resembled Prince Felix Yussupov, the second of the chief conspirators in the plot against the life of Rasputin. He too fell a victim to the universal suggestion, persuading himself that in removing the monk, even by the most reprehensible means, he was doing a patriotic action and helping in the liberation of the country. Prince Yussupov was a fashionable young man, a popular figure in Petersburg drawing-rooms, distinguished alike by personal amiability and by his prominent social position. Since the days of Peter the Great the Yussupov family, originally of comparatively obscure rank, had risen to wealth and honour largely by making successful marriages. Finally, young Prince Felix Felixovitsh had married into the Imperial family, by winning the hand of the Grand Duchess Irene Alexandrovna, daughter of the Grand Duke Alexander Michaelovitsh.

He had been personally acquainted with Rasputin for some time, having met him in the house of the widow Golovina, whose husband had been a Councillor of State. The old lady's daughter, Marya Golovina, was among the most intimate friends and the most enthusiastic supporters of Rasputin; she therefore sought continually to bring about a *rapprochement* between Yussupov and the monk, all the more so because Rasputin, at the first meeting with the Prince, had taken a decided liking to him. The haughty and pampered aristocrat, on the other hand, had from the very first conceived only a violent aversion for the simple peasant, who was so utterly different from the usual run of his acquaintance. As I have already pointed out, Rasputin had, toward the end of the year 1916, already lost much of his earlier modesty and was frequently assuming a provocative and overbearing manner.

This, combined with the preposterous reports current about the influence of the peasant, prompted the thought in Yussupov's mind of putting a violent end once for all to this disgrace. He did not stop to consider that, in so doing, he would hurt very much the Tsar, his wife's uncle, and compromise him as well. His passion made him oblivious of the fact that the deed he was meditating fitted in exactly with the plans of those people who were working systematically to undermine the Emperor's authority throughout the nation. What could have been more to the mind of the ultra-Radical agitators than to have a member of the Imperial family himself raising a hand against Rasputin, who stood so high in the esteem of Tsar and Tsarina.

Purishkyevitsh delivered in the Duma a vehement attack upon the "hidden powers," and as a result of it a meeting between the hysterical Deputy and Yussupov took place. The two men now decided jointly upon the crime and prepared for its execution, most carefully considering all details. A cavalry captain named Suchotin and a Polish doctor named Lazovyert were also brought into the plot. Yussupov undertook to decoy Rasputin into the trap, and therefore made it his business to get into touch with him again, while, up till that moment, he had ostentatiously gone out of his way to avoid him.

Golovina's house provided an obvious rallying point, and soon Yussupov seemed to be on the friendliest terms with Rasputin. He visited him on the pretext that he wanted to be treated for some ailment, and easily found his way to the heart of the guileless peasant by singing to him for hours on end gipsy songs, which Rasputin loved to hear beyond all else.

The conspirators agreed to carry out the deed on the night of December 16, 1916, and they had chosen as the scene of it the palace of Prince Yussupov in Moika Street. That immense building was at the moment not occupied by the owners, as Yussupov's whole family was staying in the Crimea. An outlying wing of the house contained a cellar, which was as a rule not in use. It was reached from the courtyard by its own little stair. This room, then, was fitted up as comfortably as possible with all sorts of furniture and carpets, for it was here that the conspirators thought of finishing off their victim. On the pretext of a little festivity Rasputin was to be enticed there, and then to be killed by poisoning his food and drink.

Yussupov delivered to him the sinister invitation, which Rasputin at once joyfully accepted. On the evening of December 16 Yussupov called for him and took him to the palace, which he was never to leave again alive.

The murderers had hoped that their participation in the deed would remain undiscovered, but, through a peculiar chain of circumstances, the Police were informed the very next morning that the crime had been committed, and, what is more, they had every reason to suspect Yussupov and Purishkyevitsh.

Before I proceed to describe the revelation of the whole case, as I came to know it—I was myself in charge of the investigation—I should like to refer briefly to a point which, for a time, very much exercised the public imagination. That was the alleged failure of the attempted poisoning, which seemed to imply a marvellous power of resistance in Rasputin's constitution to a preparation which normally is absolutely fatal.

With the utmost serenity Rasputin consumed one cake after another supposed to be dosed with potassium cyanide; he drank off one poisoned glass after another, without the expected result appearing. The murderers, looking on and waiting vainly, with their nerves all on edge, interpreted the circumstance as evidence that Rasputin's body was proof against poison, so that the poison had failed. Neither then nor afterward did Purishkyevitsh and his accomplices divine the simple truth. The physician, Dr. Lazovyert, who had been entrusted with the task of putting the chemical into the cakes and the wine-glasses, had simply been seized with conscientious scruples, and had substituted some harmless substance, such as soda or magnesia. In my view, that is the simple and prosaic explanation of the reputed miracle said to have happened before the eyes of the conspirators.

The first suspicious report that directed the attention of the authorities at once to the Yussupov Palace was that handed in by a policeman on duty in the street. I set it down here as it appears in the record of the proceedings made, at my order, by Lieutenant-Colonel of Gendarmerie Poppel.

On the night of December 16 [related this policeman, Vlassiyev] I was standing at my post at the corner of Moika Street and Maximilian Lane. At four o'clock in the morning I heard three or four shots following each other in quick succession. Judging by the sound, they appeared to come from the right side of the German Church in Moika Street. I went to Post Bridge and called to Policeman Yefimov, who was standing in Morskaya Street in front of number 61. When I asked him where the firing had come from, Yefimov answered that the shots had come from my side.

Thereupon I went to number 94 Moika Street, the Yussupov Palace, to ask the house-steward who had been firing. He called out that he had heard nothing. However, I looked through the railing and I saw two men, bareheaded and in loose smocks, crossing the yard obliquely toward the gate. Soon I recognized in them Prince Yussupov and his steward Bushinsky. I inquired of Bushinsky what had happened, and he replied again that he had not heard any shots, but that possibly someone, in high spirits, had been firing in the air just to amuse himself. I think I also remember that the Prince stated that he had not heard any shooting. Then both men went away, and I was left alone. I took the trouble to make a thorough examination of the yard, but as I found nothing of a suspicious nature, I went back to my post.

About a quarter of an hour later the aforementioned Bushinsky came up to me and informed me that Prince Yussupov invited me to go to his house. I acceded to this summons, and Bushinsky took me through the front entrance of number 94 Moika Street into the Prince's private study.

I had scarcely crossed the threshold of this room when Prince Yussupov stepped forward. He was accompanied by a gentleman who was a stranger to me. The latter was wearing a cloak, military green in colour, and to judge by his epaulettes he occupied the rank of Councillor of State. He had close-cropped reddish whiskers, and a moustache of the same hue.

This stranger asked me whether I was an Orthodox Christian, a true Russian, and whether I loved the Tsar and our country. I answered in the affirmative, whereupon he asked if I knew him. "No, I do not know you," I answered.

"Have you ever heard of Purishkyevitsh?"

"Yes," I said, "I have heard of him."

"I am he. And Rasputin, you've certainly heard of him, haven't you? Do you know him?"

I declared that I did not know him, though, of course, I had heard of him. This stranger then said to me:

"This Rasputin has just been dispatched, and if you love the Tsar and your country, you must keep silent about the matter, and must not say a word to anyone."

"I understand, sir!" I said, whereupon the gentleman signified that I might go. I left the house and returned once more to my post after subjecting the street to a thorough examination.

About twenty minutes later the inspecting officer for my district, Superintendent Kalyaditsh, came up to me, and to him I reported exactly all that had taken place. Then, along with Kalyaditsh, I went to the front door of number 94. At the entrance we found a motor standing ready. We asked the chauffeur for whom it was waiting, and he replied, "For the Prince."

Kalyaditsh then continued on his round of inspection leaving me there, with instructions to observe who should drive away in the car. Before very long Prince Yussupov left the main entrance and drove off in the direction of the Potseluyev Bridge. I waited for some time longer in front of the house, and as I saw nobody else, I went back again to my post.

Towards six o'clock Kalyaditsh came to me again and summoned me to the office of the Superintendent of the Division, Colonel Rogov, to whom we delivered our report of all that had happened. Thereafter I went home.

As I had not noticed any traces of a murder, I regarded the conversation I had had in the Prince's private room with the strange gentleman as an attempt to put me to the test, to see whether I knew what the Service required of me. Neither in the Prince nor in the other gentleman did I observe a trace of excitement or confusion, unless it was that the latter spoke very rapidly. Whether the gentlemen were intoxicated I cannot say either with assurance.

This deposition made by Policeman Vlassiyev was, to a certain extent, supplemented by the observations of the second Policeman, Yefimov, who stated in evidence:

At 4 A.M. I heard a shot, and three or four seconds later there followed in quick succession three more shots. My impression was that the sound came from Moika Street, from somewhere about number 92. After the first shot there was audible a half-suppressed cry, as if uttered by a woman. I heard no other noise.

A short time after a motor-car came down Moika Street in the direction of Potseluyev Bridge; I did not see it stop anywhere. I reported the shooting to the office of the Third Kasan Police District, using the telephone. Then I went myself toward the place from which the sounds had come.

On the Post Bridge I met Policeman Vlassiyev, who was on duty on his beat. He had likewise heard the shots, but was of opinion that they had been fired in Morskaya Street. I told him that they had probably come from Moika Street, number 92, and at once returned to my post, where I observed nothing more to report. Apart from the motor-car already mentioned no motor vehicle of any kind passed along Moika Street till between five and six in the morning.

These reports seemed grave enough to set in motion at once the entire machinery of the Police in the capital. Everyone knew that Rasputin had many bitter enemies, and so, from the very start, it was a natural thing to suppose that the strange words spoken by Purishkyevitsh, apparently on the false assumption that they would induce the policeman to keep silent, had a foundation of truth.

The Kasan Police Station, therefore, informed the Chief of the City Police, Balk, who immediately got into touch with me. I considered the case so serious that I lost no time in ringing up Protopopov, the Minister of the Interior, expressing my fear that, during the previous night, Rasputin had been the victim of a treacherous and murderous attack. We agreed to have a close investigation instituted at once; and Protopopov, by special command, commissioned General P. K. Popov, the officer commanding the Corps of Gendarmerie, to undertake the responsibility. I personally instructed him to take care, above all, to have a careful search made of Rasputin's dwelling, and to confiscate at once all compromising documents that might be found there. For, although I had never believed in the truth of the rumours concerning correspondence between Rasputin and the various members of the Imperial House, I considered it, all the same, my duty to take such a possibility into account, and to make sure that documents affecting, perhaps, very exalted persons should not fall, after Rasputin's disappearance, into the hands of unauthorized people.

The result of Popov's investigations, however, confirmed my

original supposition, for neither any correspondence compromising Rasputin, nor any letters from the Tsarina addressed to him, were found. I also had inquiry made to find out whether Rasputin might not have papers, valuables, or money deposited with one of the banks. This inquiry likewise produced no result—a further proof in my eyes of the stupidity of the scandal current everywhere about Rasputin.

CHAPTER XII

*The First Inquiries made by the Police—The Caretaker's Narrative—
The Mysterious "Little One"—Bloodstains—Interrogation of Manserv-
ant—Yussupov's Attempt to clear himself—The Mysterious Party—The
Shot in the Yard—The Dead Dog.*

THE very first interrogation of the members of Rasputin's family and of his servants pointed plainly to the fact that the happenings in the Yussupov Palace during the night of the 16th of December must have some sort of connexion with Rasputin's disappearance.

I was already practically convinced that he had been murdered in Prince Yussupov's house, when the minute of the deposition made by Rasputin's daughter, Matryona Grigoryevna, was placed before me. She said:

> On the 16th of December I left home at seven o'clock in the evening and returned about eleven. Just as I was about to retire to rest, my father said to me that he was going to pay a visit that night to the Little One's. That is the name that father always used to designate Prince Yussupov. Soon after I went to bed, and therefore I do not know whether father really went to Yussupov's.

That Rasputin had made an appointment with the Prince for that night was also confirmed by the evidence of his younger daughter and his niece, who agreed in stating that Grigory Yefimovitsh had expressed his intention of looking up the Little One that night.

As soon as the Police had appeared in Rasputin's home the family, in great alarm, rang up his friend Mme Golovina, who, however, assured them that there was no reason to worry if Rasputin was at Yussupov's. Then Matryona Rasputin tried to get through to the Prince by telephone, but was told that he was not at home.

What had really happened on that fateful night became a little clearer to me when General Popov passed on to me the statement made by the porter in Rasputin's house. This man's name was Korshunov. He was interrogated by a Police official, whose record of the deposition runs as follows:

> I am the caretaker at number 64 Gorochovaya Street. During the past night I was on guard duty and was standing in the street in front of the gate. Toward half-past twelve a large motor-car drove up. The body was painted a military grey; it was covered with a waterproof hood and had mica windows. The car came from the direction of Fontanka Street, turned in to Gorochovaya Street, and stopped at our gate. A gentleman, a stranger to me, got out and stepped toward the entrance. When I asked him whom he wished to see, he replied, "Rasputin."
>
> I opened the gate and showed the gentleman to the main staircase, but he said he would rather go up by the back stair. From the way he moved about the building you could see that that was not his first visit.
>
> In about half an hour he left the house with Rasputin; both men got into the car and drove off in the direction of Fontanka Street. I had never seen the man before. He was of average height, well built, about thirty years of age. He had a little black moustache, was otherwise clean-shaven, and did not wear glasses. He wore a long reindeer coat with the fur outside, a black cap, and long boots. The chauffeur, who looked a little older than his master, had an ordinary black moustache; he was wearing a black cloak with a lambskin collar, a fur cap, and long tan gloves.

The description that this caretaker had given of the nocturnal visitor, apart from trifling inaccuracies, fitted approximately Prince Yussupov. His account of the motor-car seemed to agree fairly well too. But that Yussupov and the stranger were really identical was brought out still more clearly by the evidence of Yekaterina Ivanovna Potyomkina, Rasputin's maidservant. After her deposition had been taken there was scarcely any shadow of doubt left that Yussupov had taken a very serious part in the events of that night.

> On the 16th of December [declared the servant in her deposition] very few visitors called on Grigory Rasputin, and among them none that I did not know. During the day about ten persons had appeared, of whom I remember especially Marya Yevgenyevna Golo-

vina, who arrived toward noon and did not quit the house again till nearly nine o'clock at night.

It would be about eleven o'clock when Rasputin's children, Matryona and Varja, along with his niece Anna, went to bed, while he himself lay on his bed with his clothes and boots on. I asked him why he did not undress, to which he answered, "I've got another visit to pay yet." When I inquired whom he was intending to call upon, his reply was, "The Little One; he is going to call for me." Then he told me to go to bed.

I do not know the surname of this Little One, but I do know that he is the husband of the Grand Duchess Irene Alexandrovna. I have seen him twice in Rasputin's home, on a holy day about the 20th of November and just about a week ago. Both times he came up the back stairs.

Although Grigory Yefimovitsh had sent me to bed, I first went into the kitchen again. Rasputin put on his blue shirt, the one embroidered with cornflowers, but he could not fasten the buttons at the collar, and came into the kitchen to ask me to help him. Meanwhile the bell at the side entrance rang.

Rasputin opened the door himself, whereupon the visitor asked if there was anyone about. Grigory Yefimovitsh replied, "There is no one up; the children are asleep. Step in, my dear fellow." Both walked past me through the kitchen and went into the sitting-room. I was in the kitchen recess and, pushing the curtain aside, I saw that the visitor was no other than the Little One, that is, the husband of Grand Duchess Irene. What kind of coat and hat he had on I cannot say, but I saw his face quite plainly.

I was already in bed when Rasputin went out with his visitor. Grigory Yefimovitsh whispered to me that he had bolted the front door inside, that he would go out by the side door and come in the same way. This is what I remember of the Little One's appearance: he is tall and lanky, with a thin face, straight nose, dark hair, no beard, dark rings under the eyes.

What made Prince Yussupov's behaviour appear extremely suspicious was the report that he had bluntly denied having been in Rasputin's company on the critical night. For Mme Golovina had at last got into telephonic communication with the Prince who, to her very great amazement, assured her that he had neither called for him nor been visited by him on the previous evening. As we were already in possession of sufficient evidence that this statement was false, the only effect produced by his clumsy denial was to compromise Yussupov very gravely.

During the course of the forenoon I was rung up several times by Protopopov, who was making urgent inquiries as to how we were getting on with the investigation. The Minister also informed me that the Tsarina was in touch with him, being anxious to learn what had really happened. I reported to him the stage we had reached in our inquiries; nor did I conceal from him my view that the cumulative result of all the evidence procured so far was to incriminate Prince Yussupov. At the same time I requested the Minister to authorize me to have the Yussupov Palace searched, a step that appeared to me extremely urgent. Protopopov approved of the measures I suggested, and besought me to do my utmost to have the case cleared up as quickly as possible; it was particularly important to determine what had become of Rasputin's body. In the circumstances the Minister entertained no more doubt than I did myself that we were really dealing with a case of murder.

A party of Police was sent with all speed to examine the Palace of the Prince, and discovered very distinct traces of blood, which led past the cellar-steps in the wing of the building diagonally across the courtyard. When he was questioned as to the origin of these traces, the Prince averred that during the preceding night one of his guests, obviously in a slightly befuddled condition, had shot a dog, which accounted for the blood. And the Police were actually shown the dead body of a dog that had been killed with bullets fired from a revolver. But the amount of blood shed seemed, from the very start, to be too great for that explanation to be accepted as genuine. The caretaker of the palace could not supply any information that was not already contained in the reports of the two policemen: he had heard shots during the night, and Prince Yussupov had had some conversation with a constable.

The evidence of Yussupov's servant, Nefedov, gave the impression of being neither truthful nor frank. It was quite clearly intended to confirm, as far as possible, the Prince's own statements. The servant declared that Prince Felix had given him instructions to make the necessary preparations in the dining-room for the reception of two or three guests. "At the front entrance," said Nefedov, "the house-steward Bushinsky and I kept watch by turns. During the evening I saw no one come in; but at eleven o'clock I left my post at the door for some time, and when I had returned, Bushinsky told me that the Grand Duke Dimitry Pavlovitsh had come and had gone into the dining-room. Bushinsky and I remained in the anteroom at the front door till about four o'clock. Neither of us entered the dining-room, for the Prince had forbidden us to do so, observing that there would be ladies present. Now and then we could hear the sound of doors opening or closing, and the playing of a gramophone, and that was all. Two or three times before the Prince had arranged such parties from which the servants were excluded. I did not hear, either in the dining-room or in the street, anything like shooting.

"Toward four o'clock in the morning the bell rang, and I went at once to the Prince's study. There were then no guests present. The Prince ordered me to go down to the yard and see what had happened there. I did so, but I saw nothing to report to the Prince. A few minutes after that he rang again and told me to go and find out more carefully what had really taken place, for, he said, there was a dog that had been shot lying in the yard. I went this time through the side door into the yard of number 92, and I did really find, near the railings, the dead body of a dog, which I picked up and carried into the Prince's garden; it is lying there now.

"On the morning of the 17th of December I cleared up in the dining-room and found everything there just as it should be. From the amount of wine that had been consumed it could only be concluded that all the guests had probably been drunk. The Prince himself was rather tipsy. The dog that was shot was an ordinary watch-dog and belonged to the Prince."

We were all on tenterhooks awaiting the report of how Yussupov would describe and explain the events of the preceding night. I was myself already firmly convinced of his guilt, and should have really expected him to make an open confession, for that was probably the most dignified course under the circumstances. But Yussupov was far from thinking of that; on the contrary, to the officials who questioned him, he retailed an involved and highly improbable story which was in glaring contradiction of all that we already knew.

I made Rasputin's acquaintance some five years ago [the Prince deposed] it was, as a matter of fact, in the house of Marya Yevgenyevna Golovina. This year I met him again in November, and he made a much better impression upon me than in previous years. I suffer from pains in the chest, and once, when I spoke to Mme Golovina about them, she advised me to consult Rasputin, saying that he had already cured many people and would be able to help me too. Toward the end of November I went with Mme Golovina to call upon Rasputin.

He described around me some circular movements with his hands, after which I did really think that I felt a certain relief. Some of his expressions—for example, that I must go to the gipsies and cure my pains with the aid of pretty women—made an unpleasant impression upon me, however, and I emphatically rejected that suggestion.

Once he turned the conversation on to the subject of my wife, inquiring as to our mode of life and finally expressing a desire to make her acquaintance. I gave him an evasive answer, and said we should talk of it again when my wife returned from the Crimea: in reality I was firmly resolved never, under any circumstances, to receive Rasputin in my house.

Meantime I had had a new house fitted up at number 94 Moika Street, and Grand Duke Dimitry Pavlovitsh proposed that I should give a little party there. We decided to invite also Vladimir Mitrofanovitsh Purishkyevitsh along with some officers and society women.

For obvious reasons I should prefer not to give the names of the ladies or officers in question, as the motive for their visiting me might somehow or other be misconstrued.

In order that the ladies should not feel embarrassed, I instructed the servants to make everything ready for tea and dinner, and then to withdraw. The majority of the guests were to come through the side gate, the key of which I had on my own person. Towards half-past eleven Grand Duke Dimitry Pavlovitsh appeared and soon after the other guests turned up. We drank tea, played the piano, danced, and finally we dined. Toward one o'clock in the morning I heard the telephone in my private room ringing. It was Rasputin, who insisted that I should go with him to visit the gipsies. When I replied that I had company, he said that I should quit my guests and go to him, which, of course, I refused to do. I asked him where he was speaking from, but he gave me no answer. The reason for my question was that I had heard through the telephone noises and voices, especially female voices, and concluded that Rasputin was in a restaurant or with the gipsies.

After this conversation I went back to the dining-room and told them of Rasputin's proposal. Jokes were cracked about it, and for some time we hesitated as to whether we should not all go together; in the end, however, they all remained at my place, and we went on with our dinner. About three o'clock the party broke up and they all went out by the side gate.

Suddenly I heard a shot fired in the yard. I rang for the servant and ordered him to go and see what was the matter. The servant having found nothing, I went down to the yard myself and noticed, near the railings, the dead body of a dog. In the street I heard the footsteps of a man wearing a grey coat after the style of a military uniform. He was hurrying away as fast as he could. I observed that he had a tall, slim figure, but I could not see more than that distinctly, because of the poor light. When I returned indoors, I told my man to remove the dog.

Soon after I rang up Grand Duke Dimitry Pavlovitsh to tell him of the incident. His Imperial Highness replied that he himself had killed the dog; he said it was just a silly prank, and that I was not to think any more about it. I sent out to the street for a constable and told him that my friend had shot a dog. Purishkyevitsh, who was present, entered into conversation with the policeman; I heard only a part of what was said. But I remember how loudly he called out that he was Purishkyevitsh, member of the Imperial Duma, and how he was all the time gesticulating wildly.

About four o'clock I left the house by the side gate, entered my motor-car, and drove to the palace of the Grand Duchess Xenia Alexandrovna, where I am living at present. This morning I spoke on the telephone to Marya Golovina, who asked me where Rasputin was. I replied that I did not know anything of his whereabouts, for I had not seen him, but had merely spoken to him by telephone. Thereupon Mme Golovina informed me that Rasputin's servants were asserting that I had called for him at his own house about one o'clock. This, however, is a mistake, for neither by day nor by night was I there; I spent the whole night in the house in Moika Street, a fact that my servants and my guests are able to confirm.

As I am told, Purishkyevitsh is supposed to have been saying something in my private room about Rasputin's death. I myself never noticed that, but during the night Purishkyevitsh was very drunk, and did perhaps mention Rasputin in some connexion or another.

I suppose that the people who planned this murder, if it is indeed a case of murder, have intentionally arranged things so that my name and the party I gave last night should seem to be associated with it.

CHAPTER XIII

Inquiries on all Sides—The Snow-boot on the Neva Bridge—Search for the Body—The Tsarina's Dismay—Rasputin's Burial—Yussupov lies to the Empress—Incriminating Telegrams—An Anonymous Letter —Purishkyevitsh flees to the Front—The Tsar's Decisions with respect to the Murderers—Opposition of the Grand Dukes—The Murderers exiled

LONG before midday of December 17 the news of Rasputin's mysterious disappearance had spread with lightning rapidity all over the capital, and was being everywhere eagerly discussed. Of course, there was as yet no incontrovertible proof that he was really dead, for so far the authorities had failed to find the body. Accordingly, there were still many people who thought that the monk was perhaps not killed, but had merely been abducted by political enemies.

During that forenoon I was literally besieged by countless inquiries over the telephone and by callers of every social class: members of the Duma, civil servants, Society ladies, Ministers, and quite humble people wanted to know what results had been achieved by the Police investigation. I was as reserved as possible in the information I gave them, and reported the real state of the facts, as far as we knew them, only to my superior, Protopopov, who rang me up repeatedly.

In the afternoon affairs took a new and critical turn. At one o'clock some workmen, crossing Petrovsky Bridge, noticed bloodstains on the parapet and pointed them out to the watchman on duty there. A policeman was summoned; he too confirmed the presence of bloodstains on the parapet and on the pier of the bridge, and reported the fact to his headquarters.

The superintendent hurried to the spot, and on the projecting ledge of one of the piers he discovered a brown snow-boot, which was immediately got hold of, pulled up, and secured. It was taken away at once to Rasputin's house, where all the members of his family and the agents of the Ochrana present recognized it as having belonged to the man who had so strangely vanished. So we had obtained a valuable clue to the way the murderers had disposed of the body of their victim.

When General Popov informed me by telephone of this find my first thought was to wonder what could have been passing in the minds of the assassins when they were conveying the corpse in their elegant motor-car to the Petrovsky Bridge, and afterward, when they had thrown it into the water there. What had been the thoughts of those men while they were doing their utmost to obliterate the traces of their deed of blood? Were they thinking of the advantages to their native land that would ensue upon their action, or were they intent merely on devising ways and means of evading the legal responsibility for the crime they had committed?

Our next step was to have the Neva searched for the body, although the river was very nearly frozen over. For this purpose I immediately got into touch with the harbour authorities and requested them to procure divers. When these got to work they did not take long to find Rasputin's body. It turned out that his arms and legs were tied with cords, and that, besides taking that measure, the murderers had attached a chain so as to cause the body to sink. The examination of the corpse showed that the murdered man had received a large number of wounds inflicted by shooting and stabbing.

I let Protopopov know at once what we had discovered, and the Minister immediately passed on the report to the Empress at Tsarskoye Syelo; the news threw her into the greatest indignation and dismay. Her Majesty expressed the desire that the body should be buried in the park of the Imperial Palace, and

The Tsar and Tsarina Leaving the Church

MEMBERS OF THE ST. PETERSBURG WORKMEN'S COUNCIL (SOVIET), INCLUDING TROTSKY, ON THEIR WAY TO PENAL SERVITUDE IN 1905

meanwhile instructed a nun, a faithful follower of Rasputin, to recite the usual prayers by the bier of the dead monk. On December 21 the burial took place in the presence of the Tsar and Tsarina and of Rasputin's family.

No later than December 17 the Empress had ordered Yussupov to tell her exactly what had taken place the previous night in his palace. Yussupov, who, as we know, had already been vindicating himself in anything but a manly way, was now bold enough to maintain his lying account of all that occurred in his letter to the Empress, a copy of which Protopopov sent to me at once. The letter bore the date of December 17, and this was its tenor.

YOUR IMPERIAL MAJESTY,

I hasten to obey the commands of Your Majesty and to report what occurred in my house last night. It will be my aim, in doing so, to clear myself of the dreadful accusation that is being made against me.

I had arranged a little supper as a house-warming in my new quarters and invited my friends, a few ladies and the Grand Duke Dimitry Pavlovitsh. About midnight I was rung up by Grigory Yefimovitsh, who invited me to go with him to see the gipsies. I declined, giving as my excuse the party in my own house, and I asked him where he was speaking from, for a great many voices could be heard coming over the wire. But he answered, "You want to know too much," and with that he rang off. That is all that I heard from Grigory Yefimovitsh during the night.

After this talk over the telephone I went back to my guests and told them that it was Rasputin who had rung me up. This provoked my friends to various ill-considered remarks, for, as Your Majesty knows, the name of Grigory Yefimovitsh is very unpopular in various circles. About three o'clock most of my guests took their departure, and after I had said good-bye to the Grand Duke and two ladies I retired with the others to my study.

Suddenly I had the impression that a shot had been fired close by. I called my man and ordered him to see what had happened. He came back almost at once with the report that a shot had been heard, but no one knew where it had come from.

Thereupon I went out myself to the yard and asked the caretakers and the policeman who had fired the shot. The caretakers answered that they had been drinking tea in their room, while the constable said he had certainly heard the shot, but knew nothing more about it.

I went back into the house, sent for the policeman, and meantime asked Dimitry Pavlovitsh by telephone whether it was he who had been firing. He answered me with a laugh that, as he left the house, he had fired one or two shots at a dog and that one of the ladies had fainted. When I observed that the shots had made some stir, he expressed the opinion that it could not be so bad as all that, for there had not been anyone about.

I called my manservant and went out again myself to the yard, where I did really find one of our dogs lying dead near the railings. I ordered them to bury the animal in the garden.

At four o'clock the remainder of my guests went home and I returned to the house of Alexander Michaelovitsh, where I am staying at present. Next day—that is, this morning—I learned of the disappearance of Grigory Yefimovitsh, which they are trying to connect with the little party at my house. I am also informed that I am alleged to have been seen last night at Rasputin's and that he is stated to have driven away with me. That is, however, a downright lie, for neither I nor my guests left my house all through the night. Finally, I have also been told that Rasputin is said to have remarked to someone that he was going in the next few days to call on Irene in order to make her acquaintance. That may be quite correct, for the last time I saw him he did really ask me to introduce him to my wife and inquired whether she was in town. I answered at the time that Irene was at present in the Crimea, and would not be back before the 15th or 16th of December. On the evening of the 14th I received a telegram from her in which she informed me that she had fallen ill, and requested me to go to her along with her brothers, who are setting off to-night.

I assure Your Majesty that I can hardly find words to express to Your Majesty how deeply concerned I am by all these happenings and how monstrous the accusations made against me appear to me to be.

I remain,

Your Majesty's devoted and faithful servant,

FELIX

This abortive attempt on the part of Yussupov to exonerate himself by such mendacious assertions from the grave suspicion that rested upon him gave the Empress great offence. For the time being she left Yussupov's letter unanswered and bluntly refused his petition that she should receive him in audience. Not till several days had elapsed, by which time the true facts of the case had already been established beyond any possibility of doubt, did she write to the Prince, in pencil and on a scrap of paper, a few lines expressive of her condemnation. They were as follows:

> No one has a right to murder. I know very well that many people are suffering the tortures of remorse, for it is not only Dimitry Pavlovitsh who is involved in this affair. Your letter filled me with utter amazement.

As I knew how keenly the Empress felt this crime committed against a good-natured man who had been so faithfully devoted to her, I was all the more painfully astonished by the reaction to this murder in many circles. It was natural that the party groups of the Extreme Left should be exultant; but a much more regrettable thing was the open sympathy for the murderers felt and publicly expressed even by very exalted personages.

Already on December 18 our censorship brought to my notice two telegrams dispatched by the Grand Duchess Elisabeth, the Tsarina's sister. One of the messages was addressed to the Grand Duke Dimitry Pavlovitsh; it was in English and ran:

> Just returned very late after week in Sarov and Divyeyev. Prayed for you all. Please send letter with particulars. God grant Felix necessary strength after patriotic deed.
>
> ELLA

The second telegram, which was in French, was sent to Princess Yussupov, the mother of Prince Felix, who was living at the time in the Crimea. It was in these terms:

> My earnest, heartfelt prayers for you all after your dear son's patriotic deed.
>
> ELISABETH

Thus the Grand Duchess made no attempt to conceal her conviction that Yussupov was at the bottom of Rasputin's murder, and approved of his act as a patriotic and heroic deed. A few weeks after the crime was committed the censorship also stopped an anonymous letter addressed to Prince Yussupov; it came from the Government of Nizhny-Novgorod, and in enthusiastic words lauded the assassination of Rasputin as a work of redemption and liberation. In this document we read:

> Brave and honourable men have, for a long time past, been striving to overcome the powers of darkness. In the Imperial Duma the matter has been discussed and the Tsar has been earnestly entreated to turn aside from his evil ways, to enter upon the path of truth and light, and to remember the oath he swore to our native land. But Nicholas has refused to give ear to the voice of truth and, together with his hypocritical courtiers, he has continued to pursue his disastrous course to the undoing of the country. Then the saviours of Russia comprehended that all further prayers and entreaties were doomed to avail nothing, because the Tsar is deaf, and that, accordingly, some other way must be taken.
>
> This way has now been found; the thing that the people have long looked for with yearning has come to pass: the wound has been opened and cleansed; the monster of unrighteousness has been made harmless; Grisha is dead and has left behind nought but an evil-smelling corpse.
>
> Truly there are still other things to be done. Many of the dark powers that had made common cause with Rasputin are even now still at work: Nicholas, the Tsarina, and other dregs of human society. The great men who carried out that deed of heroism are falsely called murderers; they are not murderers but saints who have jeopardized their lives for the well-being of their country. Woe be to Nicholas if he do violence to the life and liberty of these men! Like one man the whole people will then arise and do to the Tsar even as he did unto Colonel Myassoyedov.
>
> THE VOICE OF THE PEOPLE

The stupidity and baseness of this letter speak for themselves; but they are characteristic, for they show to what lengths the pernicious and inflammatory propaganda of the Revolutionaries had already gone, when people could venture to speak in such a tone of the august persons of the Emperor and the Empress. Of course I had this letter suppressed, so that it never reached its destination.

The investigation begun by me into the disappearance of

Rasputin was now suspended, and I handed over the whole affair to the Ministry of Justice to be dealt with according to the usual official procedure. Without waiting beyond the morning of December 17, Purishkyevitsh had gone off to the Front with the hospital train of which he was in charge, thus leaving his accomplices to face the music alone. He was very well aware that his appearance for some time to come on the orator's platform in the Duma would not be possible.

Yussupov tried as long as he could to maintain his fairy-tale of the dog that was shot, and repeated it both to the Chief of the City Police, Balk, and to the Minister of Justice, Makarov. When he tried to induce Makarov to believe that Purishkyevitsh had spoken those incriminating words to the policeman when in a state of intoxication, the Minister was in a position to counter the statement by observing that Purishkyevitsh, to his personal knowledge, abstained on principle from the use of alcoholic liquors.

Then Yussupov requested permission to leave Petersburg and to go to his wife in the Crimea; and this permission was actually granted him by Makarov in the first instance. But when the Tsarina heard of the Prince's intention, she forbade him to set off until the return of the Tsar, who was then visiting G.H.Q. Thereupon Yussupov betook himself to the palace of the Grand Duke Dimitry, and the two murderers now behaved as if they were national heroes, receiving regular visits of congratulation from those people who were so misguided as to see in their deed a work of patriotic liberation.

On December 19 the Tsar returned, and at once ordered the Grand Duke Dimitry to be placed under arrest—that is, he forbade him to leave his palace. At the command of the Tsar, Trepov, the President of the Council of Ministers, subjected Prince Yussupov to a thorough cross-examination; but this time again they failed to persuade Yussupov to describe truthfully and frankly what had taken place. Soon after the Tsar issued an order requiring Yussupov to retire to his estate in the Government of Kursk.

Grand Duke Dimitry Pavlovitsh was commanded to join the staff of the Army operating in Persia, and this decision by His Majesty called forth energetic protests from an opposition group within the Imperial family itself. Some of the Grand Dukes submitted a letter to the Tsar, beseeching him not to treat young Dimitry Pavlovitsh with such severity, as, after all, he had merely taken part in the removal of a detested and obnoxious wretch.

This letter became publicly known almost at once and gave rise to much discussion. In my view the document was both imprudent and heartless; it revealed plainly the purpose not, as might have been expected, of conserving the interests of the Imperial family, but rather of representing the special aims of the Liberal group among the Grand Dukes. The Emperor dealt with the petition with his customary sense of justice, by simply writing a marginal note to say that no one could be allowed to commit murder and go unpunished.

So the Imperial command was carried out. That same night both Yussupov and the Grand Duke Dimitry Pavlovitsh, escorted by officers, had to set out from Petersburg. During the journey they were prohibited from holding conversation and from receiving or sending telegrams.

CHAPTER XIV

From Nihilism to Socialism—Maxim Gorky's Bombing School—Revolutionaries as Patriots—Lenin works to bring about Defeat—The Ochrana suppresses a Revolutionary Meeting—Gutshkov's Disastrous Activities—Rise of a Pushing Politician—Gutshkov's Hatred for the Tsar—Case of the Yoffe Sisters—Order No. I

THE murder of Rasputin formed a prelude to those melancholy events that were destined to occur within an ever-widening sphere and to lead to the collapse of the Russian Empire. Before I turn to the description of the Revolution, I should like, however, on the strength of experience acquired in the service of the Political Police, to make one or two observations as to the development and aims of those parties and personalities whose accursed work it was at last to bring about that Revolution.

Systematic revolutionary agitation had begun in Russia in the sixties of the nineteenth century, when a group of intellectuals and innovators first made the attempt to shake and to undermine by violent measures the existing order of the State. It was at that time that the Netshayev conspiracy was formed, the conspiracy of which Dostoyevsky gives such a dreadful and such a thrilling picture in his *Demons*; it was then, too, that Peter Krapotkin was disseminating his insidious doctrines in the minds of Russian youth. It was the period of that mental aberration which is commonly indicated by the word Nihilism, and it is sad enough to reflect that, from that point onward, the whole world grew accustomed to regarding Nihilism as a specifically Russian phenomenon.

The sanguinary consequences of Nihilist propaganda were not long in making themselves manifest. In a short time repeated attempts were made on the lives of the Tsar and his

Ministers. The revolutionaries began against all the representatives of the established order a ruthless campaign that soon claimed many innocent victims. A fanatical Nihilist named Vyera Zassulitsh may claim the unhappy distinction of having been the first woman to be accused of a political crime and to be acquitted. A sentimental jury allowed itself to be swayed into returning that disastrous and mistaken verdict; and it may be said that the verdict appeared in consequence to sanction, as it were by the voice of popular approval, the violent suppression of servants of the State who happened to be disliked. Soon after that the Chiefs of the Police in Kiev and Petersburg, the Governor of Charkov, and other high officials were murdered. Nay, even in the lecture-halls of universities professors fell victims to the revolutionary madness of their hearers.

The life of the Tsar was no longer safe for one moment. After two vain attempts had been made to kill Alexander II a Nihilist named Stepanov succeeded in making his way into the Winter Palace and in secreting there a charge of dynamite. The dining-room of the Imperial family was destroyed by the explosion, and only by a miracle did the Tsar and his relatives escape for that time a horrible death. The Nihilists did not hesitate in their proclamations to assume responsibility for this criminal attempt, and to announce that it would be repeated. And, indeed, one year later Alexander II, one of the kindliest and greatest of the rulers of Russia, who had liberated his people from serfdom, was torn to pieces by a bomb.

The storm of indignation provoked throughout Russia by this deed of horror made it clear to the revolutionaries that they would have to set about their work differently if they wished to awake a popular response. Individual acts of terrorism continued as before, but with them was associated a systematic campaign, in which the people were worked up by the aid of revolutionary cries and catchwords. The secret association called the Liberation of Labour was formed, tending more and more in the direction of Socialism.

Then, in the nineties, the doctrines of Karl Marx made rapid headway in Russia, spreading with desolating effect, especially in the circles which have been called the *Intelligentsia*, the cultivated classes, above all among university students. At the same time the Revolutionary Socialists began a dangerous agitation among the peasants, stimulating among the ignorant country-people a hankering after the estates of the great landed proprietors.

At that time the real leader of Social Democracy in Russia may be said to have been L. Martov. His ambition was to become a second Marx and to work out the theory of the revolutionary teachings, while, at the same time, realizing them in practice. In the year 1898 a secret congress was held at Minsk, at which the Russian Socialist Labour Party was founded. In the year 1900 Lenin too began his disastrous activity by publishing the revolutionary organ *Iskra*—"The Spark."

The progress made by Socialism in a short time was revealed in the most astounding fashion on the outbreak of the Revolution of 1905. Already the workmen showed that they were willing to follow *en masse* the summons to the general strike issued by the Socialists. And if, by bringing to bear its utmost energy and resources, the Government did succeed for the time in suppressing the insurrection, the fact remains that the authorities saw, from that moment, that the Socialists had now grown to be their deadliest enemies. Even the Army had already been to some extent infected by Socialist ideas in 1905, a strong Socialist organization of officers and soldiers devoting itself particularly to the undermining of discipline. The Warsaw branch of the Ochrana, after much arduous labour, was able to reveal the threads of this conspiracy and to lay some of the plotters by the heels. For a certain time after that it looked as though the ferment had died down in the Army. It was not till the World War came that the military authorities realized clearly on what a slender basis of truth that optimistic assumption of theirs had rested.

It was in 1911 that my duty first brought me into touch with the group of extremists that was afterward to play an important part in carrying through the Revolution. These were the emissaries of the Bolshevik School of Capri, and I was then entrusted with the task of keeping them under observation. Maxim Gorky, along with A. N. Pyeshkov, had founded in the island of Capri a sort of revolutionary training college, on the teaching staff of which were, among others, Lunatsharsky and Alexander Kollontay. The Bolshevik party leaders sent there regularly some dozens of young people to master the art of political agitation, and, at the same time, to learn how to handle revolvers and bombs.

In the Police Department our confidential agents kept us informed of the existence and activities of this unique institute, but, of course, we could do nothing as long as the individuals involved remained abroad. But whenever the graduates from this bombing school endeavoured to get into Russia, they were arrested at the frontier, and my business was to examine the arrested persons in Petersburg.

One of those who attended Gorky's school was a workman named Gusakov, who had the appearance of a cretin and a criminal. Another was a good-natured fellow of genuine Russian disposition, who lived in Italy and was obviously suffering very seriously from home-sickness. He had become quite convinced, so he told me, of the hopelessness of the Utopian ideas with which they had tried to inoculate him, and during the course of a few days he readily supplied me with

particulars of the methods of instruction employed in Capri.
I was especially interested by what he had to say of the way
it was always impressed upon young revolutionaries that they
must cultivate a severe, self-denying, Communistic mode of
life. My informant confessed to me that he had felt most deeply
and painfully the contrast between those teachings and the
comfort, not to say luxury, with which the 'Professors' in
Capri had surrounded themselves.

After repeated discussions that took place at the time between
the Public Prosecutor and the Police it was decided that no
legal measures could be adopted against the arrested persons,
as they had not committed any punishable offence on Russian
territory. We therefore were restricted to adopting the process
of administrative banishment, and to condemning the Bolshevik leaders whom we managed to secure to a few years
of exile in Siberia.

When the War broke out I was second in command of the
Political Section of the Police Department. At that time it
seemed at first as if, from the moment the mobilization began,
all party strife, including the activity of the revolutionaries,
had ceased. During the early days of the War the patriotic
fervour was so great in all sections of the population that the
propaganda of the various Socialist groups not merely failed
to awaken a response among the masses, but actually appeared
to call forth a reaction.

Considering the patriotic enthusiasm general throughout
Russia, the Socialists determined to suspend for the time being
their agitation and to support the popular attitude. They
marched away waving the national flag like the others, ostensibly to defend Russia from the enemy; in reality they had
set before them quite another goal. They hoped by using patriotic shibboleths, or under cover of this or the other military
service, to make their way to the Front, and once there, in the

very midst of the troops in the trenches, to find better opportunities than ever before of pushing their pernicious and disloyal propaganda. And while they were operating among the fighting units, they aimed also at inciting to mutiny the men of the transport services, the wounded in hospitals, and the workmen in the factories.

As later events have shown, these calculations on the part of the destroyers of Russia were by no means without practical basis in fact. As time went on the revolutionary agitators did really succeed in undermining with their lying catchwords the morale of whole bodies of troops, especially of young classes who had recently been called to the colours and were in no sense inured to the military spirit. And by achieving that they created beforehand the conditions necessary to ensure the success of the Revolution.

Typical of the manner of this 'patriotic action' taken by the revolutionaries was the speech delivered by the leader of the Revolutionary Socialists, Tshernov, in the first and last sitting of the so-called Constituent National Assembly. By that time the Revolution had already gained the upper hand, and consequently there was no longer any reason for dissimulation, so Tshernov thought it incumbent upon him to stress particularly his anti-patriotic attitude during the War and to boast of his efforts to prevent the victory of the Russian armies.

Of course a very important part in organizing the anti-militarist propaganda was taken by Lenin, the leader of the Bolsheviks, whose real name was Vladimir Ulyanov, and who had already been in conflict with the authorities several times. In the year 1912 Lenin had preferred to quit Russia and betake himself to Austrian Galicia, where he settled in the neighbourhood of Cracow. From there he directed the actions of his comrades who had remained in Russia.

After the outbreak of war the heads of the Austrian Gen-

SCHLÜSSELBURG FORTRESS

Used as a State Prison for Revolutionaries

COURTYARDS IN THE FORTRESS OF SCHLÜSSELBURG
Where political prisoners were allowed to have their daily exercise

darmerie had him arrested, but the President of the Council, Count Stürgkh, recognized at once that Lenin might do much more good than harm to the German-Austrian cause, and therefore ordered his release. Thereafter Lenin entered into negotiations with the German Government, the intermediary being a Jew named Helfmann. In consideration of generous financial reward, Lenin undertook to foment disorder and strikes, and, in general, to prevent by any and every means the success of the Russian armies.

Lenin's general instructions were then at once published in the forbidden Press in Russia, and thenceforth the Socialists united their forces, concentrating all their efforts on making a Russian victory impossible. The War was now decried as an Imperialist adventure, and the order of the day was that Socialists of all nations should strive to bring it to as speedy an end as possible, and work for the World Revolution that was to follow. These principles were later on confirmed in due form at the famous Zimmerwald Conference.

Not very long after the War broke out a secret meeting of leaders of all the Russian Socialist organizations was to take place, with the object of deciding upon one coherent revolutionary plan of campaign. The Police Department had learned that such a deliberative council was being prepared, and all the individuals who were to take part in it, so far as we knew, were kept under most careful observation. Despite all our efforts, however, we did not succeed in finding the date and place of the projected sitting.

Early one morning General P. K. Popov, the Chief of the Defensive Section, came to me very crestfallen and disappointed, and announced that his agents had lost sight of all the persons who were being shadowed, for the latter had left their homes at a very early hour before the arrival of the police officials. From this fact Popov made the logical deduction that

that was the day on which the conference was to take place, without our knowing where it was being held.

After the lapse of an hour I got word from the Chief of the Moscow Ochrana that one of his secret assistants had received, the evening before, an invitation to be present at the meeting in question. Immediately I rang up General Popov, passing on the message I had just received from Moscow. He at once detailed a patrol for duty, hurried to the locality indicated to us, arrested the whole company, and seized the documents and minutes.

An ordinary workman had placed his house at the disposal of the conspirators. When General Popov suddenly appeared with his people, the man explained quite coolly that a few guests had come together to celebrate his birthday. Naturally General Popov did not allow himself to be hoodwinked by any such pretext. The affair was handed over to the judicial authorities and all those arrested were exiled to Siberia, where they remained until they were brought back in triumph after the Revolution.

The subsequent activities of the disloyal agitators are inseparably associated with the person of Gutshkov, member of the Duma. This man's plotting and scheming more than aught else led to the success of the Revolution, and that is why, not merely by me but by all patriots who love the Russian Empire, the name of Gutshkov is and always will be utterly detested.

During the war years I frequently had occasion to have Gutshkov watched by my agents, and, judging by the reports that came in to me, I became more and more convinced that the man I was dealing with was an adventurer, a self-seeker, and a traitor. Supplementary information which I obtained afterward from refugees abroad has tended only to confirm and intensify my first impression. The goal he strove by all possible means to attain was not, as might have been suggested, the welfare of Russia, but rather all the time only his own personal advantage. Even when, as far back as 1900, he took part in the Boer War in South Africa, that had been nothing more than an attempt to advertize himself in the public Press; all he cared for was that, day in day out, at home and abroad, the newspapers should talk of *him*.

And in that way he did succeed in keeping his name before the public. This proved to be to his advantage when, shortly after, he began to take a prominent part in the social activities, which at that time had become fashionable among our intellectuals. As in all mass movements it is never ability, but always merely insolence and cheek that count, it was not long before Gutshkov was elected by his friends to the Duma. In this body he soon drew attention to himself as leader of the Octobrist[1] Party, and he even managed to establish certain relations with the Prime Minister, Stolypin, who for a time sought the support of that group. Like every adventurer, Gutshkov plunged head over heels into any kind of officious activity, and thereby secured his election as President (Speaker) of the Duma.

But Stolypin was much too shrewd not to see through Gutshkov before very long. He recognized how unreliable and suspicious a character he was, and soon withdrew from association with him. Gutshkov was not able to maintain himself for very long in the position of President of the Duma; he was obliged to renounce this influential position, on the pretext of having to undertake a very urgent excursion to the Far East. That brought his parliamentary career to an inglorious close, at least for some considerable time. It did not, however, oblige him to interrupt his active participation in

---

[1] So called because the basis of its programme was the manifesto of October 17, 1905. It ultimately became rather reactionary.—Translator.

intrigue; and it was at that very time that he established friendly relations with Polivanov, afterward Minister of War, with whom he thenceforth worked hand in hand for the destruction of Russia.

Gutshkov, the upstart and adventurer, had the audacity to describe himself publicly as the personal enemy of the Tsar. The fact is that, at a reception given to the members of the Duma, His Majesty had once asked him whether he was the representative of the city or of the government of Moscow; and the circumstance that the Emperor was so poorly informed as to his personality had most deeply offended Gutshkov who, as has been indicated, was a very vain man. Whenever, after that, the Tsar was mentioned in his hearing, Gutshkov was impudent enough to make use of low and insulting expressions; and as far back as 1915 he is said to have announced, "If I do not die beforehand, I shall arrest the Tsar myself!"

And it was indeed ordained by an inscrutable fate that the offended vanity of that man should receive its highest satisfaction, for Gutshkov was actually one of the two members of the Duma to whom was entrusted the disgraceful task of intimating to the Tsar that he would have to abdicate.

It was as early as 1909 that the course of my official duties brought me into contact with Gutshkov, and on that occasion I was able to send him about his business in a manner befitting the man. The Ochrana had at the time arrested two sisters named Yoffe, one of whom was librarian to a district group of Socialists. The search of the library premises made by the Police brought to light some revolutionary pamphlets and a manuscript catalogue of them. On closer investigation I was satisfied that one of the two Mlles Yoffe had entered all the titles of these pamphlets in her own hand into the catalogue. When she was cross-examined, the woman also admitted, almost at once, that she had received a parcel of revolutionary books from a person whose name she would not mention; and she refused to make any further confession. On the strength of the material evidence to hand and of her avowal I passed the affair over to the Public Prosecutor, and released the other Mlle Yoffe.

When things had reached this stage, Gutshkov unexpectedly called upon me and announced in a high and mighty tone that he had come on behalf of the Yoffe family, that he protested against the arrest of the two ladies, as they had had no connexion with any political affairs whatever. Evidently it was again a deliberate piece of provocation staged by the Ochrana, and he thought the conduct of the Police strange in the highest degree.

"What is there strange in all this?" I replied coldly. "Are you aware that Mlle Yoffe here, in this office, has herself admitted that the forbidden books found in her possession were taken over by her and were entered by her in her own hand in the catalogue?" Gutshkov could not fail to see that this time his attempt to play the part of influential patron and protector was not succeeding as he had hoped. With a few words of apology he withdrew like a whipped dog. One month later the court pronounced sentence upon Mlle Yoffe; she was condemned to one year's confinement in a fortress.

During the years that followed Gutshkov was not much in the limelight, until the outbreak of the War at last gave him the long-looked-for opportunity to crown his deadly work and to hurl Russia into the chaos of the Revolution. It was now that he had the immense satisfaction of personally receiving the Tsar's abdication, and after he had entered the Revolutionary Government, he at once promulgated the shameless Order No. I, by which the Russian Army was shaken to its foundation and utterly demoralized.

This unprecedented document ordained what amounted, as far as the officers were concerned, to the complete deprivation of their rights, for it practically denied them all disciplinary powers. Soldiers were no longer required to salute, and the whole army became in all respects the plaything of the newly introduced Soldiers' Councils. The disastrous effects of that decree are known only too well; the condition in which our poor country lies to-day affords overwhelming testimony to the activities of the traitor Gutshkov. The patriotic Russian officers still living who have remained loyal to the Imperial cause will never forgive Gutshkov for his Order No. I. And for that reason, even among the refugees from Russia, many ex-soldiers have considered it their duty to bring this man to account. I can understand very well indeed the feelings of young Ensign Shabelsky-Bork, who challenged Gutshkov to a duel in Berlin. Unfortunately this encounter was prevented by the very superfluous exertions of various persons; senior officers forbade the ensign I have named to fight with Gutshkov. Thereupon another ensign, named Taboritsky, shouted out so that all might hear him that in future he would refuse to recognize Gutshkov. The latter pocketed without a word this insult from the officer who, though he was a young man, had the courage of his convictions. But that was not the end of the affair. Two years after, Taboritsky happened to run across Gutshkov in the Berlin Underground and gave him a sound drubbing. To the passengers who witnessed the scene he explained that the man he was chastising had brought Russia to ruin, whereupon the patriotic Germans applauded him heartily.

A. GUTSHKOV, WAR MINISTER UNDER
THE PROVISIONAL GOVERNMENT

JERZHINSKY AS A CONVICT
See Page 275

FORTRESS OF PETER AND PAUL

CHAPTER XV

*My Appointment as Chief of the Police—Conversations with Proto-
popov, Minister of the Interior—Varied Impressions made upon me by
Members of the Government—How Protopopov became Minister of the
Interior—Jealousy of Certain Members of the Duma—Intrigue against
General Kurlov—Reform of the Ochrana—Audience of the Tsarina—
Machinations of Milyukov and Rodzyanko—Vileness of the Press*

IN THE autumn of the year 1916 a series of significant
changes were made in the Government and, in close association with these, my promotion to the headship of the Police Department took place. This increase in rank I owe, above
all, to the kindly intervention of General Kurlov, who proved
to me again on this occasion the sincerity of the friendship
he felt for me.

On September 13 Kurlov called upon me and informed me
that the Tsar had just appointed the Vice-President of the
Duma, Protopopov, to be Minister of the Interior. Now, as I
have already mentioned, it was the custom in Russia that
each Minister of the Interior, on his accession to office, should
make a fresh appointment to the position of Chief of Police,
filling that important post with a man in the full enjoyment
of his personal confidence. So Protopopov, immediately after
his audience with the Emperor, had asked General Kurlov for
his advice as to the likeliest person to consider for the headship
of the Police Department, and Kurlov had proposed my name.

A few days later Protopopov invited me to dinner, and in
the course of a long interview gave me an opportunity of
expressing my views upon various questions concerning Home
Affairs and upon the general political situation. Later this
conversation was reproduced in a mutilated and distorted
shape in an anti-Government pamphlet; you may be sure that
the actual course of it was really very different from the form

given to it by the agitators. Protopopov dismissed me without making any definite promise, so that for a short time I did not know whether I could count upon my being appointed.

On October 1 the Minister, who had returned the same morning from G.H.Q., summoned me again and handed to me a lengthy document containing the command of His Majesty appointing me expressly to the control of the Police Department. Protopopov inquired what I proposed to begin with in my new sphere of activity. I then expounded in detail my immediate intentions, which were especially concerned with the internal reorganization of the administrative machinery of the Police; and I had the impression that my suggestions had Protopopov's complete approval. To conclude, I observed that I had up till then always fulfilled my duty according to my conscience, the best of my ability, and the state of the law, and that I should continue in future to do the same. "I should like to assure you at once," I added, "that I shall never do anything behind your back, that I shall rather keep you constantly informed of all I am doing, that I shall always consult you and submit to your instructions."

This assurance was not just such a matter of course as the reader might perhaps think, for it had sometimes happened that the official in charge of the Police had ignored the Minister, and had acted independently of him, nay, even in opposition to him. In my talk with Protopopov I had in my mind especially the behaviour of my predecessor Klimovitsh, who had at every turn treated Stürmer, the President of the Council of Ministers, in the most cavalier fashion. In Stürmer's reception-room Klimovitsh had spoken in a loud tone, audible to all, in criticism of the Prime Minister's measures. More than that, he had actually gone so far as to arrest, on his own responsibility and over the head of the Minister, the latter's private secretary, Manassyevitsh-Manuilov. Under the circumstances, therefore, there was some point in my spontaneously assuring Protopopov of my complete devotion and loyalty. And the Minister did not fail to put a proper value upon my assurance; he embraced and blessed me, and then invited me to enter upon my duties that same day. In accordance with an ancient custom, this involved, first of all, my paying calls upon the members of the Government.

The best impression was made upon me by the Ministers A. F. Trepov and N. M. Pokrovsky, undoubtedly both shrewd men of solid character. I liked very much too Admiral I. K. Grigorovitsh, who was in charge at the Admiralty. In conversing with him I must say I quickly felt that it was very much against his will to hear anything about revolutionary propaganda in the Fleet. However, I told him I should at once communicate to him very frankly whatever information on the matter came to my knowledge.

In contrast to the three members of the Government I have named, the Minister of War, Shuvayev, made a perfectly deplorable impression upon me. In talking with me, he emphasized quite unnecessarily the fact that he was of plebeian descent, and knew how to appeal to the people, as he had shown a few days before in a Petersburg factory. While he himself was convinced of the splendid effect produced by that speech, I knew from the reports of my agents that the appearance of the Minister had not merely not confirmed peace in that factory, but that, on the contrary, it had given rise to new difficulties in the establishment of order.

Nor did my visit to Count Ignatiyev, the Under-Secretary for Education, afford me any satisfaction whatever. I received the impression that this Department was being worked on decidedly Liberal lines, and by no means in the patriotic way that it should have been.

At the time of Protopopov's appointment to the Ministry

of the Interior such a vast deal of nonsense was current that I should like to say a few words by way of correcting errors and slanders that have gained a wide publicity. One particular assertion was made repeatedly: that Rasputin had exercised the chief influence in bringing about the appointment, and that it was only due to his intervention and his appeal to the Tsarina that the Tsar had agreed to it. In reality things happened quite otherwise.

Protopopov had been for some time Vice-President of the Imperial Duma, and in this capacity he had, by his outstanding qualities, especially by his exceptional personal amiability, won many friends. When the suggestion was made that two members of the Duma should be sent abroad for the purpose of making commercial and economic investigations, it was agreed to entrust Protopopov and Milyukov with this mission. After the return of these two Deputies, the Emperor wished to receive one of them personally, in order that he might hear from him the results of their inquiry. His choice fell upon Protopopov.

As I learned afterward, the invitation to this audience was quite unexpected, and it put Protopopov into a state of the greatest excitement. Nevertheless he made an excellent impression upon the Tsar, so that, when the Ministry of the Interior fell vacant shortly afterward, His Majesty resolved to appoint Protopopov to the post.

What ensued was very characteristic of the spirit that dominated the Duma. Till that moment Protopopov had been generally esteemed and respected, but his appointment as Minister sufficed to make him in one hour a detested man. General Kurlov told me how in his presence Protopopov, immediately after returning from the decisive audience, rang up his friend and colleague Rodzyanko, the President of the Duma, in order to give him the great news. Protopopov was utterly taken aback, when Rodzyanko answered him very coldly that he had no time then to talk with him.

The bitter hostility which, from that time onward, was shown by the Duma toward Protopopov had an extraordinarily depressing influence upon him, and the changed attitude of his former friends he could never understand. Once, when he asked me why he had become so suddenly an object of detestation in the Duma, I was able to answer him with complete conviction: "Since the Tsar invited you, and not the ambitious Milyukov, to report upon your foreign travels, Milyukov has been your enemy, and he will do everything in his power to harm you."

And, indeed, the Duma never missed an opportunity of disparaging and traducing its former Vice-President, and of placing difficulties in his way. Thus it was only a short time after I had entered upon my duties as Head of the Police that I witnessed the disgraceful clamour raised by the Duma against General Kurlov, mainly because Protopopov wished to have him as Under-Secretary. The Emperor's approval of this appointment had already been obtained, but the enemies of Kurlov and Protopopov had managed, by secret intriguing, to prevent the edict in question from being submitted to the Senate for registration, which, with such Imperial decrees, was obligatory.

This mistake in procedure, which had been deliberately brought about, served the Duma as a pretext to make General Kurlov look ridiculous in the public eye, the question being suddenly raised whether Kurlov had any right to act on behalf of the Minister of the Interior in submitting departmental reports to the Senate, seeing that the Senate had no official knowledge of Kurlov's appointment as Under-Secretary. According to the strict letter of the law this complaint was justified, but what seems difficult to understand is that no one at the right time could summon up courage simply to correct the mistake in procedure. Instead of that being done, the Senate and the other authorities yielded to the Duma, and returned to the Police Department all the papers signed by General Kurlov. Thereupon Protopopov requested the permission of the Emperor to have the functions of the Under-Secretary transferred to me. His Majesty graciously approved of this suggestion, whereupon I had all the documents bearing Kurlov's signature drawn up again, and signed them myself.

One of the first measures I undertook in my new office consisted in the attempt to carry out certain reforms in the organization of the Ochrana that had been planned long before. As was to be anticipated, my measures were to be brought up in the Duma in the form of an interpellation, and I waited thereafter from one sitting to another for the opportunity of personally defending before the House the reforms I had introduced. But over and over again the question bearing upon the matter was removed from the Orders of the Day. I was curious to discover the reason for this, and was not long in learning that the postponement of the debate on this subject had been brought about by the left wing of the Duma. The truth is that the Liberals were quite unable to produce any serious objections to my Police reforms, while it would have gone too much against the grain to have to give their sanction to any step taken by the Government, and in order to avoid this painful necessity, they sought to prevent the irksome Police debate from taking place at all.

It was quietly conveyed to me at the time that Kerensky was reported to have stated: "The Ministry has settled the Police question better than the Duma would have wished. They have cut the ground from under our feet, and this time we cannot raise any objections."

One of the most important questions of the time was the

appointment of a Chief for the City Police in Petersburg. This post had become vacant through the retirement of Count Obolyensky. When Protopopov broached the matter with me, I told him very bluntly that, in that responsible position, the only sort of man who could render effective service was one who possessed a thorough acquaintance with the Police routine and who was energetic, hard-working, and absolutely honest. In this connexion I mentioned Major-General A. P. Balk, the Assistant to the Chief of Police in Warsaw, and recommended his nomination. Protopopov took up my suggestion, set about making the necessary inquiries, had a personal interview with Major-General Balk, and finally resolved to propose him for the appointment to the Emperor.

I still remember very well how long Balk hesitated; he was not sure that he was morally justified in accepting promotion to so exalted a position, for he had not in the least been expecting it. He called upon me and submitted to me all his scruples. At the close of a long talk he actually asked me if I did really think him competent to fill so responsible an office to the satisfaction of the Emperor, and whether it was not rather reckless to fall in with the Minister's proposal without his fitness having been properly put to the test.

That was the attitude of persons of eminence under the old *régime* when they were offered the prospect of a brilliant career! Afterward, it must be admitted, when the Revolution had taken place, with the new men new customs were also introduced into Russia: then it became a matter of indifference to those who had the power whether they were to go to one Department or another, the Admiralty or the Ministry of Agriculture; it was all the same, provided only they were in a position to rake in money, lots of it.

Major-General Balk, immediately after his appointment, took an iron grip of the Police in the capital. He saw to everything himself and never waited too long before he intervened. He also bore full responsibility for the provisioning of the city. All the affairs that came under his purview he settled with exemplary dispatch and ability, although they must have caused him many an anxious moment.

His administration earned for him the encomiums of almost all. I continually heard the opinion expressed that the new Chief Constable was a stern, upright man and a chief familiar with every detail of the Police Service. Only subordinates who had previously been disposed to accept bribes from the civilians were dissatisfied with his strict instructions, and consequently passed an adverse judgment on their superior.

Balk's attitude after the Revolution was also characteristic. For a good while the Provisional Government kept him under arrest, and then they wanted to release him; but he declared that he would not leave prison until it had been proved that all the officials who had been his subordinates had acted strictly according to the law.

About a month after my appointment to supreme command of the Police I had the honour of being received in audience by the Tsarina. At the appointed time I appeared at Tsarskoye Syelo and was shown into a fairly large private room, where Her Majesty was awaiting me, in the garb of a hospital nurse. After I had respectfully kissed hands, she invited me to take a seat, and then inquired whether I had already got quite accustomed to my new sphere of action. With a smile she observed that, in her view, most officials busied themselves far too much with papers and documents, and lost sight the while of the real, living interests of the day. She thought that one should always watch the events of the moment, especially in the present difficult times. After all, the possibility of a revolution had to be taken into account, and one must know what was to be done in such a case.

I replied that a revolution, as such, was quite impossible in Russia. There certainly existed among the people a certain nervous tension due to the prolonged duration of the War and to the heavy burdens it entailed, but the people trusted the Tsar and were not thinking of rebellion.

"That is how I feel about it too," said the Tsarina almost in a whisper, "and I would fain believe that it is so."

I proceeded to state that the Government must not, of course, lose sight of those internal foes who were working with might and main for the destruction of the Empire, and that, for that purpose, the active assistance of the Ochrana was required, for its task was to find out the agitators and to prevent their treacherous work. I also hinted at my regret that among the Ministers there did not prevail that perfect unanimity that was so necessary, and that the Government sometimes came to decisions that sounded like the echoes of decisions already arrived at by the Opposition parties in the Duma.

In conclusion, I assured the Empress that the Ministry of the Interior had taken all necessary steps to make certain that any possible troubles would be quickly suppressed. I informed her that plans were already drawn up for the demobilisation of the Army on the conclusion of the War, the intention being to disband the infantry units first, while the cavalry, which was necessary for the maintenance of internal order, would have to be kept longer under arms.

When I had finished the Empress remained silent for a few seconds, as if she were turning over in her mind the dispositions I had been detailing, and then, in the most friendly tone, she wished me complete success in all my undertakings. Finally she said she had an important request to make: would I see to it that, at her desire, disabled officers were taken into the Police Service? This request Her Majesty expressed in the most considerate and the most modest way. Of course, I issued the very next day to all governors of provinces and cities a circular, in which I brought to their notice the desire of the Empress, and laid it down that, whenever vacancies occurred, disabled officers were to be preferred to all other candidates.

My audience had lasted seventeen minutes altogether. The Tsarina dismissed me most graciously, and once more wished me all success in the performance of my duties.

On November 1 the Duma began its session, and from now onward attacks upon the Government came fast and furious. Within a week the Duma managed to bring about the fall of Stürmer, the President of the Council of Ministers. I still remember how Milyukov appeared on the orator's platform to address the House, and asserted that he had in his pocket irrefutable documentary evidence to convict the President of the Council of treachery and of assisting the Germans, but that he intended to submit these documents only to the judicial authorities. Later developments showed how much of substance there was in this monstrous accusation. Stürmer died in bitter torment, while Milyukov is to-day well and hearty, and suffers no sort of distress; but Milyukov never produced a single one of these alleged documentary proofs, for the simple reason that they never existed. Subsequently the Provisional Government appointed a Committee of Inquiry, and the president of that committee expressly declared to Stürmer's wife that the most careful investigation into the crime of which the former President of the Council was accused had failed to reveal any evidence whatever.

After Stürmer's dismissal the Duma continued its attacks, and every day another high official was accused of treachery or espionage; not even the person of the Tsarina was spared by this shameless agitation. In such wise did Gutshkov, Milyukov, Polivanov, and company systematically prepare the way for the catastrophe.

In succession to Stürmer, A. F. Trepov had been appointed, but he too had to look on helplessly while the Duma continued its baiting and intrigue. Milyukov enjoyed the special patronage of Buchanan, the English Ambassador, and often actually spent his nights in the British Embassy. If the Foreign Office in London should ever allow the publication of its archives, the event will, I dare say, probably shed a new and not especially creditable light on Milyukov's 'patriotism.'

The same agents who informed me of Milyukov's visits to the British Ambassador also reported to me his appearance in a secret meeting of the Cadet [1] Party, of which he was the leader. There Milyukov uttered very serious warning of the dangers of revolution, declaring that, if the peasants were promised land to-day, the promise would have to be kept to-morrow, and that that would involve a revolution the end of which no man could foresee. On that occasion he made use of the expression that to make such promises to the peasants was, so to speak, waving a red rag under the nose of a wild bull. Nevertheless Milyukov continued his pernicious action and obliged Rodzyanko, the President of the Duma, to reproduce all his phrases like a gramophone. Acting as a catspaw for Milyukov, Rodzyanko in those days did his utmost to get into touch with the Association of the Nobility, and draw them into a conspiracy directed against the Tsar. The negotiations which he carried on at that time with Bazilyevsky, the President of the Moscow Association of Nobility, with Somov, who occupied a similar position in Petersburg, and with Samarin, the Marshal of the Nobility, can hardly be characterized as anything else than high treason.

---

[1] This was up to the time of the Revolution the group that might have been called Constitutional Monarchists, and after the Revolution, Bourgeois Republicans. Their Russian name was *Konstitutsionalisty-Demokraty*, the initials of which name, Ka-De, make approximately the French word *cadet*, afterward current with the *t* heard as in English.—TRANSLATOR.

Without any justification in fact, Milyukov suddenly feared
for his life, affirming that the right wing of the Radical Party
was planning an attempt upon it; he requested me to have
him protected by secret agents. Although, when the matter
was thoroughly inquired into, these fears proved to be groundless, I did, all the same, place at his disposal a few officials
attached to the Ochrana, who never let him out of their sight.

Now, as ever since his appointment the principal object
of all attack was the unfortunate Protopopov. Although positively not a single failure was brought home to the Minister
of the Interior, the hue and cry was kept up without inter-
mission; no one, they declared, could work with Protopopov.
Even his immediate subordinates left him shamefully in the
lurch: both his Assistant-Secretaries, Volkonsky and Balts,
quite openly spoke against their superior, and yet, if they
were not in agreement with the Minister's views, it would
have been their obvious duty simply to give up their offices.
They did not do that, and so I was not astonished when Balts,
who, in the year 1906 as Public Prosecutor had represented
the authorities in the charge brought against the Council of
Workmen's Representatives, took service with the Bolsheviks
in 1918.

Now, it is certainly not to be denied that Protopopov had
little aptitude for the purely bureaucratic ways of settling official business that are to a certain extent requisite in every
Government Department. His too active imaginative powers
misled him sometimes into the fault of coming to decisions
in an erratic fashion and of then giving them up again, which,
at times, rather tended to confuse the staff of officials serving
under him. However, there were no grounds at all for speaking of Protopopov's "incapacity." He might have been lacking
in his attention to business routine and in his conduct of departmental affairs, but, on the other hand, he possessed vision

PROTOPOPOV, LAST MINISTER OF THE INTERIOR UNDER THE TSAR

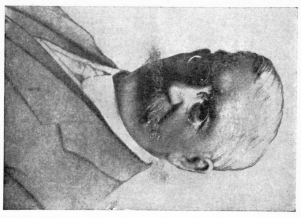

MILYUKOV, FOREIGN MINISTER UNDER THE FIRST REVOLUTIONARY GOVERNMENT

TSHERNOV

RODZYANKO, PRESIDENT OF THE DUMA

in a far higher degree than many of his colleagues in office, and was, above all, a personality of incorruptible uprightness and candour.

In the noisy agitation against him a peculiarly active part was taken by the Press of the various shades of extreme Radicalism; and, unfortunately, the Minister, being the high-minded man he was, would not condescend to put a stop to this disgraceful campaign by simply suppressing the newspapers in question. Such a proceeding appeared to him to be beneath his dignity, and he persistently rejected every proposal to adopt such a policy. At this time there appeared in a paper, which Protopopov had once very actively assisted to bring into being an article consisting of utterly meaningless and disconnected words. Only on closer inspection did the fact emerge that the initial letters of all these words when put together composed a scurrilous and insulting attack upon Protopopov.

To begin with, I often used to wonder at the equanimity with which the Minister accepted all these offensive and senseless attacks. Soon, however, I recognized that it was only on the surface that he preserved this apparent calm, for in private conversation he would often lay bare the bitter inward struggle that was going on. As a convinced Monarchist he did not wish to quit his post without the express permission of the Tsar, but at the same time he did not know how to convey clearly to the Tsar what was the real reason why he, and no one else, should be made the object of such general and bitter hatred.

Protopopov was, as I have already pointed out, a perfectly honest man of chivalrous character, who did not know the meaning of personal ambition and who was anxious to serve his Emperor to the best of his knowledge and ability. Perhaps nothing testifies so clearly to his unselfishness as the circumstance that, out of his own income, he had fifty thousand roubles divided among the civil servants in his own Department, who were feeling the pinch in those hard times.

But the campaign carried on against him finally assumed such forms that even Trepov, the new President of the Council, and otherwise so dignified and correct in his attitude, began to avoid Protopopov, and made it more and more obvious how glad he would be to have another Minister of the Interior in his Cabinet. Apparently Trepov hoped, by sacrificing Protopopov, to appease the ill-will of the Duma. About Christmas of 1916 Protopopov at last decided to present his position clearly to the Tsar and to ask for his dismissal. The Emperor listened sympathetically to what he had to say, and finally advised him, in the meantime, to take a brief leave of absence. He hoped, and hoped in vain, that after a little time had elapsed the general excitement would have died down.

CHAPTER XVI

Disintegration of the Army at the Front—Absurd Rumours among the Troops—Gutshkov's "Workmen's Group" arrested—A Commission from the Ministry of Foreign Affairs—Discussions as to the Suppression of Probable Rebellion—Treacherous Proceedings of General Russky—Watch kept upon Correspondence between Duma and G.H.Q.—Why Kryzhanovsky did not become Minister of the Interior—Threatening Excitement in Petersburg—Arrest of Bolshevik Leaders—Last Cabinet Meeting before the Revolution

IN THE autumn of 1916 the Ministry of the Interior was receiving more and more serious news as to the spirit prevailing in the Army, and especially among the Army Service Corps on the Southern Front. The staff of officers had been absolutely decimated by the long-drawn-out and extraordinarily sanguinary fighting, and in consequence younger and younger reserve officers had stepped into the vacancies left by the seasoned regular officers. They, however, had neither the experience nor the authority necessary to maintain proper discipline among the units under their command and to counter all revolutionary tendencies with the requisite energy.

Further, the younger classes of recruits who, from the summer of 1916 had been sent to the Front, proved to be insufficiently trained and very unreliable as to their morale. In these circumstances the pacifist agitation, aiming at a speedy conclusion of the War, was continually gaining ground. Already there had occurred gross cases of refusal to obey orders, especially in battalions fighting on the Rumanian Front. These incidents pointed very plainly to the parlous condition of military discipline in many units.

It seemed to me that it was high time to inquire very carefully into the causes of the demoralization among the troops, and to find out the identity of the agitators under whose influence the soldiers had lost their faith in the possibility of ending the War by an early victory. For this purpose I sent to the Southern war zone Lieutenant-Colonel of Gendarmes, A. P. Kubitsky-Petuch, a steady, trustworthy officer. The information which Kubitsky submitted to me on his return had the most discouraging effect upon my mind. According to his statement, it was throughout the Army the subject of common talk that the Tsarina was a traitor in alliance with the Germans, and was trying to bring about the defeat of Russia. That being so, the soldiers thought it was no wonder that the Russian Army should suffer one reverse after another.

I considered it my duty to bring this grave report to the notice of the Minister of the Interior, who laid it before the Tsar himself. The monarch read through the document, waved his hand in hopeless resignation, and never said another word about the matter.

About that time Gutshkov founded in Petersburg a Workmen's Group in the War Trade Committee, without anyone's having an idea of the purpose this group was intended to serve. It turned out that it was evolving the most amazing schemes for completely changing the whole body of social legislation, and soon it was beyond possibility of doubt that, under cover of a patriotic organization working for a Russian victory, Gutshkov had simply founded a revolutionary fighting group destined to form a tool for his treasonable aspirations. By dint of keeping them under observation for some time, I was able to acquire sufficient evidence; and getting into communication with the Commander of the City Police, I ordered the arrest, without more ceremony and on the grounds of antipatriotic intrigue, of the whole of this Workmen's Group.

Of course Gutshkov immediately rushed from one authority to another trying to obtain the release of his collaborators. The damnatory evidence which was available against this group was, however, so plentiful that I insisted upon handing over the affair at once to the appropriate tribunal. The information I had collected in this case I owed in the main to a secret agent named Ambrozilov, whom the Provisional Government subsequently exiled to Siberia, apparently in revenge.

Not long after this I was summoned to attend N. N. Pokrovsky, the Foreign Minister, who gave me instructions, in the name of the President of the Council, to organize an intelligence service for the special purpose of acquiring precise information as to the economic situation and the spirit of the people in Germany. The sums necessary for this enterprise, the Minister explained to me, would be paid out of a special fund. Pokrovsky was greatly astonished when I replied that no money whatever was necessary, for the news service desired by the Government had already been instituted some considerable time before. As a matter of fact, Krassilnikov, the Chief of the Foreign Branch of the Ochrana, had discovered a very able agent who had managed to make his way to Germany, and then kept us regularly supplied with interesting and detailed information about the prevailing spirit and the general situation in the German Empire. This evidence had up till that time been collected in the Police Department, and was now at once laid before the Minister for Foreign Affairs.

The disquieting news that was coming in to us from all sides obliged the Minister of the Interior to give his attention to the counter-measures that would have to be taken to meet popular disturbances that might arise. To that end the Minister got into touch with the Commander of the City Police and the Military Governor. The Governor, General Chabalov, worked out, in co-operation with a special commission, detailed plans for the combined action of Police, Cossacks, and other troops with machine-guns. Various plans of operation were provided for use, according to the extent of the rebellion.

Unfortunately General Chabalov was short-sighted enough to count upon the absolute trustworthiness of all the troops garrisoned in Petersburg; he obstinately refused to order out of the capital all reserve units that had been recently called up, urging as a pretext that there were no vacant barracks at his disposal in the neighbourhood of Petersburg. This circumstance, along with the strange attitude adopted by General Russky, contributed mainly to the fatal course that things subsequently followed.

Protopopov thought it his duty to draw the Tsar's attention to the ferment in the capital. After consulting Shabalov, the Emperor then commanded four regiments of Cavalry of the Guards to be dispatched to Petersburg. A few days passed in restless expectation, without the troops that had been requisitioned putting in an appearance. Then it turned out that General Russky, the commander on the Northern Front, had simply ignored the Tsar's commands; instead of sending the Guards regiments, Russky transferred a detachment of seamen to Petersburg. This behaviour of Russky's bordered upon open treason; and already at that time I had serious thoughts about the striking intimacy that existed between Russky and Gutshkov.

Accordingly I had a careful watch kept upon the correspondence between the members of the Duma and the Chief Command of the Army, and soon I received information that increased my anxiety in the highest degree. For it appeared that Gutshkov, Milyukov, and Rodzyanko were quite unmistakably working with the object of bringing the whole of the Chief Command, and, to be precise, Generals Russky and Alexeyev first of all, over to the side of the Duma. It was not long before I noticed that the bulk of the correspondence concerned was not passing through the post, but was being carried on by the agency of special confidential messengers, and was therefore not accessible to me. But if I had had nothing to go upon but the scarcely veiled hints in the letters that I did manage to see, they would have sufficed to afford me an insight into the treacherous ongoings of the whole company. It was simply amazing to note the tone adopted by these people: it was a matter of course with them to speak of the necessity for "making changes in the State."

In none of the belligerent States has anything of this kind happened. Everywhere, even in Germany, all parties were united in the desire first to bring the War to a victorious conclusion before they took in hand internal reform. But in Russia, at the very time when affairs were most critical, people gave less and less attention to the War, and more and more to political revolution. And, meanwhile, the blockade had been bringing Germany close to the brink of collapse, and, consequently, the prospects of an Allied victory seemed very much nearer.

It is true that in Russia the murder of Rasputin had for a short time diverted the attention of the Duma from Protopopov, but soon the attacks upon the Minister of the Interior began again. It has been already pointed out that Trepov had signified his desire to drop Protopopov, but, as a matter of fact, Trepov had gone into retirement before his unpopular colleague, and Prince N. N. Golitsin had taken his place. The latter repeated the attempt made by Trepov to get rid of Protopopov. In his efforts to conciliate the Duma as far as possible, the new President of the Council of Ministers decided upon a somewhat unusual step; he began negotiations behind Protopopov's back with S. E. Kryzhanovsky, with a view to inducing him to take over the Ministry of the Interior. He could scarcely have made a better choice, for Kryzhanovsky was a shrewd, energetic, and experienced official, who possessed a most intimate knowledge of the whole administration. Things might have developed very differently if Kryzhanovsky had been placed at the head of the Home Office some months earlier. But Prince Golitsin was not able to realize his intention. It is said that the Tsar had no particular liking for Kryzhanovsky. So things remained as they were until it was too late.

General Kurlov told me that Kryzhanovsky had made it a condition that Kurlov should be appointed General Commanding the Corps of Gendarmerie. But as Kurlov was, if possible, even more detested by the Duma that Protopopov, Prince Golitsin did not dare to fulfil Kryzhanovsky's wishes, and that is perhaps another of the reasons why Kryzhanovsky's appointment never took place.

In spite of the threatening excitement in certain classes of the population, I am of opinion that the crisis would never have come just as it did if the Imperial Adjutants-General Russky and Alexeyev had done their duty. However, instead of suppressing with a hand of iron all revolutionary manifestations in the Army—which could still have been quite easily done—these two commanders, under the influence of the Imperial Duma, not only did nothing of the kind, but, in addition to that dereliction of duty, left the Emperor right up to the end in the dark as to the real situation. It is significant enough that, after the victory of the Revolution was assured, the Tsar expressly stated that he was ready to forgive all his enemies, but for General Russky he could not bring himself in his heart to feel any forgiveness.

Later, when the Revolution, for the outbreak of which he had been greatly responsible, assumed its most catastrophic form, General Alexeyev tried to repair some of the wrong he had done, by leading his army against the Bolsheviks. What this meant in fact, however, was that he drove under the fire of the Red troops an army consisting of youths, partly unarmed and without transport, and thereby sacrificed in vain countless numbers of strong, healthy men.

The most ridiculous and pitiful part was played in those fateful days by Rodzyanko, the President of the Duma. He was hypnotized by the attractive prospect of becoming President of the Republic, and behaved himself like a boy who has undertaken some job without understanding the sense of his instructions and without having the necessary strength to carry them out.

In February 1917 the disquieting symptoms indicative of approaching trouble among the people and especially in the Army, which till then had been more or less sporadic, became more frequent and more dangerous. I was now almost continually receiving reports about petty or serious offences that had been committed by recently called-up reserve-men belonging to the Petersburg garrison. Every day the Police were arresting military men guilty of picking pockets at the tramway stopping-places. The prisoners would then be handed over to be dealt with by the Army authorities; but as, even then, the military prisons were marked by the absence of reliable supervision and guards, the men would often make their escape after a short period of confinement, and, after perpetrating some fresh misdeed, would once more fall into the hands of the Police.

About that time, too, greater or smaller bands of demonstrators began to make their appearance in the streets of the capital, noisily demanding bread. Naturally, whenever these manifestations assumed serious proportions, they were broken up as quickly as possible by the Police, but such demonstrations took place again and again, indeed almost incessantly. Rumours of threatening famine were systematically spread among the population, being generally believed and calling forth the spirit of panic and terror. In order to check this sinister development I summoned Balk, the Commander of the City Police, and requested him to lose no time in determining what supplies of flour and bread actually existed in the capital. After consultation with the official in charge of the Food-control, General Balk assured me that the stocks on hand were adequate to feed the entire population of Petersburg for more than three weeks, even if no new deliveries of any sort were to be made. There was, accordingly, no immediate risk of starvation.

At my request this state of matters was made known by means of proclamations detailing the facts, and drawn up in the clearest possible language so as to be understood by the people, and this measure had at least a temporary effect in calming the excitement prevailing in the capital. However, there were still some hundreds of idlers and vagabonds who were organized by the agitators into a crowd, and went roaring through the streets.

On February 18 a strike broke out in the Putilov works; the management replied to this with a lock-out. The result was that some thirty thousand men were suddenly deprived of the means of subsistence, which materially increased the unrest in the working-class districts. Moreover, the employees of the Putilov works endeavoured to induce those engaged in other Petersburg industries to join in a sympathetic strike. In the Vyborg district workmen's demonstrations were held, and the crowd, getting out of hand, were guilty of violence that could no longer be considered insignificant. Some of the street cars were stopped and overturned by the mob, a Police official of some importance was knocked down, and the demonstrators tried to make their way across the Neva into the centre of the city; they were, however, prevented by mounted Police.

Four days before the outbreak of the Revolution, General Chabalov, without previously coming to an understanding with the Minister of the Interior, proclaimed martial law in Petersburg. In all Government buildings troops were quartered; the guard assigned to the Police Department was composed of a company of the Pavlovsky Guards Regiment.

On February 24 the numbers of the strikers had already grown to about two hundred thousand, and the Police were no longer able to keep the crowds from forcing their way into the central districts, especially as the Ministry had issued instructions to refrain, as long as ever it was possible, from the use of firearms. On the other hand, the mob bombarded the men of the Police force ruthlessly with stones and pieces of old iron, by which a number of brave policemen were severely wounded. When the attempt was made to relieve the Police by employing detachments of Cossacks, a very serious state of matters was revealed: the Cossacks, who had once been the terror of a riotous crowd, now actually fraternized with the mob and gave not the least sign of taking serious measures against it. This occurrence was not only a belated warning for the authorities, but a great encouragement to the revolutionaries, and was therefore at that moment a peculiarly critical fact.

Till then we had had no hint that the revolutionary parties had secured the control of this proletarian movement. Now, however, I instructed General Globatshov, the head of the Petersburg Ochrana, to make inquiries; and it appeared that the Socialist organizations had determined to exploit the unrest in Petersburg for their own ends, and to prepare by systematic propaganda for the general strike and for demonstrations in the streets. On receiving this report from General

Globatshov, I decided to proceed quickly and to the purpose. I gave orders to arrest the revolutionary leaders at once, and General Globatshov managed to capture in a private dwelling the whole of the Petersburg Committee of the Bolshevik Party, so that that dangerous organization was for the moment completely paralyzed.

Unfortunately, Kerensky, of the Revolutionary Socialist group, was protected by his immunity as a member of the Duma. I had had him watched by some experienced agents when he was on a journey to Saratov, and they had observed him in a restaurant handing over certain papers to an individual, who was at once arrested, and confessed that he had received from Kerensky the seditious proclamations found upon him. Thereupon I had applied to the Ministry of Justice to have Kerensky deprived of his immunity, so that the Police might lay hold of him. Fate willed it that, a few days later, Kerensky himself should become Minister of Justice, and in this capacity should take cognizance of the proposal I had made to restrict his liberty.

On the evening of February 26 Protopopov came to dine with me. After we had dispatched our official business, we chatted for a long time in company with my wife, my brother, and my friend Gvozdyov, who was afterward butchered by the Bolsheviks. The Minister showed his best side that evening, as a charming companion and gentleman.

At ten o'clock Protopopov left me in order to take part in a sitting of the Cabinet. After midnight I was myself summoned by telephone to go to Golitsin's house. There I found the whole of the Government assembled, and I was asked to give a detailed report of the present political situation, the way the revolutionary movement was developing, and the counter-measures taken by the Police Department. So far as I was able to do so without documents, I explained at great

length to the Ministers the ominous relations subsisting between the Duma and the Chief Command of the Army; I
made some observations on the revolutionary propaganda
among the reserve units and the transport service; and concluded by affirming that now that I had had the leaders of
the actively seditious organizations arrested, the only body
offering any danger to the maintenance of order was the
Duma.

Protopopov advocated in most urgent terms the dissolution
of the Duma, making special reference to my report, and after
a fairly long debate the Council of Ministers decided to sanction the proposal of the Minister of the Interior. In view of
the possibility of such a decision being taken, the Tsar had
signed beforehand a decree that was now to be published the
next morning. It ran: "Founding upon paragraph 99 of the
Fundamental Law of the State, we order the prorogation of
the Duma from the 26th of February, and command that it
be convoked on a date to be appointed, but not later than the
17th of April 1917."

The events of the day that had already begun brought it
about that this decree of the Tsar was the last order that he
was to issue concerning the Duma. Who knows whether
things might not have taken a different turn had this edict
been proclaimed a few months before!

CHAPTER XVII

*The Morning of the Revolution—Mutiny and Murder in the Barracks
—The Mob storms the Prisons—The Police Headquarters in Danger—
Criminals destroy Records—The Revolution completely Victorious—
Traitors among the Generals—Gutshkov's Revenge—The Tsar abdi-
cates—Two Loyal Commanders*

IT WAS already getting toward three in the morning when
I returned home from the Cabinet meeting in Prince Golitsin's house. The Ministers had all been irritable and at the
same time depressed, obviously suffering under the consciousness of the burden of responsibility weighing upon them, and
their mood had affected me too. Although I was unusually
tired, it was long before I could go to sleep, I was so excited.
I was awakened again at six o'clock by the telephone bell. It
was the Commander of the City Police, Balk, ringing me up to
say that in the barracks of the Volhynian Guards Regiment
a sergeant-major named Kirpitshnikov had shot his superior
officer, Captain Lashkyevitsh, attached to the training section.
The murderer had thereupon vanished, leaving no trace, and
the temper of the regiment in question was very dangerous.
This communication of Balk's filled me with dismay, for one
could see from it how far the anarchy in the military barracks
had been already carried.

As the crime had been committed within the sphere of the
military authorities, I was not able to take any direct steps
myself, but I tried to get into touch with the Military Governor, Chabalov. All my attempts, however, to speak to him
by telephone were unsuccessful; to all inquiries as to his
whereabouts I never received any but vague and evasive
answers.

Kirpitshnikov, the sergeant-major before mentioned, after-

ward published his reminiscences abroad, and frankly acknowledged that, once he had done the deed, he had fled from
the barracks, not having even the slightest idea whether, an
hour later, he would have been hailed as a hero or hanged on
a lamp-post. And, indeed, that naïve observation was in keeping with the situation at the moment: no one in all Petersburg had any notion whatever of how things were going to
develop in the next few hours.

From my window I could see that the streets were extraordinarily busy for the hour of day. Soon military motor-
cars appeared, rushing at breakneck speed in all directions,
and then isolated rifle-shots were heard in the distance.

The telephone bell rang again; it was Balk once more with
another piece of alarming news: Major-General Dobrovolsky,
the commander of the Engineer Guards Battalion, had just
been murdered by his men.

Subsequent events happened with alarming rapidity. After
Captain Lashkyevitsh had been shot, the Volhynian Regiment
had mutinied, the men had driven the other officers out of
the barracks, and the mutineers had marched to the neighbouring barracks of the Preobrazhensky and the Lithuanian
Guards Regiments, the men of which had likewise joined the
revolt. In the barracks of the Lithuanians the rebels seized
the arsenal, and now the soldiers, armed with rifles and
machine-guns, raced in motor lorries at frantic speed all over
the town.

A crowd stormed the remand prison and set free all the
prisoners; the same thing happened in quick succession at all
the other prisons in the capital. Police officers in the outlying
quarters of the city were stormed by the mob; the policemen
who did not manage to make their escape in civilian garb
were butchered in the most inhuman fashion and the buildings were fired. In the eastern, the Lityeiny, quarter this pil-

laging of Police officers assumed particularly serious
proportions. Soon the news reached me by telephone that the
released criminals had set fire to the records department in
the Petersburg District Court; that meant the destruction of
a great number of precious and irreplaceable documents.

There was no longer any room for doubt as to the extraordinary seriousness of the situation. For some days past, as
has been already indicated, Petersburg had been supposedly
in the hands of the military authorities. But these had shown
their inability to prevent the murdering of officers by mutinous troops, or to suppress the revolt of the rank and file with
an iron hand. It was quite evident that the men had simply
ceased to obey their superiors. This fact received confirmation from every successive scrap of news that reached me.
The mutineers were disarming all the officers they could lay
their hands upon; any attempt at resistance was immediately
followed by death. A detachment of Pioneers that had remained loyal and made an attempt to withstand the mutineers
was overpowered, and in the same way the latter succeeded
in storming the Military College in Kirotshnaya Street and
in disarming the inmates. The numbers of the rebels grew
steadily, for the mob from all parts of Petersburg joined them
in countless swarms, so as to make sure that, if there was any
plunder and pillage going, they might not remain empty-
handed.

The bridge that connects the Lityeiny district with the
Vyborg district that lies north of the Neva was defended for
some little time by some plucky Police officers armed with
machine-guns, but in the end the rebels stormed the bridge
and made for the barracks of the Moscow Guards Regiment
situated in the Vyborg quarter. This regiment was still waver-
ing; in particular the training section offered armed resistance

PRISON OF THE OCHRANA FIRED BY REBELS

GENERALS ARRESTED BY MUTINEERS
Painted by Vladimirov

to the mutineers. Soon, however, the loyal troops were over-come, whereupon the Moscow Regiment also joined the revolt.

I was thinking of hurrying to the headquarters of the Police Department with the special purpose of looking up Minister Protopopov, who had his residence in the same building, but at the very moment when I was about to leave the house I was detained by a messenger who informed me that desperate machine-gun firing was going on in the Lityeiny Prospekt. This was the attempt, already referred to, that was made by the Police to prevent the mutineers from crossing the Lityeiny Bridge. As I should have had to cross the Lityeiny Prospekt on my way to the Police headquarters, the messenger im-plored me not to expose my life uselessly, but rather to stay at home and wait till things had quietened down again. So the only thing left for me to do was to establish telephonic connexion with the office. My secretary informed me that the service was being carried on as usual, but that, as was very comprehensible, everyone in the building was in a restless state of nervous excitement. As I had every reason to fear an attack by the mob upon the Police headquarters, I gave orders to have the staff sent home at once.

A very short time after evidence was forthcoming that this measure had been very justifiable, for my secretary, who was still faithfully at his post in the office, rang me up again to report that a howling mob had already forced its way into the courtyard of the building. I gave instructions that the books with the addresses of the officials employed in the De-partment and especially of the secret agents should be burned at once which fortunately they were able to do just in time.

As I learned later, the 'liberated people' searched every flat in the building, and some of the leaders, who apparently had very good reason for doing so, took a great deal of trouble to discover the Criminal Register and to destroy it. All the archives of the Special Investigation Branch, with records of finger-prints, photographs, and other data concerning thieves, forgers, and murderers, were dragged down into the court-yard and there solemnly burned. Further, the intruders also broke open my desk and appropriated twenty-five thousand roubles of public money, which I had had in my keeping.

From the Police headquarters the crowd invaded the residence of the Minister, Protopopov, and ransacked it from top to bottom. According to the statements of eyewitnesses, there were among the mob women who looked like persons of better education; they were wearing Persian cloaks, and were seen carrying off great bundles of stolen goods from Protopopov's home.

I shall not make special mention of numerous inquiries by telephone which I had to answer in the course of the following hours. Above all, I was besieged by the Moscow authorities with inquiries as to what was really happening in the capital. I replied to Colonel Martynov, the Head of the Moscow Ochrana, that a serious mutiny had broken out among the troops in Petersburg, and that I should send him further information as opportunity presented itself.

It is characteristic of the general confusion prevailing that morning that, for quite a time, neither the military authorities nor the mutineers thought of occupying the Telephone Exchange. Thus it came about that it continued to function undisturbed, preserving, as it were, strict neutrality, so that the revolutionary leaders on the one hand and the members of the Government on the other were able to maintain communication by telephone. Gradually, however, it became more and more difficult to obtain the connexion required, apparently for the simple reason that the girls at the exchange were, in increasing numbers, thinking it preferable to quit their posts of duty and to seek refuge from the storm by going home. Finally even the direct wire to the Imperial Palace ceased working, and I could not even be put through to the Commander of the City Police or to the Ochrana.

I was therefore very much surprised when I was suddenly rung up by Protopopov from the Mariensky Palace. I reported to him the entire course of events so far as I was informed, and added that the Higher Command was apparently quite powerless, as the troops, the overwhelming majority of them at least, were making common cause with the revolutionaries.

Thereafter I left my house, accompanied by my wife and my friend Gvozdyov. Strictly speaking, I did not myself know which way I was to turn, although I had with me a passport for abroad, as well as another passport bearing a name that was not mine. On the way I thought of calling on my brother, who was then living in the Astoria Hotel, but on second thoughts I did not do so, as I foresaw that the hotel would be attacked, which, indeed, did actually happen. I therefore betook myself to the abode of a good friend, an engineer named A., who lived in the neighbourhood of the hotel mentioned. There we were hospitably welcomed, but, of course, sleep was out of the question. In the streets there was the rattle of rifle and machine-gun fire, motor lorries manned by armed hooligans kept passing incessantly, and we heard the wild shouting of the disorderly rabble. Under such circumstances we spent a sleepless night.

It became ever more obvious that meanwhile there was no possibility of suppressing the revolt. In the whole of the capital there were only very few military units that remained aware of their duty, and these were far too weak in numbers to adopt any active measures against the rebels. General Chabalov had to confine himself, for the time being, to the defence of the Government quarter of the city.

While I was pursuing my melancholy thoughts, I saw them

plundering like vandals the house of Count Fredericks, the Controller of the Household. And all that was, in the last resort, the work of General Russky, who had failed to carry out the Emperor's commands! With a few reliable regiments order in Petersburg could have been quite easily maintained; instead of obeying instructions, the miserable traitor had transferred a body of seamen to the capital, thus adding fuel to the flames. With my whole heart and soul I cursed that General, whom the Tsar had pampered and spoiled, showering upon him tokens of his favour.

At the same time I taxed my memory to ascertain whether I too, perhaps, had not done things for which I should not be able to answer to a just judge. But I could not recall a single illegal action; and even when I went back in my mind over all the so-called ambiguous cases that had occurred during my period of office, I could not but decide that I was in a position to give a good account of each one, to my own conscience and before any impartial tribunal.

What was I to do now? Really the most sensible thing would have been at once to make my escape abroad; the means to do this, as I have already suggested, were in my possession. But I regarded it as a dishonourable piece of conduct to make off, while my Minister and other high Government officials were helpless in the hands of the rebels.

For two days I remained with A., the engineer, and then I moved over to the quarters of another acquaintance living close by. Of course I had to make my way there on foot, for in those days there were no vehicles of any kind available. On the way I was accosted by a stranger in an officer's grey overcoat. He pointed excitedly to the Fortress of Peter and Paul, shouting out that he had been confined there for five months, and, what was more, that the Ochrana alone was responsible for it. I asked him what offence he had committed,

and he confessed without any more ado that he had em-
bezzled monies belonging to the State, because he had required
funds to keep up a second family he was maintaining unknown to his wife. According to him, the meanness of the
Ochrana action lay in the fact that the police had caught him,
when he was fleeing the country, quite close to the frontier
between Finland and Sweden. It was, after all, rather annoy-
ing to have spent so much money on that long journey and
then to be arrested in the end. And in conclusion he delivered
for my benefit a long speech, the general effect of which was
that, under the Tsar, his bones might have rotted in prison,
but that the free people had conquered now, and that he was
awaiting the moment when he would be able to take his share
in laying the foundations of a new, free Russia.

After this little episode I reached safely the residence of
my friend I. K., where I spent the following two days. Meanwhile, it became hourly more obvious that the Revolution was
about to gain a complete victory. In the year 1906, at the time
of the Moscow disorders, the Semyonovsky Regiment had
greatly distinguished itself in suppressing the troubles; on
the evening of February 27 that regiment also joined the
revolutionaries, and one more hope of General Chabalov's
had gone.

The plight of this unhappy officer grew more desperate from
hour to hour. By noon of that day he had had to report with
a heavy heart to the Tsar that it was beyond his power to deal
successfully with the revolt, and he pleaded most urgently for
reliable troops to be sent to reinforce the garrison. In the
course of the afternoon Chabalov then assembled the few
loyal troops left to him upon the square in front of the Winter Palace, to wait there for the arrival of the hoped-for relief.
Active measures against the revolutionaries were out of the

question, for the attitude of Chabalov's men was quite passive, and we had to be glad that they did not go right over to the side of the mutineers. During the evening Chabalov decided to terminate the occupation of the square, as there was reason to fear that the revolutionary troops meant to bombard it, and he was anxious to avoid endangering the palace. So the Imperial forces now abandoned the palace, and withdrew to the vast building occupied by the Admiralty, situated on the Neva embankment.

With the following morning there arrived a great body of well-armed troops, who, at first, were believed to be the relieving forces that had been sent in from the Front. Unfortunately this sudden flicker of hope almost at once gave way to bitter disappointment when it became known that the newcomers were soldiers of the Machine-Gun Regiment from Oranienbaum, who had also mutinied. They had gone over to the Revolution on the evening of February 27, and had immediately set off, with their machine-guns, for Petersburg, where they were now triumphantly welcomed by the other rebels.

And there was no further sign of the expected loyal troops. All attempts by G.H.Q. and General Ivanov, who had meantime been appointed dictator, to initiate counter-action against the rebellion in Petersburg met with failure. At midday on February 28 the Peter and Paul Fortress capitulated, so that its guns now threatened the Admiralty Buildings facing it. Under these circumstances, and considering the temper of his own troops, there was no course open to Chabalov but to surrender likewise to the revolutionaries. He was secured, as I heard later, and taken into the Duma building.

On the morning of February 28 the Tsar had left the quarters occupied by the Higher Command to betake himself as quickly as possible to Tsarskoye Syelo; but in the night his special train was stopped and compelled to turn back, for the news coming to hand of the threatening state of matters prevailing in Petersburg was becoming more and more disquieting, so that the officer commanding the train, General Voyeikov, did not dare to go any nearer to the capital. Instead of doing that, Voyeikov decided to take the Tsar to Pskov, the headquarters of the Northern Army, where, in the midst of his troops, he would at least be assured of personal safety.

In Pskov the base intrigues of Alexeyev and Russky,[1] the two generals who were in sympathy with the Duma, now began to be revealed in plain colours. Instead of recommending His Majesty to adopt energetic measures against the Revolution in Petersburg, which, if capably organized, would certainly even then have had much prospect of success, these two generals did the very opposite, and by their action contributed very materially to the fall of the Tsardom. For Alexeyev telegraphed to the Emperor that the anarchy which was growing every moment in the country, and especially in the Army, could be kept in check only by forming a Government of men enjoying the confidence of the Duma. General Russky, for his part, submitted this message of Alexeyev's to the Tsar, and adjured him to suspend all military action that had been initiated with a view to crushing the revolt, and to begin direct negotiations with the members of the Duma. The Emperor, in this fateful moment, was good-natured enough to yield to the advice of the two generals. He actually renounced the attempt to assert his authority by force of arms, and in coming to this decision what weighed with him especially was the desire to avoid all useless bloodshed. He had no suspicion that this surrender to rebellion, more than all else, would plunge Russia into far greater terror and bloodshed

[1] Alexeyev was at G.H.Q., and communicated by telegraph with Russky in Pskov. —TRANSLATOR.

than would have been entailed by energetic suppression of the Revolution and the subsequent speedy restoration of orderly and constitutional conditions.

Then General Alexeyev collected expressions of opinion from the various army commanders on the question whether the Tsar should abdicate; and again it was General Russky who submitted to the Tsar a skilfully compiled selection of the answers sent in. Under pressure from Russky, the Tsar did actually make up his mind to intimate by telegraph to Rodzyanko, the President of the Duma, that he was ready to agree to abdication. In the telegram sent by His Majesty to Rodzyanko he stated:

> There is no sacrifice that I should not be willing to make for the salvation and the well-being of our beloved Russia. I am therefore ready to abdicate in favour of my son under the regency of my brother Michael Alexandrovitsh. The only condition that I make is that, till he reaches his majority, my son shall remain in my care.

On March 2 there appeared in Pskov the two deputies, Gutshkov and Shulgin, who had undertaken the shameful task of accepting the deed of abdication. The Tsar received them at once, and Gutshkov naturally used the opportunity to deliver a long speech. It is characteristic of the man that, as Shulgin afterward reported, during the whole interview Gutshkov did not have the courage to look straight into the eyes of the Tsar, whom he had betrayed and from whom he was now exacting vengeance for his injured vanity. His oration he concluded with the insolent words, "If you wish to consider the matter a little longer, I shall withdraw meanwhile and await your decision; but in any case the whole business must be settled without fail to-night."

The Tsar behaved as if he had not noticed the effrontery of the tone, and intimated to Gutshkov with grave dignity that he was prepared to abdicate in favour of his brother, the Grand

Duke Michael. Thereupon he entered the saloon carriage which was standing near by, and there dictated the final form of the historical document, which he signed with a firm hand.

What passed in the mind of the Emperor on that evening is indicated in his diary. On March 2 His Majesty wrote:

> In the morning Russky called and read aloud to me long telegrams exchanged between him and Rodzyanko. According to the latter's account, the state of matters in Petersburg is so grave that, even if a Government appointed by the Duma takes office, that alone will not suffice to establish order. They are demanding my abdication. Russky sent these telegrams to G.H.Q., and Alexeyev passed them on to the commanders of the armies at the Front. At two o'clock the answers from all the generals were received, and their purport was that, to save Russia and to preserve order, I must make up my mind to this step. I announced that I was ready to agree, whereupon they sent me from G.H.Q. the draft of a manifesto. In the evening Gutshkov and Shulgin arrived from Petersburg. I had an interview with them and handed to them the manifesto with my signature attached. At one o'clock in the morning I departed from Pskov with a heavy heart. Treachery, cowardice, and deception are all around me!

And, indeed, the Emperor had been pitifully cheated and betrayed by the responsible men who surrounded him, for, as subsequent events have proved, the abdication which His Majesty was so urgently pressed to sign in no sense helped to re-establish order; on the contrary, it was really the first step toward final disaster and ruin.

Only two army leaders, General Count Keller and the Tartar Khan of Nachitshevan, had shown themselves in this dark hour to be the loyal servants of their Tsar. They were the only ones who did not advise the Tsar to abdicate, but offered to place themselves and the forces under their command at his disposal to suppress the rebels by armed force. May their names be mentioned here in grateful remembrance!

CHAPTER XVIII

The Difficult Plight of the Imperial Officials—I go to the Duma—My Arrest—Companions in Misfortune—A Disturbed Night—Kerensky asks Questions—Transference to the Fortress of Peter and Paul—From Prison Governor to Prisoner—My Quondam Subordinate searches me —Kerensky as a Comedian—Prison Régime then and now

THE nerve-shattering news of His Majesty's abdication, which was followed immediately by the announcement that Grand Duke Michael, named by Tsar Nicholas as his successor, had likewise renounced the throne, brought all the officials who had served the Imperial *régime*, and consequently myself among them, face to face with the difficult question of the attitude they should adopt toward the duties they had sworn to carry out. After thinking the matter over for some time, I reached the conviction that the Tsar's abdication implied at the same time that all officials were now released from their oaths and must submit to the new Government. This appeared to me to follow clearly enough from the wording of the deed of abdication, in which it stated:

> In the name of our beloved native land we summon all her loyal sons to fulfil their sacred duty, to obey the Tsar in this time of great difficulty and trial, and to assist him, as well as the representatives of the people, so that the Russian Empire may be guided along the path of victory, happiness, and glory.

The Grand Duke Michael, again, in his act of renunciation had summoned all citizens of the Empire to place themselves at the disposal of the Provisional Government, until the Constituent National Assembly had reached a final decision as to the future form to be given to the Russian State.

Accordingly I wrote a letter to Rodzyanko, informing him of my readiness to place my services at the disposal of the

Soldiers Outside the Duma in March, 1917

PETLYURA, HETMAN OF THE UKRAIN

new Government, if it could find employment for them. For, at that time, I was firmly resolved to co-operate honestly with the men then in power, however little in other ways I shared their political views. In my opinion every good Russian was under an obligation at that critical moment to support the only authority that existed, and so to prevent the Revolution, which had now become an accomplished fact, from being immediately followed by anarchy.

I betook myself, then, with the letter to Rodzyanko in my pocket, to the Taurian Palace,[1] where I knew the Duma was in permanent session, an executive committee being entrusted with the business of the Provisional Government. It had never occurred to me that this walk was the last I was destined to make for some time on my own initiative and as a free man.

In front of the Taurian Palace the mutinous soldiers were thronging in thousands, awaiting the instructions of the newly appointed Military Commissions of the Duma. From time to time a non-commissioned officer would appear, rushing out of the building, looking very excited and shouting to the expectant crowd that any man willing to join in the occupation of this or that railway station or Government office was to report at once! Then a few dozen men would gather round the 'group-leader' in question, and hurry off with him in one direction or another. All this gave me the impression of absolute chaos, and I could not forbear from indulging in a smile of pity as I observed the primitive methods adopted by the revolutionary Government in executing its strategical measures.

After watching these proceedings for some time I overcame my reluctance and made my way as best I could through the densely packed crowd, who eyed me suspiciously, and arrived at the entrance to the vast building. At the gate some ragged

[1] Tavritshesky Palace.—TRANSLATOR.

and obviously tipsy soldiers of the Preobrazhensky Regiment were on guard, and asked me roughly what I wanted there. When I explained to them that I wished to speak to the President, Rodzyanko, I was allowed to pass in. After taking a very few steps I was stopped by a reserve officer, who had torn off the badge from his cap and who looked as if he might be a member of the Liberal Intelligentsia. He asked me my name. When I gave it, he twisted his face into a grin of triumphant malice and, "in the name of the people," declared me under arrest. A few soldiers whom he summoned seized my person, rummaged my pockets, and then dragged me away to what had been the retiring room of the President of the Council, where I found quite a number of companions in misfortune. In the corners of the room were posted four guardsmen with loaded rifles, who kept an eye on every move made by the prisoners.

Then it dawned on me that, instead of making sure betimes of my safety by coming to the Duma, I had simply walked into the trap. For, meanwhile, Kerensky had issued the instruction that all Ministers and higher officials of the fallen Government were to be secured and interned in the Duma building. The first to be arrested was Shtsheglovitov, the former Minister of Justice and afterward President of the Imperial Council. He had been followed soon after by Stürmer and Goremykin, both one-time Presidents of the Council of Ministers, by the former Minister of the Interior, Maklakov, by my friend General Kurlov, by General Suchomlinov, and by Archbishop Pityirim. These and many other exalted dignitaries of the State had fallen into the hands of the revolutionaries.

Protopopov too had presented himself of his own accord to the Duma on the night of February 28, making use on the occasion of these simple words, so characteristic of his honest patriotism, "I am Protopopov, Minister of the Interior. As I care only for the well-being of our land, I place myself voluntarily at the disposal of the Duma." Of course he was at once arrested by his triumphant enemies.

Thus all of us who had for many years past been working together to maintain public order and obedience to the law in Russia, now met again as prisoners in the committee rooms of the Duma. Certainly we had meanwhile no opportunity of exchanging sentiments and opinions, for we were strictly forbidden to hold any conversation; so we walked silently to and fro like dumb beasts in a cage. From time to time we were visited by a lieutenant named Znamyensky, a young man of pronounced Jewish type, who was responsible for keeping us under observation, and who insolently took advantage of every appearance among us to jeer at our unfortunate plight.

As no sort of sleeping accommodation was provided, we found ourselves obliged to pass the night seated on the chairs, still guarded by four soldiers, who kept an unfriendly eye upon us and noted the least movement. An incident that befell was to show us, moreover, how dangerous our situation was. From the next room we suddenly heard rifle-shots followed by a cry of pain. It turned out that Rear-Admiral Kartsev, who had been confined there for some days, had out of sheer nervous excitement almost lost his senses, and had unconsciously grabbed at the bayonet of one of the sentries. The soldier, thinking that Kartsev was going to attack him, had fired two or three shots, wounding the Admiral in the shoulder. A patrol under the command of a drunken N.C.O. of the Preobrazhensky Regiment, hurrying up, re-established order in the room. The Admiral was removed to a hospital, and so the incident was closed. But I must say it made our frame of mind only the more nervous and depressed. When the window-curtain in our room was drawn back in the morning it appeared that a pane of glass had been shattered by a shot. The soldier, when he was shooting at Admiral Kartsev, had fired in the direction of our room, the bullet had passed through the door, and must have come within an inch or two of my head in its flight toward the window.

The day was spent in deadly monotony, broken only by the unwelcome clowning of Lieutenant Znamyensky. Every now and then the door would be opened and another prisoner introduced. In the evening Kerensky, the Minister of Justice under the revolutionary Government, appeared. He addressed us in condescending tones and inquired 'graciously' as to our wishes and complaints. When he was informed that, during the preceding night, one of the prisoners had become almost insane, he did at least grant us permission to talk to each other, which indeed meant a great relief.

I was disagreeably surprised when he turned to me and invited me roughly to follow him to an adjoining room. There he asked me abruptly what political personalities had been in the Secret Service of the Police Department. Of course I was not disposed to betray to him the secret agents of the Police, and therefore answered evasively that I personally had had no secret agents. That seemed to annoy Kerensky very much, for he fell into a state of obvious excitement, shouting angrily at me, "You are trying to conceal something from me! I should like you to understand that you will have to answer for it!" With that I was taken back again to the other persons under arrest.

Scarcely, however, had I reached my chair there when we received the order to hold ourselves in readiness for removal to the Fortress of Peter and Paul. This command, which naturally came to us with an unpleasant shock of surprise, affected along with myself two more of those who were confined in our room: the President of the Council of Ministers,

Prince Golitsin, and the Assistant to the Minister of the Interior, Kukol-Yasnopolsky. Escorted by soldiers, we stepped toward the exit from the Duma building, and there saw quite a lot of other prisoners gathered, who were likewise awaiting their removal to the Fortress. Four motor-cars drove up to the gate. We all got in. In the same vehicle as myself sat the Governor-General of Finland, Z. A. Zeyn, and Senator N. I. Trusyevitsh, my predecessor at the head of the Police Department. The fourth passenger in the car was a soldier holding a loaded rifle in his hand.

In another car bound for the Fortress was Sovyeshansky, Colonel of Gendarmerie. This officer had certainly never had anything to do with political action, but it had been his duty to superintend the execution of capital sentences. Kerensky, who was present while we were being removed, now showed what vileness he was capable of, by telling the soldiers who formed our escort of that fact, warning them in derision to keep a specially sharp look-out on this Colonel of Gendarmerie, for his had been a "dirty business." Kerensky forgot to add at the same time that the Revolutionary Socialist Party, to which he had belonged for so many years, had likewise practised for long the equally "dirty business" of carrying out, by their own hands, the 'death sentences' passed by them upon members of the Imperial family, Ministers, and other loyal officials.

The moment of departure was approaching. But just before it actually arrived a lieutenant of artillery opened our car door, raised his hand to the salute, and said with ironical politeness, "Gentlemen, during the journey conversation of any kind among you is forbidden. Any attempt at flight will entail the immediate use of the rifle." After making this friendly intimation he shut the door and our procession moved off.

Never before had the way down Shpalyernaya Street, along the bank of the Neva to Suvorov Square, seemed so long as it did that day. The strangest feelings stirred within me when our car turned to cross Troitsky Bridge and I saw before me the vast pile of the Fortress of Peter and Paul, destined for an indefinite period to form the place of my involuntary sojourn. Under the Imperial *régime* the State prison within the Fortress had been controlled by the Police Department, so that I had been, in the last resort, the supreme head of this establishment, into which I was now being cast as a prisoner! It was inevitable that, at that moment, this irony of fate should call forth within me a melancholy mood of grief and despair.

Immediately on our arrival we were subjected to treatment which was as senseless as it was humiliating. In the middle of the night, with the thermometer showing 27 degrees of frost, we were obliged to line up in the great courtyard of the Fortress, turn our faces to the wall, and stand thus for about half an hour. What purpose that was supposed to serve we never knew, unless the commandant was merely making it his business to torture and degrade us.

After that the unfortunate Colonel of Gendarmerie, Sovyeshansky, was led away by himself, the soldiers who formed his escort mocking him and telling him that he was going to be imprisoned in a cell on the ground floor, where the damp was so dreadful that the floor was covered with water. I knew that this detail was founded on fact: the cells in the ground floor had therefore hitherto been used only as places of confinement for habitual criminals of the worst class.

The remaining prisoners, myself among them, were taken to an upper story, where there was a number of half-habitable individual cells. No conversation was allowed here either, and even talking to the sentries was, as we were informed, strictly prohibited. In other respects the previous routine of prison arrangements had suffered no change; you were allowed to wear your own underclothing, and, if you had money at your disposal, you might have necessaries sent in from the town.

The cell allotted to me was Number 68, and there I was to remain until the further course of my fate had been decided. About two o'clock in the morning, Ivanishin, a Guards Colonel, visited me; he searched me, removed my necktie and braces, but left me my purse.

This Ivanishin had previously commanded the Trubyetskoy Bastion, and consequently had till then been my subordinate. Now he was wearing diagonally across his chest a red sash with long bows, in order to proclaim thereby his loyal devotion to the Revolution. That, however, did not prevent him from addressing me with my title of "Excellency" and from treating me in other respects also with something approaching politeness and consideration.

A soldier brought me some hot tea, and I drank greedily the warm fluid, which was doubly welcome after that long wait in the bitter cold of the prison-yard. Colonel Ivanishin then left me, and closed the door of the cell behind him, leaving me under no delusion now as to my situation: I was no longer head of the Ochrana, but a prisoner in this gaol.

Soon I noticed that some of the window-panes were smashed and that the cell was icy cold. But mere weariness told: I wrapped myself in my cloak, pulled the fur-cap down over my ears, and sank into deep sleep. Next morning I was wakened by a soldier who brought me hot water for tea. When he inquired why I had spent the night in my furs, I drew his attention to the panes that had been shot to pieces. A few hours later I was transferred to cell Number 44, which faced the south; and there I remained for the whole six months of my captivity.

After some little time I was informed that Kerensky had come to the Fortress and wished to speak with me. I was taken out to the corridor, where I found the former Ministers, Maklakov, Makarov, Stürmer, Shtyeglovitov, and Protopopov already assembled. Kerensky strode pompously to and fro before us, and began a pathetic oration in which he made continued and bombastic reference to "freedom," "the newly won rights of the people," and "atonement for the sins of the Tsardom." In conclusion he made known to us that the new Government had appointed a Special Commission, whose task it would be to show up all the crimes and acts of illegality that we had committed. He urged us, when we were being examined by that Commission, to be open and frank, for the further duration of our imprisonment would depend upon the extent of our straightforwardness.

The subsequent course of events was soon to show that this statement of Kerensky's was nothing more than one of his numerous and plausible lies. In reality our imprisonment had nothing in the world to do with "the extent of our straightforwardness." The truth is, that we were kept prisoners only because the new *régime* had to have "crimes of the Tsardom" at all costs: it needed them. We might be as straightforward as we would in our depositions; that did not reduce the duration of our imprisonment by one day.

It was very striking to note the frequency with which Kerensky, in the course of his speech, emphasized the fact that he had decided upon this or the other course "in his capacity of Procurator-General."[1] You could not fail to see how proud this quondam petty lawyer was of the resounding title, which

---

[1] This title is sometimes rendered in this book as "Public Prosecutor" according to the usual convention. But this seems to be really an inadequate rendering. It corresponded to Attorney-General, approximately.—TRANSLATOR.

Peter the Great had once created for the Minister of Justice, and which Kerensky had now adopted of his own authority. Altogether the newly fledged Minister missed no opportunity of parading his freshly acquired dignity before us, and of impressing us as painfully as possible with his power and our complete dependence upon his mercy. Thus he turned with an imposing gesture to Colonel Ivanishin who accompanied him, and inquired about our food: were we not being worse looked after than prisoners under the Tsarist *régime?* Colonel Ivanishin, saluting with cringing subserviency and his voice trembling with awe, could think of nothing better to say than: "Your Worship, the prisoners are having much better food than in the time of the Tsar!"

I have already stated that we were privileged to buy whatever food we chose, provided we could afford to pay for it, and to wear our own clothes. To that extent, then, we were indeed not so badly off at first. It must, however, be pointed out that, even before the Revolution, that had been the general practice with prisoners on remand; indeed they were better off under the old *régime*, inasmuch as they were allowed to order wine, which we were now forbidden to do. Altogether it is a thing to be noted that there was no justification for associating with the name "Fortress of Peter and Paul," or even specially with the name "Trubyetskoy Bastion," the idea of a sinister dungeon. As a matter of fact, this Trubyetskoy Bastion was one of the best, and, in the way it was managed in the time of the Tsars, one of the model prisons not merely of the Russian Empire, but of Europe. With the exception of the damp cells on the ground floor, which under the Imperial Government were in any case used only as special punishment cells, the rooms assigned to prisoners were clean, bright, and airy, while the management was in its time to be characterized as exemplary. During the first days we spent under arrest we still enjoyed the amenities of the old system, but, unfortunately, that tolerable state of matters was not to last very long; it soon underwent changes that were notably for the worse.

CHAPTER XIX

The Revolutionary Régime in the Fortress—The Psychological Effect of Solitary Confinement—Easter in Prison—Cross-examination of Proto- popov—The Extraordinary Commission—I write my 'Confession'—The Socialist Member of the Duma as Agent of the Ochrana—Protopopov's "Nonsense"—Purposeless Inquiries

ON MARCH 20 the Fortress was occupied by a section of Finnish soldiers, who immediately set about lording it over us and introducing in the prison a "revolutionary *ré- gime*." They began by removing from our cells all that made them semi-habitable and left us only the bedsteads. Till then we had been permitted to wear our own underclothing; now it was taken away from us, and we were supplied with a kind of hospital garb of coarse sackcloth.

The right to provide our own food was also abolished, and our guards now fed us alternately with dreadful, evil-smelling soup and an equally repulsive hash made of all sorts of un- speakable offal. Our bedding consisted of straw mattresses and pillows stuffed with hens' feathers. Finally, we were com- manded to wear dressing-gowns in our cells, and they were to be exchanged for ordinary clothes only when a prisoner was summoned to the office. The cell floor we had now to clean every day ourselves.

Once a day we had a walk in the yard. This lasted alto- gether perhaps ten minutes, during which all conversation was most strictly forbidden. Every fortnight we were allowed to have a bath, and how we did not all contract some fatal trou- ble in the process, God alone knows, for there were draughts in every direction, especially as the doors in the anteroom could not be shut, so that in the bathroom itself the air was always freezing.

The complete isolation of the solitary confinement to which we were now subjected became in the long run very hard to bear, and produced fits of extreme nervous excitement which alternated with a condition of dull apathy. The hardship of our condition became more intense as the season of Easter approached, when, of course, every Russian feels an urgent need of friendly intercourse with his fellow-men. Under the old arrangements Easter had always been celebrated as a festival even in the prisons, and at that time of the year the warders had been in the way of treating their charges with brotherly kindness and love. On this occasion, during the night before Easter, Smirnov, the N.C.O. commanding the guard, came thundering into my cell accompanied by two of his men and smelling strongly of wine. I noticed this because he kissed me and shouted in my ear, "Christ is risen." And for all of us who were then shut up in the Trubyetskoy Bastion that was the beginning and the end of the Easter celebrations.

Some days later I was suddenly called to the presence of Kerensky in the office of the gaol. When I arrived there, accompanied by my soldier escort, I found him engaged in conversation with Protopopov. I soon noticed that Kerensky was doing his utmost to get out of the former Minister whether N. E. Markov, the leader of the Right Wing in the Duma, had been in receipt of Government pay for the support he gave to the Right, the more conservative section of the Radical movement.

For a long time Protopopov tried to avoid making a direct reply to this question; his answers were framed so as to suggest that the actual facts of the case were more ambiguous than they really were. However, I was seated between the two of them, and I could see that Kerensky was holding in his hand documents with the contents of which I was quite well acquainted, and which made it clear that certain sums *had* been paid to Markov by the Ministry of the Interior. Under the circumstances it appeared to me that it served no purpose to refuse to admit the truth; and when Kerensky turned to me and asked whether I knew if Markov had received anything in the way of material consideration, I replied that the documents lying on the table contained a sufficient answer to the question.

During the whole of this interview Protopopov betrayed most astonishing timidity and lack of assurance. It really seemed as if he were ashamed of having given financial assistance to Markov. I was all the more surprised by this, because I myself, as late as the end of the year 1916, had frankly declared my view that the Government could not afford to dispense with the assistance of the patriotic parties, and must therefore contribute something to support them. As I saw the matter, there was no need to be secretive about it, for there was nothing in the transaction that anyone need have been ashamed to admit.

However, Kerensky used it as a pretext to lecture Protopopov in the most insolent fashion, as if he had been a schoolboy. Unfortunately, the situation was such that we were absolutely in his power, and that he could take the liberty with impunity. He jeered at Protopopov, asking him how he, who after all was a popularly elected member of the Duma, could have justified his action in spending State funds in subsidizing the National Union, which had been notoriously and in the highest degree undemocratic, and had shown itself extraordinarily malignant in its action. The manner in which Kerensky was rating Protopopov so excited my repugnance that I at last stood up and asked in rather a categorical tone whether my presence was necessary for the remainder of the inquiry. When Kerensky said that it was not, I requested the soldier who had brought me to the room to take me back again to my cell. And that was the end of my first cross-examination, which was to be followed by many others.

Once a week prisoners were permitted to receive visitors, and I need not say how much I looked forward to the meetings with my wife. Before the first occasion I did not know under what painful circumstances that interview would take place; but I was not to be long in learning that our gaolers had made sure that any joy we might have in it would be embittered. The first time my wife called I asked in all innocence how my friend Gvozdyov was getting on, and I was at a loss to understand my wife's embarrassment when I put the question. She made a scarcely perceptible sign with her eyes, and when I turned round I saw an N.C.O. standing behind me and apparently writing down in his notebook a word-for-word report of our conversation. Not till then did I fully understand how dangerous it was to mention any names. I was terrified by my unintentional indiscretion, and fell into such a state of confusion that I jumped up hurriedly, took leave of my wife, and returned in haste to my cell.

Life in prison passed in utmost monotony, for not only were we severely isolated from each other and thus deprived of any opportunity of exchanging thoughts, but we had neither books nor newspapers, and consequently had not the slightest means of indulging in any intellectual activity. And with that we were permanently hungry, for our food, under the new prison order, was more than inadequate. The one distraction we had, if I may call it so, was provided by the cross-examinations we underwent at the hands of the Extraordinary Commission entrusted with the investigation of the 'crimes' that had been committed by the officials under the old *régime*.

The helplessness with which this Commission set about its business would have been positively amusing if the matters at issue had not been so serious, and if, in the last resort, the Commission had not been settling my own fate, which depended absolutely upon its decision. First of all we were questioned narrowly about all manner of absurd details connected with our former service; but as apparently this procedure had revealed nothing that our judges could exploit for their purposes, we were commanded to draw up statements of our own, indicating therein any acts that we had ever committed "against the people." I, for example, was required to give a written account of all the measures I had initiated for the suppression of the revolutionary movement, of my conduct in the Jewish question, and of various other points arising out of my official career. It seemed that the new authorities, who at every turn were in the way of talking at large to the people about the "crimes" of the Tsarist officials, had at bottom no clear idea of what charges they should bring against us. And now they hoped that our own confessions would supply them with the evidence that would enable them to bring us to book.

To begin with, I did not know in the least what attitude to adopt with reference to this strange order. At first I did my utmost to search my conscience in all honesty, and for some days and nights, which I spent in solitude in my cell given over to my own thoughts, I tried to recall all the instructions I had ever issued in my different official positions. With the best will in the world I could find nothing in my memory that could have been described as a 'crime.' I could indeed recall, I must say, errors of omission and commission of which I had been guilty, and which I was ready and willing at any time to admit very frankly.

The Commission had granted me for the composition of my 'confession' no more than the space of two weeks. But, owing to the tumult of excitement that possessed me I was absolutely unable for fully five days to put anything whatever down in writing. Whenever I tried to make a beginning I was assailed by the disagreeable thought that every word I wrote would be set in a false light by distortion and wrong interpretation. I was very well aware that the aim of the Commission was in no sense to arrive at a just and unbiased decision, and that they would, on the contrary, certainly examine whatever I set down, with a view to seeking and finding material on which to found accusations against myself or other officials. That being so, I felt very little inclined to be myself the agent supplying my accusers with the evidence they required.

Finally, however, I did make up my mind to write down in accordance with the true facts whatever I had to say about my long years of service in the Police Department. I therefore began by describing in general terms the conception I had formed of my duties, and the manner in which I had been accustomed to deal with my subordinates and with petitioners who came to call upon me. Then I set down in all possible detail the measures adopted by me against those revolutionary organizations that, in my opinion, had pursued their destructive activities, thinking nought of the well-being of Russia, but only of their own interests. I also wrote a very complete account of the subdivision of the various tasks and duties allotted to the Police and of the spheres of action assigned to the separate sections that were under the control of the Chief of the Department.

While I was still busy compiling this document, I was summoned several times for examination by the Commission. The most amazing questions were put to me; and the whole character of this ordeal strengthened the impression I had received from the start, that the Commission was not seriously concerned to inquire into real offences perpetrated by former officials, but that, with the object of constructing 'crimes' at any cost, they were listening to the most senseless, the silliest gossip. For instance, they asked me on one occasion whether it was true that, when I was in the position of second-in-command at the Police headquarters, I had spoken over the telephone to Belyetsky, the former Chief. Naturally I answered that I did not know to which conversation they were referring. The president thereupon informed me, with hesitation and with obvious reluctance, that the Commission was investigating the affair of the Duma member, Malyinovsky. Now I knew which telephone conversation they were talking about.

For the enlightenment of the reader I should like to explain that Malyinovsky, a member of the Bolshevik Central Committee, had in the year 1910 fallen into the hands of the Moscow Ochrana. As his conspicuous gift of oratory and his great organizing power were well known, the head of the Ochrana for the time being determined to make an effort to win over Malyinovsky, and he succeeded too, for Malyinovsky resolved to serve the Police Department in the capacity of secret agent. To avoid exciting suspicion, he was kept under arrest for some time after the arrangement was made, and then he was released on the ostensible ground of the insufficiency of the evidence against him. From that time onward Malyinovsky regularly supplied the Ochrana with information about the proceedings of the Socialist Party, and the intelligence he brought was, as a rule, reliable and useful. When he was afterward elected to the Imperial Duma, of course, the value of his secret co-operation was enhanced. Then Belyetsky, the Chief of the Police Department, hit on the idea of making use of Malyinovsky for the purpose of carrying out a bold political stroke.

At his instigation Malyinovsky provoked a violent discussion among the members of the Socialist Party in the Duma, and guided it so skilfully that a split took place, an event that, at the time, gave rise to great excitement and consternation among the Socialist leaders all over Europe.

When, however, Belyetsky subsequently retired from the post of Chief of the Ochrana, his successor did not continue the relations with Malyinovsky, who, in consequence, was deprived of the five hundred roubles he had been drawing monthly, a circumstance which, very naturally, he found extremely disagreeable. He therefore applied to Belyetsky, requesting him to put in a good word for him with the new head of the Police Department, recommending that he be reinstated in the service of the Ochrana. This request Belyetsky had passed on to me, and that had formed the subject of the conversation over the telephone in which the Commission of Inquiry was manifesting such interest.

The part I had myself played in the whole affair had been very simple: on behalf of Belyetsky I had spoken to Trusyevitsh in favour of Malyinovsky. My intervention, moreover, was unsuccessful, for Malyinovsky's petition was turned down. He thereafter went abroad, where he found new patrons in Lenin and Zinovyev. As Burtsev had accused him of maintaining relations with the Ochrana, a tribunal was constituted by the Bolshevik party to investigate his case, but it acquitted him. From the time he left Russia the Germans made use of Malyinovsky in the organization of revolutionary propaganda among Russian prisoners of war interned in German camps. Further, after the Bolshevik Revolution, Lenin had Malyinovsky shot when the latter returned to Russia.

I described in brief to the Extraordinary Commission all the facts known to me about the affair, and my cross-examination, as far as this Malyinovsky business was concerned, was at an end. What was supposed to be the real purpose of making a new 'inquiry' into this long-forgotten, and in itself trifling, affair I have never been able to learn to this day.

A short time after that experience I was once more called up for examination. This time the president of the Commission, with very black looks, pushed over to me a document about which I was required to tell all I knew. It was an old memorial sent in by the Marshal of the Nobility in the Government of Simbirsk, and addressed to the Minister of the Interior, Protopopov. It complained of certain irregularities alleged to have been committed by the local Police authorities in that government. At first I could not think what were the intentions of the Commission in dragging up this utterly insignificant matter, but they pointed out to me that Protopopov had written in blue pencil upon the memorial the word "Nonsense." Upon this fact the 'Judges' were basing the charge of "neglect of duty" against the Minister who, according to them, when information was sent him of abuses in the Police Administration, had simply ignored it.

I had no sooner glanced at the document than I managed completely to rebut that accusation. I drew the attention of the examining magistrate to the important circumstance that, along with the word "Nonsense," Protopopov had also marked the paper with the two letters "P.D.," which, according to the usage accepted in the Ministry of the Interior, meant, "To be passed on for consideration to the Police Department." So that, although Protopopov had been of opinion that the complaint in question was unfounded, he had nevertheless not omitted to have the thing sent on to the Police Department, in order that it might be officially looked into. As a matter of fact the document *had* reached me, whereupon I had set about having the necessary investigation carried out, the final result, moreover, being a complete confirmation of the Minister's verdict: the complaint had indeed been nonsense.

The embarrassment of the individual who was directing this cross-examination was plain and unmistakable when I was able to produce this striking proof that neither the Minister nor his subordinates had been guilty in this matter of any neglect of duty. Apparently that meant that yet another bright hope of the Commission's had miserably failed them.

No less characteristic of the senselessness of the entire procedure of the Investigating Commission was my examination on April 8, which I have retained almost word for word and shall here set down, so that the reader may form his own picture of the hopelessly futile process to which we were subjected.

After I had been brought in before the Board one of the assessors asked me to state what had been the system in use for maintaining telegraphic communication with foreign countries and with G.H.Q. I answered that, to the best of my knowledge, between the Ministry of the Interior and the Army Command there had been direct connexion, but that I was not quite sure of the facts. As for the foreign service, the Ministry had always made use of telegrams in cipher.

"So that means," said the president of the Commission with an air of great self-importance, "that the Police Department had no direct communication with countries abroad?"

"No," I replied; "our telegrams were drawn up in code, and were dispatched through the Postal Section number 35, which was installed in our head office. What happened to the telegrams after that I do not know, but I assume that they were sent on by the Post Office by the usual routes."

Thereupon the president asked me if I knew anything about the relations between Protopopov and a certain Charles Perrin. I answered, as the truth required, that Perrin had been an acquaintance of Protopopov's, to whom the latter had once telegraphed. "I believe," I added, "that Perrin had applied to Protopopov for a permit to enter the country, but the inquiries instituted in the Police Department about Perrin yielded very unfavourable results, for it turned out that the military authorities suspected him of espionage." Then I was asked if I could remember when those inquiries had been made. "I think in November," I replied, "but I cannot say exactly. In any case, they *were* made, and Protopopov received all the data we had referring to Perrin. A fortnight or so later Perrin again telegraphed to Protopopov, asking once more for permission to come into Russia. At Protopopov's desire, however, we put together a polite form of refusal, and this, in the form of a telegram, was then sent off by Protopopov himself."

That was all I knew about the Perrin business. Then the president of this tribunal wished to be informed whether there had existed in the Police Department a special section to deal with matters of espionage. I said there was not. One of the assessors put a question to me as to what the facts were concerning the "Danish cable," to which I truthfully made answer that I had not the slightest idea. And with that this cross-examination, like those that had preceded it, came to an end— a classical example of utter futility. I was then permitted to return to my cell.

CHAPTER XX

Days of Terror—Awaiting a Catastrophe—The July Bolshevik Revolt —The Provisional Government wishes to have my Assistance against Lenin—My 'Crime' is discovered—Senseless Accusations—My Defence

IN THE early days of July 1917 we prisoners noticed that something unusual was happening in the city. The officers and soldiers in the Fortress appeared to be in a state of nervous excitement that we could not understand; and very soon, too, the customary weekly visits paid by our relatives were stopped.

Suddenly we heard coming across to us from the city the rattle of rifle and machine-gun fire, and as we still had no idea of what it really meant, we tortured ourselves for hours on end with the most fantastic theories.

Of course the first thing I thought of was a revolt of loyal supporters of the Imperial cause against the Republican Government. However much I might have rejoiced at that in the interests of Russia, our own situation was likely to become only the more dangerous, as, after all, we were there in prison, in the hands of the revolutionaries. For all that, I hoped with my whole heart that the fighting that was going on outside might end with the victory of the Monarchist Party. From some veiled hints let fall by the guards, however, I soon had to recognize that it was apparently not a Monarchist insurrection that was in progress, but a revolt of some kind on the other side. Any further details we could not find out by any means at our disposal.

All conversation with our gaolers had again been most strictly prohibited, but in the state of inner excitement that possessed me I at last could endure the strain no longer, and asked the soldier on duty, when he entered my cell, what was really going on, and what was the explanation of the continual explosions that I quite plainly heard through the open window. But when the soldier heard my question, he twisted his face into a mocking grin, looked me up and down, and then replied that in the town—all was quiet! After giving me this patently false information and making me only more puzzled than I had been before, he locked the door behind him and remained out of sight and hearing for hours.

Not till late that night did I manage to get a little sleep, but I was soon awake again, starting up in terror, for in the corridor I heard the hurried steps of men obviously very excited and rushing to and fro within the Fortress. In a condition of utmost nervous tension I listened to every sound, and the panic in which I was reached its height when I heard a voice in close proximity to my cell door inquire: "Have you your revolvers loaded?" The sentry's voice replied in the affirmative, whereupon the unknown whispered, "If they get into the Fortress, none of the prisoners must be left alive." You can imagine my state of mind when I caught those words. I understood that the fate of us all was hanging on a thread, and the worst of it was that I did not yet know which party was on the point of storming the Fortress. In this mood of hopeless despair, and to be prepared for any issue, I hastily wrote a farewell note to my wife, making what speed I might in doing so, for I thought that at any moment I might meet with a violent end.

This nerve-racking situation was prolonged for three days and nights, and it is really a miracle that not one of us prisoners lost his reason under the strain. It was July 7 before things calmed down again and the firing ceased. Once more the prison doctor made his round of the cells, and relatives were again permitted to resume their visits.

A good while elapsed before I learned all the particulars of what had actually taken place in those days, which had been for me so full of terror. The coward Kerensky, in spite of his big talk, had not in all the months of his 'rule' in Russia summoned up courage to arrest the leaders of the Bolsheviks; on the contrary, he had looked on passively while they steadily increased their influence upon the demoralized Army. The lamentable failure of the offensive undertaken by the Provisional Government on the Galician Front had then contributed still further to the complete destruction of the authority of that Government, which was already shadowy enough; and thus, by the beginning of July, the Bolsheviks were able to carry out their first attempt at an armed revolution. Certain units which should have left Petersburg for the Front bluntly refused to take the field, and, instead of doing so, went to a meeting where they were incited by Trotsky to rebellion against the Provisional Government. Soldiers and an armed rabble again took command of the streets and made a noisy demonstration in front of the Taurian Palace, demanding with loud shouting the fall of the Government and the proclamation of the Dictatorship of the Soviets.[1]

The sailors and soldiers from Kronstadt, the most Radical of all the revolutionary units, immediately marched upon Petersburg, where Lenin, who had taken up his quarters in what had been the mansion of the dancer Kshessinskaya, held a regular parade. The absolute lack of authority on the part of the Government was well shown by the fact that the Kronstadt seamen captured and were going to lynch Tshernov, the Minister of Agriculture, a leader of the Revolutionary Socialist Party, who tried to calm them by making a speech. Tshernov owed his life solely to the intervention of Trotsky, who at that time still deemed it expedient to prevent the mob whose passions he had aroused, from committing deeds of bloodshed that would have excited too much horror.

[1] The Russian word means simply 'councils.'—TRANSLATOR.

As by a miracle, the Provisional Government was able for that time to get the better of the Bolshevik revolt, mainly because certain Cossack regiments unexpectedly proved loyal and opposed the badly organized bands of the rebels.

How critical our position had been in those days was revealed by a circumstance which likewise did not come to my knowledge till later—namely, that the Fortress of Peter and Paul had also been occupied by the Bolshevik seamen from Kronstadt. Apparently during those hours when the excitement was at its height, literally no one had given us prisoners a thought, so that we had been spared the worst. Then in the night of July 5–6 victory decided for the Government, and soon after the seamen in the Fortress also had had to capitulate.

I was still completely unaware of all these happenings when, a few days later, I was summoned to the prison office. There I found an examining magistrate present, who addressed me in unusually affable tones, saying: "You are the late head of the Police Department, and should therefore be in a position to assist the Government by throwing light on some important matters. I therefore invite you to let me know your views on the incidents that occurred from July 3 to 5."

This mode of address rather astounded me. I replied that I had no idea of what *had* happened in those days, as we prisoners had not received any news whatever. Then the official explained to me briefly that a revolt had broken out among the Bolsheviks in the capital, but that the Government had completely suppressed it by force of arms. After supplying me with so much information, he let me see plainly what was in his mind by requesting me to communicate, with all possible detail, the evidence concerning the personality of the Bolshevik leaders and their treacherous activities that had come to my knowledge during the time I had occupied the post of Director of the Police Department.

Thus I had temporarily exchanged the situation of suspect under arrest for that of counsellor to the Provisional Government, a situation which, even in the serious plight in which we all still found ourselves, entertained me not a little.

Now, Kerensky and Company I detested with all my soul, but, however disinclined I was otherwise to support them by presenting them with all the information I had acquired in the Service, I thought it expedient in this case to comply with the request. I knew that, in face of the threatening Bolshevik danger, the Provisional Government was a lesser evil; and therefore I let the examining magistrate have the benefit of all that was known to me about Lenin, Trotsky, Zinovyev, and the other leaders of the Bolshevik party. I also directed the attention of the Government to the extensive collection of information to be found in the secret archives of the Ochrana about certain of those persons—I was assuming that the documents in their cases had escaped the general destruction of the February Revolution.

It would have been rather simple on my part to expect from that turn of events any permanent improvement in my situation. In spite of the consideration shown to me for a few days, I continued to be suspicious as before, and subsequent events were to prove that I was perfectly justified. For, no sooner did the Provisional Government feel that the Bolshevik danger had been averted, no sooner did they begin to think that they had escaped disaster, than the Extraordinary Commission of glorious memory resumed its activities.

It was in the days of the July troubles that the Government had deemed it necessary to have recourse to my assistance. By August 1 the Commission had at last discovered, with much labour that 'crime' of which I had been guilty during my official career, and for which I was now to be called to account. On that date I was summoned for examination by the magistrate Yodlovsky, who solemnly informed me that I was now definitely in the position of an accused man: the Commission charged me on the one hand with neglect of duty, and on the other hand with abuse of official authority.

Naturally I at once sought to learn what this strange double accusation was based upon; the first part of it appeared to be in patent conflict with the second. When I asked a direct question on the point, this is what Yodlovsky told me. Toward the end of the year 1916 I had sent out to governors, captains of town Police, and Gendarmerie authorities circulars in which I had instructed them to find out whether and where proclamations were being prepared for January 9, the anniversary of the first Russian Revolution. These circulars also contained orders that all appropriate measures should be taken betimes, so that, in any case, such intended demonstrations should be prevented or, if need be, suppressed by military force.

You can understand my amazement when I was taken to task for that circular. According to my own conviction, I had simply done my duty, by taking steps for the maintenance of order; and I therefore asked the Commission very bluntly, if in their view I ought, let us say, to have looked on in silence at anti-Government demonstrations. The answers I received, however, very speedily convinced me that the Commission's conception of the official duties of a Russian Director of Police under the Tsar was altogether too peculiar to make any rational explanation of such things possible between us. So, with what resignation and equanimity I had at my command, I soon abandoned the attempt to prove to these gentlemen how untenable their position really was.

In the course of later examinations it became more and more obvious that the 'crime' of which we imprisoned officials of the Police and Gendarmerie were being accused was, more than all else, our co-operation with the secret agents of the Internal

Agency. They were trying now to interpret this entire method of procedure in criminal investigation as abuse of official power.

The arguments with which the Commission tried to support this view were as simple as they were childish. The Tsarist Government had made use of information supplied to it by members of prohibited political organizations, and in return for their services these secret agents not merely were in receipt of money payments, but were assured of immunity from arrest. It was on that very fact that our enemies were founding the charge they brought against us of exceeding our powers. For, the Commission maintained, the duty of the Police would have been to hand over their own agents to the judicial authorities, as their mere membership of illegal societies should have made them amenable to the law. The failure to secure the proper punishment of the agents was construed by the Commission as "neglect of duty" on our part, while these same judges interpreted the employment of the agents in the collection of information as "abuse of official powers."

This extravagant sophistry, of course, would not have borne legal criticism any better than the test of ordinary human logic. But the men who were sitting in judgment upon us were anxious to convict us at any price of some crime, and as nothing better could be found, this absurd interpretation of the law had to serve as a basis for the accusations made against us.

Naturally I replied that the Internal Agency had not been brought into existence by me, but that it had been created many years ago, and that, further, no Political Police in the world would find it possible to do its work without making use of secret agents. Moreover, I pointed out, the granting of exemption from punishment was, after all, one of the first conditions if confidential assistants were to be won over from the revolutionary camp, and consequently such secret assistants would never be obtained at all if that condition were not fulfilled. But when it became more and more patent that the Commission was not in the least inclined to accept my justification, nay, that my having ever occupied the office of Chief of the Police was in itself accounted to me for sin, I desisted from any further effort to sustain my defence, and determined to bring it forward later on, abroad, in the form of these memoirs.

In addition to my other crimes, I was also charged with an offence because I had arrested that famous War Trade Committee of Gutshkov's and had permitted the postal Censorship. In both cases I was alleged to have transgressed the legal limits of my powers. As I have already indicated, I owed my information as to the treacherous and disloyal activity of the Workmen's Group in the Trade Committee to a certain Ambrozilov, and the essence of the charge was, as in the general indictment against me, that the employment of intelligence procured by such an agency amounted to "abuse of official powers." As for the censorship of letters, I was in a position to inform the examining magistrate that it had been instituted at the command of the Tsar, and that consequently the Police Department could not be made responsible for it.

After countless cross-examinations the Commission evidently became convinced that it was not possible to bring any serious charge home to me, for it decided at last to accept bail for a large sum and to release me from prison. I was, as a matter of fact, transferred from the Fortress to another prison.

CHAPTER XXI

Some Pleasant Recollections of my Imprisonment—Kindly Guards—
A Revolutionary against his Will—The Other Side of the Picture: in
the Power of a Murderer—Dismissed from the Fortress—The Bolshevik
Revolution—Flight of the Investigating Commission—Liberated at Last
—Vicissitudes in Kiev—Pursued by Fate—Proposal from the Tsheka
—A Railway Porter in Paris—Spirit of the Russian Emigrants

I DO not wish to conclude my recollections of the time I
spent as a prisoner in the Fortress of Peter and Paul without devoting a few words also to the agreeable impressions I
received there.

No doubt the soldiers who composed our guard were in the
main coarse, brutal men intoxicated with their newly acquired
power and only too willing to wreak upon us prisoners their
hatred of the old *régime*. Nevertheless there were among
them, too, good-natured fellows who, whether by little gifts
of tea, sugar, and cigarettes, or even merely by a few kindly
words, many a time put new courage into our sinking hearts.

It must not be supposed that the long-drawn-out torture
inflicted upon us by the Investigating Commission, with the
senseless indignity of those cross-examinations, failed to produce its effect upon our nerves. Often did I go back to my cell
after such an ordeal utterly exhausted and collapse upon my
bed, holding my hands to my head in blank despair. More
than once at such a time the cell door opened and an ordinary soldier would come in to cheer me up. With kindly,
simple peasant speech he would tell me to pluck up courage
and not give up hope, but wait patiently till all that disorder
that they called "Revolution" should come to an end of itself.

With unfeigned gratitude I recall the really touching behaviour toward us prisoners shown by an Esthonian soldier,

named Meisling, who was one of our guards. He was always pleasant, cheerful, and considerate, and this, combined with his rather imperfect command of Russian, often moved me and, I daresay, many of my companions in misfortune, exerting upon us a wholesome influence and lifting us out of the depression which, when we were left to ourselves, was often more than we could endure.

And that Little Russian, too, who so often came into my cell, was another touching figure. He told me in a friendly way that he had once, under the Tsardom, spent ten long months himself in some provincial gaol, and therefore knew only too well what it felt like to be under arrest, and especially in solitary confinement. With kindly thought he suggested to me that, if ever I felt especially depressed, I should at once knock on the cell door and call him in. Whenever I did so he did actually come to me at once, and would frequently chat with me for hours on general topics, for, of course, the regulations in force forbade all discussion of the political events of the day.

Once—it was one Sunday in the summer-time—he knocked politely at my cell door; then he came in and said he had just received a letter from home and did not know how to answer it properly. Would I draft an answer for him? He read the letter aloud to me. His relatives were complaining bitterly that the communal and judicial authorities were now simply packed with Jews. However much it would have attracted me to fulfil the soldier's wish by dictating a reply to him, I thought it more prudent to refrain: in those troublous days you could never know what consequences might arise out of any apparently innocent but yet inconsiderate step. I explained to the soldier that I knew too little about the situation to be able to express an opinion in the matter, and was therefore not in a position to offer him any suitable advice.

The most likeable of our guards was a seaman attached to

the Gendarmerie, whose name, unfortunately, has slipped my memory. He was a good-looking, intelligent, and unusually well-educated young man, who distinguished himself in all respects by his decent, gentlemanly attitude to the prisoners. In course of time he developed a special preference for conversing with me about political questions of a general character, which was certainly in breach of prison rules. He was circumspect in his observations on those subjects and never defended the Socialist point of view, giving me thus quite plainly to understand that he was a revolutionary entirely against his will.

In a general way the Rifle Regiment was very unfriendly in its attitude to us, but one soldier even of that unit showed us many a little kindness. He was the man who, whenever it was at all possible, supplied us with cigarettes; and only one who has spent some time in prison can have any idea how much a cigarette can do at times to revive drooping spirits!

It must be admitted there were, among our guards, a fair number of individuals of a more disagreeable type. One of the worst of these was a certain man named Kulikov, a coarse, degenerate fellow, with a bald pate and cold eyes, almost like those of a beast. He belonged unmistakably to a criminal type, and I have no doubt that in earlier days he had had frequent opportunities of making the near acquaintance of the inside of the Tsar's gaols, not, of course, as a warder but as an inmate. He inspired me with a strong feeling of repulsion, and I looked forward frankly with terror to the days when he was on duty in our corridor. How well founded that feeling was became evident only a few months later, just after the Bolshevik Revolution took place. Kulikov was one of those four men who, in January 1918, forced their way into the Lityeiny Hospital, and there brutally strangled Kokoshkin and Shingaryov, two imprisoned Cadets, *i.e.*, Moderate Republican Ministers under the Kerensky Government.

Another person who made himself noticeably unpleasant was an N.C.O. of the Preobrazhensky Guards Regiment, whose behaviour was exceptionally rough not only to us prisoners, but even to his own comrades. He was very fond of making a great din by banging doors and rushing with his noisy boots through the passages in the Fortress, issuing at the top of his voice all sorts of more or less trivial orders.

On September 6, 1917, I was at last removed from the Fortress of Peter and Paul to solitary confinement in the ordinary prison, where I soon entered hospital. There I spent the next two months. Compared with the severe conditions I had known in the Fortress, the prison hospital was a much more comfortable place to live in, and while I was there I suffered far less from those fits of disconsolate apathy that had so often got the better of me before.

While I was still lying in the prison hospital, the long threatened Bolshevik Revolution broke out, on October 25. That glorious Government of Kerensky's had managed still to get the better of the Bolsheviks in July, but now it collapsed utterly within a few hours. This time the insurrection was better organized, and, besides, not a single regiment in the Petersburg garrison took up a determined stand on the side of the so-called Government. Trotsky was able by his own unaided efforts to bring the Fortress of Peter and Paul over to the rebel side: he simply went and delivered to the troops occupying it one of those speeches of his that were as unscrupulous as they were effective, inciting them to mutiny. That one stroke practically sealed the fate of the capital, for, in the Fortress, the revolutionary troops and workmen found the stores of arms and ammunition of which they stood in need.

Scarcely had the situation begun to look dangerous when Kerensky left the city in a motor-car with all the appearance of a fugitive, ostensibly to bring relief from G.H.Q., most probably his real and immediate object being to seek safety for his own precious person. The victory of the Bolsheviks was quite decided before the day of October 25 had closed, and they lost no time in proclaiming the Soviet Republic.

The Investigating Commission upon which our fate had depended till then broke up in a panic, for most of its members had more or less reason to fear their own arrest at the hands of the Bolsheviks. We, the Tsarist Ministers and officials, however, remained prisoners as before, the only difference being that now the Bolsheviks, instead of the Provisional Government, looked as if they would sit in judgment upon us and punish us for our 'crimes.' So we had good grounds for anxiety as we thought of our future prospects.

Our situation did not take a turn for the better until the Left Wing of the Revolutionary Socialist Party formed a coalition with the Bolsheviks, and sent members to join the Soviet Government. The Revolutionary Socialist Steinberg took over the office of People's Commissary for the Administration of Justice, so that our fate was now in his hands. Whether it was that Steinberg had some sense of justice, or whether he had some political reason for shielding us from the bloody *régime* that the Tsheka was inaugurating, the fact is that he proved relatively accessible to rational argument, and ordered the release of a number of imprisoned Tsarist officials on payment of considerable sums as bail. On the other hand, the Ministers of the fallen Kerensky Government now replaced us as scapegoats, and were treated by the Bolsheviks just as they had previously dealt with us.

While I was still in prison, my wife had not been idle. She had plied the Bolshevik authorities with memorials and petitions for my release, until she did at last induce the Commissary of Justice to set me free, as I have stated, the sum fixed as caution money being ten thousand roubles.

Then followed a difficult and dangerous time, during which I did not know from one day to the next whether I should not suddenly receive a visit from the agents of the Tsheka, sent by their chief, Jerzhinsky, to arrest me. As by a miracle that fate, which at the time befell so many of my former colleagues, was spared me, and I lived quite unmolested in Petersburg till July 1918, when I took advantage of an opportunity that occurred of quitting the capital, which was growing too hot. The Ukraine had, under German protection, declared its complete independence of Russia, and whoever had been born on the territory of this new republic was now treated as a foreigner in Soviet Russia. Thanks to the circumstance that I had first seen the light of day in Kiev, I was able to claim foreign nationality and to go with my wife to that city.

On my arrival there my first business was to look about me for suitable employment that would at least provide me with a livelihood, and I was very glad when the Hetman Skoropadsky offered me a post attached to the Kiev Court of Appeal. I thought that I had found a new sphere of useful activity and a new and comparatively assured foundation upon which to build up my life. In reality, however, my sorrows were only now about to begin.

The rule of Hetman Skoropadsky was of only short duration, for the Entente Powers soon found ways and means of making difficulties for this pro-German Dictator by setting up in opposition their own tool, Simon Petlyura, who, having plenty of money at his disposal, quickly obtained a numerous following. The German troops which had, to start with, provided Skoropadsky's main support, having by now become demoralized by the Soviet system, adopted a neutral attitude, so that Petlyura was able to enter Kiev on November 14, 1918.

If I had become in the eyes of the Russians an Ukrainian,

under this new Petlyura *régime* I had been turned once more into a Muscovite, and that meant not merely the loss of my position, but almost the complete withdrawal of all rights and elementary protection. All the same I waited on in Kiev, not least because I saw no chance at the moment of getting out.

But Petlyura's rule was not to last long either. As early as the beginning of February he had to flee before the Bolshevik army of the renegade General Klembovsky. That was the end of his career in the Ukraine, and he lived thereafter in Paris, till he was murdered in the year 1926 by a Jewish fanatic named Schwarzbard.

Just before the Bolsheviks entered Kiev I managed, with the devoted assistance of a few faithful friends, to flee from the city and to make my way to the Hungarian frontier. I arrived there with nothing but the clothes I stood up in, for I had had to leave all I possessed otherwise in Kiev.

But one would have thought that I was being pursued by a relentless fate, for I had hardly settled in Budapest when the Bolshevik insurrection broke out and Bela Kun instituted his reign of terror. I was obliged to continue my flight, and this time I made for Prague, where my brother, who was then employed at the university of that town, was able to grant me temporary asylum.

Thence I went on to Berlin. After staying there for some little time I betook myself to Munich in the vain hope that the Bavarian Government, which had only a short time before overthrown a system like that of the Soviets in Russia, and was still having to struggle against Russian emissaries of that political hue, might be able to employ my services. I had been labouring under a delusion, however, and all my efforts to obtain an appointment under the Munich authorities were of no avail.

On the other hand, a man from Berlin called on me one day.

He was an envoy from the Tsheka, and did me the honour of proposing that I should enter the service of the Bolshevik Government as a spy. The sum of money offered as a bribe was quite considerable, but I have seldom in my life experienced such satisfaction as I felt at the moment when I had the privilege of throwing that gentleman downstairs.

After that my wife and I passed through very difficult times. The depreciation of the mark drove us out of Germany, and as, on the occasion of Poincaré's visit to Petersburg in 1913, I had received the distinction of being included in the Legion of Honour, I now cherished hopes of finding an abiding-place in France. We therefore turned our faces toward Paris, where for some time I was permitted to earn eighteen francs a day as a porter, looking after luggage in the St. Lazare terminus.

One day, however, the higher authorities discovered that I was a foreigner, and I had to resign that extremely lucrative job in favour of a native-born Frenchman. My wife had meantime found a post as bottle-washer in a perfume factory. That was fortunate. As for myself, I should literally have starved to death in the streets if I had not managed to find refuge in the "Russian Homes" maintained by a philanthropic young English lady in Sainte-Geneviève-des-Bois, where I am still living to-day.

But, however difficult and unhappy my personal situation may be, I am much more concerned by the attitude of so many of my companions in misfortune, whom I have come across here in Paris, and on whose minds the events of the last few years have produced such disastrous effects. M. Milyukov's conduct caused me no surprise. After all, his share of responsibility for the collapse of the Tsar's Empire would appear to be by no means the smallest, and when, as far back as 1921, after the failure of Wrangel's enterprise, Milyukov and his followers officially proclaimed their decision to give up once for all any idea of opposing the Bolsheviks by force of arms, that was only what was to be expected. But it seemed to me all the more disconcerting that he should have found so much support among the emigrants when he committed this act of treason against the Russian idea, and that there should not have arisen one courageous man to put Milyukov in his proper place.

That incident showed once more how deep and strong is the intimate connexion between the Russian *intelligentsia* and the revolutionary chaos, and how slight, in the last resort, is the intellectual difference that separates the present rulers in the Kremlin from their *bourgeois* predecessors. From the very beginning the intellectualism of the Russian 'Liberals,' which was absolutely opposed to the national spirit and arose out of foreign influences, was to prove fatal to the Russian Empire, and it is fitting that that *intelligentsia*, now living abroad, should have again betrayed its native land.

I should like to state that, in my wanderings through Western Europe and, finally, also during my stay in Paris, I have found quite a number of loyal, sincere supporters of the old *régime*, men who have sworn to endure every hardship and privation, nay, even to suffer death, rather than to compromise with the Bolsheviks and to accept, lying down, the present condition of things in Russia.

Further, I have even met men who were once opponents of the Tsardom, who consequently had come up against me in my official capacity, but who had learned to understand how mistaken their revolutionary opinions had been, how little the Revolution had profited the Russian people, how frightful and disastrous, rather, it had proved. Is it not significant that Peter Struve, once the father of Russian Marxism and the personal teacher of Lenin, has to-day repented and abjured his former views and recognized the Grand Duke Nikolai Nikolayevitsh as the true leader of Russia? How far this man, openly acknowledging his previous aberrations, towers above those lukewarm patriots who have not the pluck to deduce from the events of the last ten years the only possible conclusion and associate themselves whole-heartedly with the Monarchist idea!

CHAPTER XXII

The Tsar's Pocket-handkerchief—False Notions about the Ochrana current abroad—Real Significance of Banishment to Siberia—Humane Treatment of Political Prisoners in Old Russia—Ochrana and Tsheka—How the Bolsheviks mislead Foreign Visitors—Burtsev recommends that the Ochrana should be maintained—Unsuccessful Recruiting

ONCE in Tsarist Russia, when the Special Corps of Gendarmerie, the predecessor of the Ochrana, was being founded, Count Benkendorff, who had just been appointed to the command of this body, appeared before the Emperor, Nicholas I, and asked for more detailed instructions. Instead of making any formal reply, however, the monarch pulled out a white handkerchief and handed it to the Count, saying, "Dry the tears of the oppressed. May your conscience and the conscience of your subordinates ever remain as stainless as this linen!"

The Political Police of Tsarist Russia, from that time onward, always acted in keeping with those truly sublime words spoken by the ruler, and if the Empire of the Tsars, like every other state, did have to protect itself from the underground intrigues of hostile powers, yet the Ochrana, in the means it adopted, never went beyond the methods in use in other lands.

It must be admitted that, from the start, the Russian Police had a much more difficult task to perform than the Police of any country in Western Europe. I do not mean because the Russian people in the mass was more troublesome to rule, or because the institutions of the Empire were to be maintained only by force. But while in England, France, and America the intelligent classes of the people in earlier times were always genuine patriots and fought to uphold the national institutions, that was in Russia unfortunately not the case, and had not been so from the first years of the nineteenth century.

Ideas derived from foreign sources and misunderstood early permeated the educated classes in Russia and filled them with quite erroneous notions. Instead of considering that the circumstances in our country were entirely different from those prevailing in the West, and that the mechanical transplantation into Russia of European conceptions of liberty could do nothing but harm, as these ideas had grown up under quite other conditions and were in conflict with the spirit of the Russian population, the *intelligentsia* at once set about slavishly moulding Russia anew in accordance with the schemes of Western theorists. And, with this end in view, their first concern was to destroy utterly all that the Tsars with their counsellors and servants had laboriously built up in the course of ages.

In face of those incessant attempts to undermine the order of the State, the Tsarist authorities really practised leniency to excess; and if the Government of the Empire can be justly reproached with any dereliction of duty, it is only that it stood too much upon its dignity and showed too much restraint in neglecting to enlighten people abroad, as it might have done, as to the real conditions existing in Russia. Consequently public opinion in the West was wholly at the mercy of those purveyors of false information who sought to further the success of their own delusions by persistent and, alas, only too successful propaganda. Otherwise it would be beyond comprehension that, to this day, in Europe and America such completely false and perverted opinions still exist as to the actual conditions under the rule of the Tsars.

What misunderstandings have been caused by one thing alone—the practice followed in Russia of banishing criminals to Siberia! Many and many a time I have met educated persons in Germany and France who believed in all seriousness that "the horrors of Siberia" of themselves morally justified the Revolution.

Now what were the facts with regard to these 'horrors'? First of all it must be stated emphatically that real hard labour in the mines was never inflicted except upon such criminals as in other countries would have suffered the death penalty. For in our 'backward' land of Russia capital punishment had long ago been abolished in the cases of ordinary offenders and replaced by exile to Siberia. The only crimes punishable by death were the murder or attempted murder of any member of the Imperial family, and even with such criminals, and they were unfortunately only too numerous, the sentence was often enough commuted by special grace to banishment.

When people abroad hear any allusion to convicts in the Siberian mines, they usually think at once of political offenders. But these, as a rule, were condemned merely to "administrative relegation," and this penalty, which was really nothing more than a measure of self-protection adopted by the State against its enemies, did not in any sense come up to the lurid conception that people in the West used to entertain of exile to Siberia. This "administrative relegation" meant merely that those falling under the sentence were obliged to reside for a certain period in some locality East of the Urals; without permission from the authorities they were not allowed to leave the district, but within the prescribed limits they were able to move about in perfect freedom. Consider, moreover, that the places to which political offenders were exiled were mostly situated in regions where the climate was rather favourable, and that the exiles were permitted to enjoy ordinary social intercourse among themselves, to read, write, and carry on their trades or professions as they chose, and it will be seen that this system, applied by Tsarist Russia for the temporary

Political Exiles in Siberia Under the Tsardom

POLITICAL EXILES IN AKATUISK PRISON

In the centre is the famous woman conspirator, M. Spiridonova

removal of its most dangerous foes, must be characterized as extremely humane.

It should suffice to point out that almost all the men in power in the Russia of the Revolution had been in their time exiled to Siberia. That fact alone shows how little the punishment was in truth calculated to undermine the vigour of those upon whom it was imposed. Not one had had even a serious illness during his banishment, not one had suffered ill-treatment, and they all came back from Siberia with energy enough to carry to success their sinister work.

With such "merciless measures" did we, the officials of Tsarist Russia, seek to defend the State, until the revolutionaries took the helm and proclaimed that now barbarism would give way to humanity, and oppression be replaced by freedom. It has been shown how the first step taken by the new *régime* was to cast into prison many conscientious servants of the Emperor, with a view to bringing them to justice, the result of this first manifestation of 'liberty' being simply to prove clearly that no illegal act could be brought home to any one of us.

When, with the October Revolution, the Bolsheviks came into power, no one henceforth took the trouble to adopt any formality at all with representatives of the old order: they were merely arrested and slaughtered wholesale, and all in the name of liberty and humanity. Whoever had once belonged to the Ochrana was now regarded as the lowest criminal among the people; to persecute him, to murder him, was the duty of every honest and loyal Communist.

But at the very time when a barbarous war of annihilation was being waged against those unfortunates who, inspired by the best intentions, had once striven to serve the State and the common weal, a new Ochrana arose differing from its predecessor only by its use of means a thousand times more objectionable and unscrupulous. This was the infamous

Tsheka,[1] which to this day, under the new name *G.P.U.*,[2] is carrying on its unparalleled reign of terror all over Russia, and by which every year thousands of innocent men and women are sacrificed.

By a fortunate combination of circumstances I am in a position to give absolutely authentic and reliable information about the working and organization of the Tsheka, and thus to show the European public how things really are in the Communistic State of freedom and equality. For, while the majority of the Ochrana officials have fallen victims to the fury of the Red Terror, the new rulers deemed it expedient in some cases to compel officials of the Tsarist Police Service, by threats of death, to continue their work in the Tsheka. One of the men who thus agreed, against their convictions, to act as policeman for the Bolsheviks made it his business not merely to mitigate the evil brought upon Russia by the Tsheka, but also by roundabout ways to convey abroad evidence of the activities of the "New Ochrana."

That is how I have come into possession of important documentary proofs, which I hesitate the less to make public because my informant has meanwhile paid for his boldness and his enterprise with death. He died in the prisons of the Tsheka, remaining to the end faithful in his devotion to the Old Russian Idea, and his communications should serve to enlighten European public opinion as to the true spirit of Soviet rule.

This is all the more necessary because the 'unbiased' newspaper reporters, publicists, trade-union members, experts, and merchants who, for some years past, have continually been visiting Russia bring back with them impressions that are quite ill-founded. Very few of them are aware of the net that,

[1] Tshe and Ka are the initials of two Russian words meaning Extraordinary Commission.—TRANSLATOR.

[2] The initials of the Russian for State Police Department.—TRANSLATOR.

POLITICAL EXILES RETURNING FROM SIBERIA IN 1917

Trotsky in Prison

Nadeshda Konstantinova Krupskaya
Lenin's Wife

from the moment they cross the frontier, surrounds them all the time, preventing them from catching a glimpse of anything, from even hearing a word, that might not suit the men in power in the Kremlin. If the world had to depend only upon such accounts of Soviet Russia, then there would be little hope that the truth would ever come to light, for Europe would never learn anything but what the Soviet Government intends or desires to publish. All the impressions received, all expressions of opinion heard by the foreign visitor, are carefully staged and disseminated, so that the stranger naïvely believes that he is making "unprejudiced study" of the facts, while he is really being shown round by the Tsheka and deceived at every step. What foreigner is there who has ever been able to peep behind the scenes devised for him? What he sees are hygienic and humanitarian arrangements intended for his edification. What he hears are the words of paid agents, or terrorized citizens, who would never dare to utter a criticism that would involve them in trouble, imperilling their own lives and those of their dependents. And thus it is that the dark side of Bolshevik rule, with its medieval prisons and torture-chambers, with its unheard-of terrors of every kind, is concealed from the eye of the visitor; and only he who knows the Tsheka and its secrets from within can declare the truth about them.

When, after the Revolution of February 1917, the revolutionaries returned in troops from banishment or from abroad, Burtsev was the only one who advised the new rulers to preserve the Ochrana as an institution, staffing it with men of "revolutionary convictions." He thought that even 'liberated' Russia would very soon require a Secret Police for its defence. But Kerensky, with his sentimental swagger, declared that, with the Revolution, the "shameful" Ochrana had ceased to exist for ever, and that the free Republic would get along without such an instrument. So the Ochrana Sections were broken up, their personnel being thrown into prison or sent to the Front, and the names of the secret agents, so far as the new Government got to know them, were published in the Russian and foreign Press.

However, in a very short time the new masters began to shake in their shoes, dreading attempts upon their lives. Then, as the power of the Bolsheviks grew stronger and stronger, and the situation of the Provisional Government became more and more precarious, Kerensky was the first to open negotiations with the former heads of the Ochrana, myself included, to see whether we were willing to assist the Government with our experience in its struggle against the extremists of the Left.

Commissary Svatyikov, who had been sent abroad to wind up the Foreign Department of the Ochrana, was suddenly given other instructions, and now endeavoured to recruit the members of the former Ochrana Service in Paris for the Provisional Government, but, I must say, without finding his advances very warmly received. Evidently Kerensky and his associates had now perceived that even they could not do without the support of a Political Secret Police. They made every effort to recall to life the very organization that they had only six months before sentimentally condemned and practically destroyed. If that Government had been vouchsafed a longer life, the Ochrana, with a considerable number of its former employees, would probably have celebrated its resurrection. But then came the October Revolution, which put an end to Kerensky's brief glory and installed the Bolshevik system. Only a few weeks later in the place of the Ochrana arose the Tsheka.

CHAPTER XXIII

The Tsheka and its Founder, Jerzhinsky—Origin and First Organization of the Tsheka—Agents of the Red Terror—Commissaries of the People themselves the Prisoners of the Tsheka—Economic Espionage—Summary Judicial Procedure—"Provocation"—"Entered under Outgoings"—Postal Censorship—Siberia To-day—Hostage System

THE cradle of the Tsheka was the Smolny Institute, once an educational establishment for daughters of the nobility, after the October Revolution the seat of the Soviet Government. The men assembled there, with Lenin at their head, though devoid of all practical experience, undertook to rule the Empire along entirely new and untried lines laid down solely according to their own over-subtle political theories. And no doubt, from the very beginning they must have feared that the Russian people would not be disposed to accept all their hare-brained measures without a protest. So, during the first months of their unaccustomed authority, they were all the time in mortal fear, and they hailed with delight the cunning Pole, Felix Edmundovitsh Jerzhinsky, when he offered to look after their safety.

Jerzhinsky, a man who, for cold-blooded cruelty, could have given points to Marat, was only too pleased to seize the opportunity afforded him of inaugurating in Petersburg a reign of terror. He at once had set up an "Extraordinary Commission to deal with Counter-revolution, Speculation, and Sabotage," the personal management of which he reserved for himself. Thus arose the Tsheka, whose name is nothing more than a juxtaposition of the initials, *Tshe* and *Ka*, of the Russian words for Extraordinary Commission. Jerzhinsky took jealous care from the start that his powers should be unrestricted in every way, for the Commissaries of the People,

275

trembling for their lives, hastened to comply unreservedly with all his demands. It was decreed that the Tsheka should not, like the Police in other lands, be under the jurisdiction of the Home Office, but should be responsible directly to the whole Government. That provision alone guaranteed to it the absolute control of the whole land, and made of it an instrument a thousand times more dangerous than the Ochrana had been. In Tsarist Russia, of course, the whole Police system was immediately subordinate to the Ministry of the Interior, which exercised permanent and minute supervision over its conduct, while now the Council of Commissaries of the People was neither disposed nor competent to control in each case the measures applied by Jerzhinsky.

Soon the Tsheka began its raids in Petersburg, arresting on all sides individuals who were in any way objectionable in its eyes, and every day hurling at haphazard many innocent victims into the Beyond. For this unique authority had, from its inception, united in itself the functions of the Police and those of the Judiciary—that is, it not merely made arrests, but acted at one and the same time as judge, accuser, and executioner. From then onward no one in Russia was sure of his life, a condition that continues to this day.

When the Soviet Government migrated to Moscow, the seat of the Tsheka was likewise transferred, its notorious Headquarters being established in Lyublyanka Street. In Petersburg the chief office was removed to a block of buildings in Gorochovaya Street, and the management entrusted to the equally bloodthirsty Uritsky. This man was soon overtaken by his well-deserved fate; he was murdered by the Revolutionary Socialist Kannegiesser. Jerzhinsky immediately used this incident as a pretext to have his powers extended, and to develop still further the formidable organization of the Tsheka.

The men of the new order had almost without exception

Tsheka Headquarters in Moscow

JERZHINSKY, HEAD OF THE TSHEKA

been engaged in the work of conspiracy under the Tsardom, and in their years of contest with the Ochrana they had acquired a very wide experience. They therefore knew exactly how conspiracies had to be organized, and now that they had arrived at the helm they were able to take all precautions to ensure that any counter-revolutionary movement would be nipped in the bud. For this purpose Jerzhinsky created a machine that put the old Tsarist Secret Police hopelessly in the shade in respect of its perfection and extent.

After the first period of disorder and terror was over, the Tsheka was constituted of two main divisions: the Counter-espionage Section and the Secret Operative Section. The function of the former was to keep a careful watch upon all movements opposed to the Government, and, as under the rule of the Tsar, this task was performed, above all, by an elaborately thought-out External Agency. Thousands of persons were compelled, partly by persuasion or bribery and partly by threats of death, to assist in the counter-espionage. They included officers in the Red Army, women of every social class, politicians, clergymen, as well as workmen and peasants. Methods adopted were those that had been in vogue in the time of the Ochrana. Names of agents were also kept strictly private, being known only to those right at the top. Every week all the agents had to report to the chiefs of their Sections and to put before them the results of their work. The material reward earned by these people was very meagre, for the Soviet State had ways and means sufficient to oblige recalcitrants, in spite of poor pay, to serve the Tsheka.

In all central and local government offices branches of the Tsheka were set up as far back as 1918, so that before long there was hardly even one tiny town or village in Russia where Jerzhinsky's agents were not at work, in order that all resistance to the revolutionary order might be suppressed in blood.

And quite as remarkable as any other feature was the zeal with which Jerzhinsky from the outset had his own superiors, the Commissaries of the People, and the other principal leaders of the Soviet Government, kept under observation. When, after some time, several States, misled by the vain hope of doing a profitable trade, resumed diplomatic relations with the Soviet Republic, Jerzhinsky immediately sent out his agents to spy upon every word and act of the Ambassadors of the Soviets.

Soon the Commissaries of the People realized that they themselves were the prisoners of the Tsheka, but the mutual distrust among these "popular leaders," and their dread of possible attack upon their lives by Russian citizens of different political faith had become so great that no one dared to infringe the absolute authority that Jerzhinsky had acquired.

More and more, too, the countless Communist organizations, local party groups, associations of youth, newspaper offices, and schools were called in to co-operate with the Tsheka Espionage Service; so that not merely the actual employees of the Tsheka, but all the Communists of the whole Empire became actively involved in the observation of each other and of everybody else.

The invention of "Economic Espionage," an institution till then unknown in any part of the world, provided the Tsheka with a pretext for interfering in all, even the most innocent, concerns, of every Russian. For after it had become quite evident that the Communist trading policy, from which Lenin and Company had expected to see arise unheard-of prosperity in the land, had ended in complete collapse, attempts had to be made to suppress with violent measures the 'contraband' traffic, which kept on growing and growing, because without it no one could procure even the necessary means of subsistence.

Many dealers and peasants, whose only offence had been the purchase or sale of a few pounds of flour or butter absolutely required to sustain life, were sacrificed to the Tsheka's insane lust of persecution, being imprisoned and shot as persons who had committed "crimes against Communist public order." It hardly requires to be stated that the 'guardians of the law' made the most of the welcome opportunities to enrich themselves by 'confiscating,' on their own account, the monies or stocks of provisions which were found on hand in such cases, or by extorting large sums from their unhappy victims.

The vast proportions assumed by the scandalous state of matters in the Tsheka are perhaps best indicated by the fact that even the Revolutionary tribunals, which in virtue of their very constitution naturally had the warmest sympathy for criminals, were nevertheless obliged to pronounce sentence of death upon numerous officials of the Tsheka for abuse of authority.

But if the fury of the Tsheka was in itself an unparalleled reign of terror, the desperate plight of the Russian people was aggravated a thousand times by the power arrogated to itself by the Tsheka of not merely making arrests, but of at once sitting in judgment upon the prisoners. The procedure was a model of simplicity. There was no form of trial. The accused was merely brought in, charged with an offence, questioned about his accomplices, and then condemned, no matter whether he had confessed or not, no matter whether there was evidence against him or nothing more than groundless suspicion. If, in rare cases, the Tsheka decided to release an arrested person, that by no means provided the fortunate one with any guarantee that he would not be seized again a week later and this time condemned.

A verdict of guilty was generally followed by sentence of

death, which was pronounced under the high-sounding name of "the highest measure of social defence." The execution was regularly carried out by shooting in the Tsheka building: a revolver-shot was fired into the back of the head. The bodies of victims were not handed over to relatives, but simply buried anywhere. That was the means adopted by the Tsheka to render it impossible to check the real numbers of people butchered.

Of course there was no lack of those "provocations" with which the Tsarist Police had always been reproached, unjustly as we have seen, by the revolutionaries. As Tsheka spies very often received a reward if they managed to get hold of a 'profiteer' or a 'hoarder,' no one could feel safe. Incriminating material evidence might be smuggled into one's home, and the consequence might be death and loss of fortune. Typical of the businesslike procedure adopted by the Tsheka was the technical expression used in the Police jargon to indicate executions: the victims of their unique justice were referred to as "having been entered under outgoings."

In its method of dealing with secret agents, also, the Tsheka very quickly marked the difference between itself and the Police under the Tsars, the change being very much for the worse. While those at the head of the Ochrana had always endeavoured to take into consideration, as far as possible, the psychological difficulties of their subordinates, and rather to dismiss them from the Service than to imperil their lives in any way, Jerzhinsky abolished the dismissal of secret agents on principle. Whoever, whether voluntarily or under compulsion, once entered the service of the Tsheka could now escape from it only by death. And woe to the agent who, by a rash word or an awkward step, warned the counter-revolutionary he was watching! Such unfortunates were, as a rule, arrested at once and banished for many years to the Solovyetsky Monastery.

It is no matter for surprise that the "black cabinets" were introduced again by the Tsheka. Far from respecting the privacy of correspondence, the Bolshevik Police installed branches in all the larger post offices, whose business it was to keep an eye on all the mails. These "black cabinets" assumed special importance when postal connexion with foreign countries was resumed, for now it was a question of preventing from crossing the frontier a single word of truth concerning Russian conditions. With all modern technical contrivances, electrical and X-ray apparatus, photographic appliances, chemical means of all sorts, the whole of the foreign mail was kept under strict surveillance. If anyone had been so impudent as to write in a letter one phrase in criticism of the Soviet system, he could be quite certain of being immediately arrested and imprisoned. And, on the other hand, the importation of all newspapers and books disapproved of by the Bolsheviks was stopped in the same way, so that henceforth no one living within the Russian frontiers should be able to learn what was going on in the rest of the world, and what people in Europe and America were thinking of Soviet Russia.

The new rulers had for the most part returned from Siberian exile to enter the Kremlin. What could be more natural than that they should now send all whom they deemed objectionable to Siberia? This appeared the more expedient because meanwhile all the prisons had been crowded with victims of the Red Terror and some relief proved to be urgently required. Accordingly those guilty of 'minor' offences, such as peasants who had made known their devotion to the Church, or merchants who had carried on 'contraband' trade in provisions, were banished for some years to the most distant parts of Siberia. Those crimes, however, which under the rule of the Tsars had been punished by exile, such as the publication of forbidden printed matter or participation in the work of illegal societies, were, by the Tsheka, punished unhesitatingly by death, while at the same time the remotest connexion with one of the accused in any given case would often suffice to bring ruin and destruction upon perfectly innocent persons.

But all the horrors of this system were far surpassed by the barbarous custom of taking hostages. The Tsheka has made its own a usage known to the most uncivilized tribes and highway robbers: it has no scruples whatever in arresting the relations or dependents of a wanted man and in keeping them languishing in prison until he gives himself up. Further, every Russian who wishes to obtain a permit to travel abroad must make known to the Tsheka the names and addresses of all the members of his family residing in Russia, and it is plainly signified to him that they will at once be made subject to the vengeance of the Tsheka if he should take it into his head while he is abroad to utter one word in criticism of the conditions in Soviet Russia.

CHAPTER XXIV

Collapse of Communist Economic System—'Abolition' of Tsheka—
Revival under another Name—Refined methods of the G.P.U.—Farce
of Bolshevik Administration of Justice—G.P.U. Foreign Service—Spying
upon Russian Refugees and Foreigners travelling in Russia—"Eye of
Moscow"—Secret Section of G.P.U.—Continued Persecution of Monarch-
ists.

IT WAS inevitable that the insane attempt of the Bolsheviks
to introduce into Russia between one day and the next a
Communist economic system should end very quickly in perfect fiasco. Famine, lack of the most vital necessities, the fabu-
lous depreciation of the money, and the menace of unrest that
was steadily growing throughout the whole population seemed
to make it almost impossible to avoid the complete collapse of
the Soviet domination.

Lenin, however, was shrewd enough to recognize at the
last moment that the system could be saved only by departing,
temporarily and apparently, from original principles. As he
was not disposed under any circumstances to give up the supreme power, he determined to swerve quite definitely for a
little toward the Right, correctly assuming that he would
thereby gain time to draw breath, and that during that interval the tottering Soviet Government would once more be able
to re-establish its authority. Therefore permission was granted
off-hand for the carrying on, within certain limitations, of
private trade, which till then had been most strictly prohibited;
and every effort was made, by holding out the prospect of
exorbitant profits, to interest foreign capital in Russia. That,
then, was the beginning of the New Economic Policy, that
senseless, cross-bred invention to which the Bolsheviks owe the
continuance of their power to this day.

Meanwhile, however, despite all attempts to isolate the country, rumours concerning the existence and *modus operandi* of the Tsheka had found their way abroad. At first people had believed that what they heard was nothing more than fantastic tales of imagination, but very soon European opinion became convinced and had to recognize, with revulsion and horror, that the deeds of terror done by the Tsheka did really surpass the monstrous creations of the wildest fancy. Under such circumstances the gentlemen in the Kremlin saw very clearly that a resumption of economic relations between Russia and the democratic Western States was out of the question. That meant, as the Soviet *régime* was in dire need of moral and financial credit abroad, that the Tsheka was rather a serious obstacle. Without any more ado then, the Tsheka was abolished—at least in appearance.

Superficially altered, its powers were transferred to a new institution bearing the name of State Police Department, or, to use the initials of the Russian designation, G.P.U. Foreign correspondents were solemnly informed that the times of War Communism, and with them the days of the Terror, were now over, and that the G.P.U. would henceforth exercise no other powers than the Political Police of other lands. They even went so far as to place the G.P.U. under the control of the Home Office, or rather the People's Commissariat of the Interior, and thereby to seem to distinguish it from the Tsheka, which, of course, had not been responsible to any of the ministries. Besides, it was affirmed that the G.P.U. would no longer have the right to dispose of cases coming under its purview: arrested persons were, in accordance with the procedure generally followed in democratic States, to be handed over to the regular tribunals. This seemed a mighty step forward, considering the position the Tsheka had occupied; and the provision which authorized the G.P.U. to keep untried suspects arbitrarily in confinement for a period of not more than three months seemed in comparison to be merely a slight blemish.

In reality, however, this apparent transformation of the Tsheka, which had been made for no other reason than to conciliate foreign public opinion, effected not the least change in practice. As before, the G.P.U. operates with the same medieval inquisitorial methods, with the same cruelty and terror, with the same absolute powers as its predecessor. No doubt such officials of the G.P.U. as come in contact with a stranger visiting Russia are most charming and amiable, most convincing in the correctness of their bearing. But once the prison doors have closed behind a victim of its hate, so that all risk of 'indiscretions' has ceased, the G.P.U. drops the mask and reveals itself in its true colours: the same cruel, bloodthirsty, and unscrupulous Tsheka as it was when it reigned in terror, open and unashamed.

For, even though the pressure of foreign opinion has obliged the Bolsheviks to introduce at least the semblance of some kind of orderly administration of justice, there are numerous paragraphs in the Soviet code that are so infinitely elastic in their application that the G.P.U. may still legally deal with obnoxious individuals by inflicting the penalty of prison, exile, or death. For this purpose no more is required than the perfectly vague conception of "political" or "economic counter-revolution"; or than the provision that anyone is liable to be punished whose actions are in any sense opposed to the success of the Communist political system. Only the artless and unsuspecting foreigner will ever be so far cheated over the real character of Russian administration of the law as to accept at its face value the institution of People's Courts, which, on paper, seems to correspond to trial by jury in Western Europe. As a matter of fact, these People's Courts are so constituted that they have no will of their own and comply at once with the wishes of the G.P.U. And, besides, to this day there are still innumerable victims of the new Tsheka who are merely suppressed in the gaols without ever being brought before a judge.

Only in one respect is the G.P.U. to be distinguished from its immediate predecessor: its methods are more refined and perfected. The consequence is that Russia to-day is covered by such a close network of political espionage as never existed in the world before. In the large cities there are hundreds and thousands of secret agents in the pay of the G.P.U., watching every intellectual movement in the country. The postal censorship has been still better organized, and even on the mail-trains technical experts of the G.P.U. now travel regularly, to see to the scientific opening and examination of all correspondence that looks in any way suspicious. Their methods are so skilful that the receiver has no means of knowing that letters have been tampered with, even though the envelopes have been opened in transit three or four times. Specialists devote themselves to the reading of invisible inks, to the decoding of ciphers, and to the translation of messages in foreign languages.

The G.P.U. has also further developed the practice of keeping under observation Soviet officials and even the Commissaries of the People. It is the duty of every head of a Government office to send in a monthly report on the political leanings of his subordinates; and, on the other hand, countless agents of the Political Police stationed in the offices throughout the Empire take care that the superiors are looked after in like manner.

In comparison with this secret work, the public activities of the G.P.U. are almost insignificant. There are, indeed, also uniformed officials in the service of this authority who, like the gendarmes in Tsarist Russia, have to supervise especially the traffic on the railways and shipping, but everyone knows that, relatively to the numbers of secret agents and spies scattered everywhere, these uniformed men are only a dwindling minority.

It has been pointed out that the Ochrana used to maintain a foreign branch to keep watch upon revolutionaries living beyond the frontiers; the G.P.U. did not hesitate to imitate the system and to perfect it still further. It is amazing to note the incomprehensible unconcern shown by the European Powers in allowing Soviet 'missions,' with extraordinarily numerous personnel, to settle down in their capitals. By far the majority of the countless individuals attached to the staffs of these trade delegations, Red Cross missions, legations, and embassies have no official occupation. They are nothing more or less than agents of the G.P.U. commissioned to spy upon the Russian refugees, to arrange criminal attacks upon dangerous opponents of Bolshevism, to keep under close observation artists, scholars, and actors on 'leave of absence' from Russia, and to see that Moscow is regularly informed as to their attitude.

The Foreign Agency of the G.P.U. is always very desirous of getting into touch with any organized group of refugees, in order to find out what matters are under discussion and what decisions are being taken. Its agents are so skilful that, unfortunately, they have scored success in many an unlikely enterprise. As they have plenty of money to spend, and as, on the other hand, the whilom Tsarist officials in exile are often in the direst need, it has more than once occurred that an emigrant here and there has succumbed to temptation and accepted the suggestion to enter the Secret Service. That such a proposal was made to myself I have related in an earlier chapter; and I am still grateful to God this day that He granted me the power to reject the offer in the only proper fashion.

Another of the duties that fall to the Foreign Agency is to make preliminary and very exact inquiries into the political views, the mode of life, and the circle of acquaintance of all persons intending to visit Soviet Russia for purposes of observation and study. This espionage practised upon such foreign travellers begins before they have even left their homes, but the G.P.U., as a rule, sets about it with such adroitness that the individuals in question have not the least idea that every step they take is being noted. It does not require to be stated that the observation becomes a hundredfold more intense once the foreigner has passed the Russian frontier: after all, there is not in Soviet Russia a single railway-train that does not carry agents of the G.P.U., there is not a hotel where a majority of the staff does not consist of paid Police spies. The stranger cannot write or receive a letter without its being opened and copied; he cannot pay a visit without the fact being recorded in the notebook of the agents in attendance upon him. Every foreign subject resident in Russia has his own *dossier* in the G.P.U., containing copies of his entire correspondence, and memoranda of his conversation and movements.

All Russians know that foreigners are subjected to this minute espionage, and consequently avoid, as far as they can, having any dealings with them at all; otherwise they run the risk of being summoned before the G.P.U. to undergo a searching cross-examination on the conversation that has passed. That is why strangers travelling in Russia never happen to hear a word in criticism of existing conditions, unless it be that the critic is himself an agent of the G.P.U.

For the Soviet Government has a masterly understanding of how best to influence the minds of foreigners. It knows that here and there *some* criticism there must be, if the foreigner's suspicions are not to be aroused; so the G.P.U. provides the requisite criticism through its own channels, by bringing the stranger in an apparently natural way into touch with its agents, who, wearing the mask of ordinary citizens, merchants, workmen, or officials, represent the required 'voice of the people.'

The evidence accumulated concerning both *guests* and the doings of emigrants resident abroad is collected in a special section of the central office of the G.P.U. in Moscow, and systematically analysed. From there also are sent out instructions to the employees of the Foreign Agency, so that nothing taking place anywhere in the world, of a character hostile to the Soviet *régime*, may escape the 'Eye of Moscow.'

The struggle against the internal enemies of Bolshevism is conducted by the Secret Section of the G.P.U., with its many Sub-sections. Special departments work up the material relating to the Mensheviks,[1] Revolutionary Socialists, the Clergy, and the Monarchists. A recently invented cartographic system used by the heads of these Sections enables them to overlook quickly all the "nests of conspirators" that actually do exist, or are supposed to exist, all over Russia.

The institution of the secret rendezvous, too, as it had been formerly used to facilitate intercourse between the officials of the Ochrana and their secret agents, was taken up again by the G.P.U. Such secret quarters are looked after by special collaborators who, themselves, never go near the office of the G.P.U., and do not bear any obvious indication about them that they belong to the Police at all. To these addresses the agents of the Internal (System of) Observation bring their

---

[1] The Bolsheviks are the 'whole-hoggers,' the Mensheviks are the party of relatively moderate revolutionaries who would have been satisfied with a more restricted, a less extreme programme. *Bolshe* means 'more,' and *menshe* means 'less.'—TRANSLATOR.

reports, and there likewise they receive their instructions, so that they are not obliged either to call in person at the G.P.U.

The success which these elaborate methods have made it possible for the G.P.U. to achieve is, unfortunately, very notable. Besides, the adherents of the monarchical system had, of course, no sort of experience in secret plotting, and for that reason the conspiracies that have been hatched by them were organized on lines that were both artless and amateurish. For example, the group led by the Counter-Revolutionary Shepkin, including some three hundred persons, mostly ex-officers, was betrayed to the G.P.U. through the fact that its members omitted to use their assumed names even in private intercourse among themselves. A G.P.U. spy managed to gain the confidence of the too credulous conspirators, and then procured complete lists of the members, thereby enabling the Red Police to suppress the whole organization. The end, of course, was three hundred executions.

More astounding is the ease with which the G.P.U. was able to discover a plot set on foot by the Revolutionary Socialists, although the members of this body must have already acquired extensive familiarity with all the mechanism of conspiracy in its struggle with the Ochrana. In this case it was the Foreign Section of the G.P.U. that succeeded in securing the necessary evidence, for it managed to steal the whole of the archives of the Revolutionary Socialist "Administrative Centre," which was fixed in Paris. The documents were got through to Moscow, and that settled the fate of the party.

Although to-day, under the iron heel of Soviet oppression, the Monarchist movement in Russia has been almost completely crushed, the persecution of real or alleged followers of the Tsardom is still being carried on with undiminished barbarity. As late as June 1927 many persons accused of having been parties to Monarchist conspiracies were executed, among

Boris Savinkov, Revolutionary Socialist, Before the
Bolshevik Tribunal

Grand Duke Cyril Vladimirovitsh, Present
Claimant to the Russian Throne

them being Prince Paul Dolgorukov, who had been bold enough to make his way secretly from Rumania into Soviet Russia; Mikulin, a member of the Imperial Duma, who had placed his home at the disposal of a Terrorist fighting group of Monarchists; Prince Mestshersky, a supporter of Grand Duke Nikolai Nikolayevitsh, and some ex-officers of the White Army.

CHAPTER XXV

Social Conditions in Bolshevik Russia—New Aristocracy and New Bureaucracy—Persecution of Religion—Persecution of Jews—Symptoms of Disintegration in Bolshevik Régime—Cleavage in Communist Party— The Red Army—Discontent among the Peasants—Reasons for Continuance of Soviet Rule—Above all, Organized Fear—Europe's Responsibility—Appeal to the West.

WHENEVER the Bolsheviks are called to account for the terror practised by them they defend themselves, as a rule, by pointing out that all this frightfulness is necessary to protect the interests of the people, and to prepare the way properly for the foundation of the "future State," where class shall be unknown, and freedom and equality prevail.

More than ten years have now passed, yet that 'preparation' has no success of any kind to its credit. Even one who may not be convinced, as I am, that Russia can prosper and attain to power and wealth only under a Monarchist government will at least have to admit that Bolshevism has not fulfilled a single one of its bombastic promises. How does it stand in reality with the "land of freedom and equality"? Is the Russian nation better off to-day than it was under the Tsardom? In the Communistic "state of the future" are there really none who suffer hunger and distress? Have social differences really ceased to exist?

No! Now, as ever, social inequality does exist. The only difference is that the classes that used to be dominant have given way to a new aristocracy formed of arrogant despots, separated by an iron wall of suspicion from the real people. Behind the fortifications of the Kremlin, and closely protected by a party guard, sit the rulers of Russia, while outside, over wide areas, famine rages, disease is spreading and ravaging the country, and even in Moscow tens of thousands of beggars, cripples, and workless people are dragging out a weary and pitiful existence.

More and more the Communist Party has adopted a strictly aristocratic caste spirit. More and more jealously the influx of new members is obstructed, so that the great privileges to which partisans are entitled need not be shared among too many 'comrades.'

Complaint used to be made of the Tsarist officials, with their fussiness and red tape, though this arose in most cases only from their devotion to duty and their sense of responsibility. But the Soviet *régime* has created an unparalleled bureaucracy for its own sake: it paralyses all public life and action, and its sole purpose is to assure a care-free existence to the largest possible number of supporters of the Government.

Not even to the Jews, who nevertheless had been in their time the most ardent protagonists of the Revolution, has it brought any improvement in their position. It is true that some pot-house politicians of overweening ambition have suddenly attained to absolute power, thus placing themselves in a position to enslave and exploit millions of poor Russians. It is true that, when Bela Kun fled from Hungary to Moscow, he was able to occupy a splendid residence furnished with the goods stolen from the Grand Dukes; and that Zinovyev could lead a life of luxury, with champagne banquets and revelry of all kinds. But those Jews who did not have the luck to come to the top with the Revolution are to-day suffering a thousand times more grievously than they did under the much-maligned Anti-Semitic rule of the Tsar.

Bolshevism, which aims at the extermination of all religion, is persecuting the Jews, as well as the Orthodox Christians, for their faith, which the Imperial Authorities did not do. Moreover, among the general population, and especially among the peasants, there prevails more bitter animosity against the Jews than ever, for the Russian is inclined to make Jews in the mass responsible for the disaster brought upon the land by the leaders of the Jewish Internationale.

This hostility on the part of the people is frequently revealed in regular *pogroms,* while the Soviet Government, which needs the peasant and is afraid of him, thinks it expedient to allow free course to these outbreaks of popular passion. After all, any movement is welcome that is not directed against the Government itself, and may therefore serve as a safety-valve for the prevailing concealed ill-will.

Neither the persistent lying reports of the semi-official Soviet Press nor the strict censorship and suppression of all opposition opinion can cover up the fact that the internal disintegration of the Bolshevik system is making irresistible progress. In the last few years the Communist Party itself has split up into factions, which are in bitter antagonism to each other: the leaders of the Revolution of 1917 are ruthlessly thrust aside by new men, and the Terror does not respect even the founders of the Soviet order. The day does not appear to be far distant when this cleavage must inevitably bring about the fall of the whole structure, just as of yore the French Revolution was wrecked on the dissensions of the individual groups.

The Red Army, the one and only support upon which Bolshevism can truly count, is likewise betraying signs of dissatisfaction, a circumstance which is very little affected even by the G.P.U.'s unceasing espionage of the troops. If the Soviet Government had expected, by the systematic removal of ex-Tsarist officers serving in the Red Army, to cleanse the Army from the "counter-revolutionary plague," that measure has proved a failure too, for the new generation of 'Communist' officers, hurriedly trained at the military colleges, has come out more and more frequently with Anti-Soviet opinions.

That the peasants are deeply discontented with existing conditions can no longer be concealed. For economic reasons the growth of a class of large farmers has been tolerated, with the result that the people on the land have lost again all the apparent advantages at first conferred upon them by the Revolution, while the oppressive burden of taxation is driving them to economic ruin.

In spite of all that has been stated, the Soviet power still seems outwardly to be as firm and strong as ever. That, at first, is mysterious, but closer inspection finds the explanation in quite a number of circumstances. To begin with, the fury of the Tsheka and the G.P.U. all over the country has called forth such an atmosphere of dread that nobody trusts anyone else, no one believes himself safe from traitors, and everyone is prepared to recognize in a friend or a near relative an involuntary agent of the G.P.U. in disguise. This fear in which everybody stands of everybody else naturally makes any public manifestation of the seething discontent a very difficult matter, and thus serves to maintain the appearance of internal peace. All the more terrible will be the reaction when the day of reckoning with the Soviet reign of violence does arrive!

But, to a very considerable extent, it is other countries that must be held responsible for the continuance of the Bolshevik system, for international capital has short-sightedly preferred the interests of the moment to those of the future, and, aiming at re-establishing as quickly as possible profitable business relations with Russia, has actually sought to win the favour of the Reds. The recognition of the Soviet Government by most of the European Powers has, unfortunately, lent it very great support, and the credits granted to it by Europe have saved it from inevitable collapse.

At one time it was a tradition among the foremost merchants and traders of Europe to do business only with honest men, and bluntly to decline even the most profitable proposals made by suspicious customers. The World War has effected a regrettable transformation of this business ethic, for nowadays the commercial world does not hesitate to accord moral and financial credit to a band of robbers and violent upstarts. On the day when Europe understands its fatal error and radically changes its policy toward Soviet Russia, the rule which the Bolsheviks have established over a people of upward of one hundred million souls will break down utterly.

And what tremendous possibilities for Europe itself would the end of the Soviet system bring with it! Only then would Russia awake to new life and strength, and make up for all that it has missed under the oppression of the Red Terror. It would have to set about building up the trade that has been ruined and the manufactures that were so senselessly destroyed, and to that end it would require not merely European goods, but European brains as well, to make up for the shortage of intellectual workers.

For in Russia there are to-day no engineers, no merchants, no technical managers, no administrative officers who really understand their job. The old ones have been for the most part killed or have died of privation, and their successors, trained by the Soviet schools, are, measured by European standards, perfectly ignorant. Consequently, after the fall of Bolshevism, Russia will be actually a vast colonial territory waiting for the pioneers of European and American culture. May the West keep this consideration in view and determine accordingly its attitude toward Bolshevism!

INDEX